Local Selfhood, Global Turns

The book examines the works of Akshay Kumar Dutta (1820–1886), who can be seen as ideologically inhabiting the cusp between religion and rationalism – the two most crucial avenues of debate and discussion in the public sphere in nineteenth-century Bengal. While nineteenth-century Bengal has been an important discourse within South Asian history, major figures of reform such as Rammohun Roy, Debendranath Tagore, Iswarchandra Vidyasagar, and Keshub Chunder Sen have generally been the focus. The book attempts to rescue Dutta from the clutches of academic amnesia, and to locate him as one of the foundational figures of intellectual refashioning among the common albeit educated public in nineteenth-century Bengal.

Sumit Chakrabarti is Professor in the Department of English at Presidency University, Kolkata. His areas of expertise include nineteenth-century Bengal, intellectual history, and postcolonial and cultural studies. His most recent monograph is titled *The Calcutta Kerani and the London Clerk in the Nineteenth Century: Life, Labour, Latitude* (2020) and he is the editor of the forthcoming Oxford World's Classics edition of the short stories of Rabindranath Tagore.

SOUTH ASIAN INTELLECTUAL HISTORY

This series aims to create a cohesive set of volumes on South Asian intellectual history which will set the paradigm for an emerging academic sub-discipline. It shall indeed offer a definitive shaping of the field.

The series, about South Asian worlds of ideas, will contribute in multiple ways to realms of scholarship beyond the niche of South Asian studies. It will contribute to global history, and especially global intellectual history. South Asianist historians – of the premodern and early modern as well as colonial and postcolonial periods – have shown with remarkable clarity the problems with provincialized area studies approaches, and the necessity of studying intellectual-cultural production through transregional frames. This series will therefore mark a pioneering development in intersecting transregional, transnational, and global history with intellectual history. It will also facilitate interdisciplinary dialogue between established approaches to intellectual history and wider fields of studying subaltern, demotic, and vernacular thought, with their profound impact on South Asian history and politics. In doing so, it will play a profoundly transfigurative role, taking history of ideas beyond elite vocabularies and text-centrism.

Series Editors

Asad Q. Ahmed
University of California, Berkeley, USA

Milinda Banerjee
University of St Andrews, Scotland, UK

Farhat Hasan
University of Delhi, India

Anshu Malhotra
University of California, Santa Barbara, USA

Upinder Singh
Ashoka University, India

Local Selfhood, Global Turns

Akshay Kumar Dutta and Bengali Intellectual History in the Nineteenth Century

Sumit Chakrabarti

CAMBRIDGE
UNIVERSITY PRESS

Shaftesbury Road, Cambridge CB2 8EA, United Kingdom

One Liberty Plaza, 20th Floor, New York, NY 10006, USA

477 Williamstown Road, Port Melbourne, VIC 3207, Australia

314–321, 3rd Floor, Plot 3, Splendor Forum, Jasola District Centre, New Delhi – 110025, India

103 Penang Road, #05–06/07, Visioncrest Commercial, Singapore 238467

Cambridge University Press is part of Cambridge University Press & Assessment, a department of the University of Cambridge.

We share the University's mission to contribute to society through the pursuit of education, learning and research at the highest international levels of excellence.

www.cambridge.org
Information on this title: www.cambridge.org/9781009339827

© Sumit Chakrabarti 2023

First published 2023

Printed in India by Avantika Printers Pvt. Ltd

A catalogue record for this publication is available from the British Library

ISBN 978-1-009-33982-7 Hardback

For Professor Gautam Bhadra

In reverence, gratitude, and love

Contents

Acknowledgements

The idea of the book was born out of certain discussions with Professor Gautam Bhadra on the significant gaps in scholarship on nineteenth-century Bengali intellectual history. I am grateful for his patience and steadfast guidance during the process of writing. This book is dedicated to him.

Professor Brian Hatcher was a constant intellectual support. His interest in my project, detailed critical comments, and encouragement were pillars of strength during the writing process. I am very grateful to him.

Subir Dutta, friend and comrade for years, read the drafts multiple times and came back with critical comments that have helped me think. This is another chance to acknowledge his quiet but certain mentorship.

Soumen Mukherjee, colleague from the Department of History at Presidency University, Kolkata, was a keen participant in the thinking process. His interventions and erudite comments have helped me rethink many arguments. I wish that I had his scholarship to expand many of my debates.

This book would not have been written without the logistical support of Subhamay Mandal at the Paschimbanga Bangla Akademi, Kolkata. I am very grateful to him. Prithwish Bhusan Banerjee and Mrinmay Mukherjee at the Presidency University library were always eager to help. The National Library, Kolkata; the Bangiya Sahitya Parishat, Kolkata; the West Bengal State Archives, Kolkata; and the Centre for Studies in Social Science, Calcutta, Kolkata, have supplied useful resources without which I could not have moved ahead.

Sohini Sengupta, Sourav Chattopadhyay, and Soham Deb Barman have been student comrades whose contributions to this book are no less than mine. Resourceful and ready at all hours, invested in my work, and very much part of the process, they have always given more than I have deserved. I am grateful.

I am grateful to the anonymous reviewers at Cambridge University Press whose comments gave me both confidence and new insight. Rachel Blaifeder, Qudsiya Ahmed, Sohini Ghosh, Anwesha Rana, and Aniruddha De have been involved at various stages of the book. I thank them for being patient with me. It has been a wonderful experience to work with the Press.

I am grateful to the administration and my department at Presidency University for being cooperative and understanding throughout the process.

Most of the manuscript was written in the quiet of my study during a raging pandemic and lockdowns across the globe. Nandini, my constant companion, kept me sane, motivated, and suitably entertained with fine music, poor jokes, and anecdotes collected from various media. She was around, and I was happy.

Note on Transliteration

I have not used diacritical marks in the text to avoid clutter. Also, they are a distraction for the general reader and unnecessary for specialists. I have largely followed the common form of pronunciation rather than orthography, except for proper nouns and words that are relatively familiar to the English-speaking world – thus *shastra*s, Debendranath Tagore, and *bhadralok*. For most first instances of unfamiliar Bengali words and phrases, I have provided a translation in parenthesis. All translations from Bengali to English, unless otherwise mentioned, are mine.

Introduction

One would often, but not consistently, come across mentions of Akshay Kumar Dutta in discussions on the cultural and intellectual life of nineteenth-century Bengal. He would, on most occasions, be a cursory reference, a footnote, a character on the fringes of the larger rubric of the discussion. There was a great churning of intellectual frameworks throughout the nineteenth century in Bengal – religious and educational reforms, epistemic shifts, cultural upheavals, and much of all these have been documented with care by historians and social scientists alike. Akshay Kumar Dutta, however, has rarely featured as a crucial presence in these discussions and debates. This book asks the 'why' question by attempting to closely read some of his works and examine if such erasure has foreclosed possible complications to certain categories of critique.

Born on 15 July 1820 in the quiet hamlet of Chupi in Burdwan district, Akshay was the youngest and the only surviving child of Pitambar Dutta and Dayamayi Debi. His father worked as a cashier in Calcutta (now known as Kolkata), and Akshay's initial years were spent in Chupi, being educated in the local *pathsala* run by Gurucharan Sarkar. He also started learning Farsi with Munshi Aminuddin and Sanskrit with Gopinath Tarkalankar as a young boy while still at Chupi. His father, subsequently, took him to Calcutta, where, after a brief stint at a free school run by missionaries at Kidderpore, he was admitted to Gourmohan Auddy's Oriental Seminary. His father's untimely demise in 1839 did not allow him to finish his formal education, but as his biographers have documented, his love of learning led Akshay to train himself in both the sciences and the humanities and provoked him, at an early age, to contemplate on the epistemic disconnect between

Puranic and European forms of learning.[1] As Akshay grew up in Calcutta, the city caught in the middle of multiple reforms, he was introduced, through his visits to the Bangla Bhasanushilani Sabha (a forum for the spread and practice of the Bangla language), to the poet Iswarchandra Gupta, who was also incidentally the editor of the periodical *Sangbad Prabhakar*. The latter, much impressed by Akshay, introduced him to Debendranath Tagore, and the turn of events led to Akshay becoming the editor of the Brahmo periodical the *Tattwabodhini Patrika*. As one would understand, neither was Akshay the native Calcutta elite nor was he to be ignored henceforth as the editor of what was going to be one of the most important periodicals of the nineteenth century in Bengal. His position, as I would elaborate in further detail in the first chapter, would always remain curiously interstitial – neither the elite *bhadralok* of the Calcutta society nor the rank outsider merely receiving enlightened knowledge from the informed native elite. He was a practitioner, instrumental in producing both knowledge and opinion, yet not ensconced in either family lineage or metropolitan roots. Akshay, however, was an important presence in the cultural milieu, and I have often wondered why when so much of South Asian history writing involved nineteenth-century Bengal and critical biographies of its many actors, Akshay never became a subject. In his lifetime he had written and translated extensively, had worked tirelessly for vernacular education, had spoken at length about religion and reform, was one of the major textbook authors on popular science and morality – and thus had an impact on the consolidation of Bengali identity during the period. Yet he is conspicuous by his absence in all major narratives, critical or otherwise, on nineteenth-century Bengal. This book is an attempt to fill that gap.

A few years ago, I had almost accidentally picked up a volume of Akshay Kumar Dutta's collected works at a local vernacular library. We had an abridged version of his essay 'Palligramastha Prajader Durabastha Barnan' (A Description of the Sad Plight of Rural Subjects) in secondary school, included in the vernacular literature syllabus.[2] The essay had not left much of a mark on my mind, except for the title, and I had forgotten all about its author and the contents of the essay. It was much later that I came across occasional references to Akshay Dutta in certain histories of nineteenth-century Bengal. I brought the volume back with me and started to read his works. What propelled my interest initially was the fact that for a man who had written quite copiously for a certain period of his life, the references to him were almost always cursory, a couple of lines, a footnote, or a bibliographical reference. I wanted to understand this erasure, the perspective of constructing the narrative of Bengal in the nineteenth century in terms of the choices that historians and writers were making well into the twenty-first century.

Akshay Dutta was an exact contemporary of Iswarchandra Vidyasagar. They were both born in 1820 and died five years apart in the latter part of the century. They knew each other and worked together in the paper committee of the *Tattwabodhini Patrika* – Akshay as its editor and Vidyasagar as an invited member.[3] Later, when his health was failing and Akshay had to resign from his position as the editor of the *Tattwabodhini Patrika*, Iswarchandra had invited him to be the principal of the government teachers' training college. The latter was also instrumental in arranging for him a monthly pension of twenty-five rupees from the Tattwabodhini Sabha.[4] It is possible to find certain important similarities in their discursive frameworks and their writings, and I have discussed this in the first chapter of the book. Likewise, Akshay was also intimately connected through his work as the editor of one of the most important periodicals of the time with most of the contemporary intellectual processes and movements. As I read through the volume of Akshay's work, I wondered why, in spite of his significant presence within this milieu of Bengali intellectual and cultural churning in the nineteenth century, Akshay has remained a small voice, rarely picked up for elaborate and critical discussions on the formative years of Bengali modernity.

The year 2020 marked the bicentennial year of the birth of both Akshay and Iswarchandra. While the celebrations, seminars, symposia, and conferences mostly revolved around the contributions of Iswarchandra Vidyasagar, there was a certain revival of interest in the life and works of Akshay. Bengali little magazines and small presses began to publish issues on him, sometimes reading him alone, often in the shadow of Iswarchandra, the Brahmo Samaj, or science practice in Bengal.[5] Nevertheless, Akshay was being read once again. However, this interest was largely localized and confined to general discussions on his role as a rationalist, an educationist, an editor, or his influences, friendships, and mentors. However, two important aspects struck me in this context. In the first place, most of these discussions around Akshay were taking place within the confined space of the Bengali cultural milieu in spite of the fact that nineteenth-century Bengal has been a focal concern for the historians of South Asia across the globe almost since the seventies of the last century; second, the understanding and assessment of Akshay Dutta's role as an intellectual was not being opened up to or connected to the larger concerns of intellectual history and epistemic paradigm shifts across the major debates within historical, cultural, and social studies in the global academia. As I read Akshay's works, comparing them to the works of his contemporaries and trying to examine what he was reading and why, I realized that a larger intellectual canvas was perhaps necessary to place Akshay's works in context. At the same time, most of the works on nineteenth-century Bengal written within the Anglosphere, as I have already mentioned earlier, had rarely engaged in depth with Akshay. Also, a reading of his works revealed eclectic interests, epistemic concerns, and a range of scholarship that needed a detailed critical engagement in terms of their role in the shaping of the modern Bengali mind. In many ways, this was crucial to my initial interest in taking up Akshay Dutta and his works for a close critical analysis. My attempt in this book will largely be to engage with some of his important and foundational works that according to me significantly influenced the ideological mores of a colonized Bengali society in transition.

Another aspect worth pointing out is that somewhere between the events of the early part of the nineteenth century and the later part, the middle years have sometimes not been adequately represented in terms of their intellectual churning and the figures that were instrumental in this. Rammohun Roy, for example, gave the necessary reformist push in the early years of the nineteenth century, followed immediately by the likes of Debendranath Tagore, both much-discussed figures within South Asian historical scholarship. Likewise, from the eighties onwards, the onus of intellectual representation was carried on by the likes of Keshab Chandra Sen, Bankimchandra Chattopadhyay, and later on by Rabindranath Tagore. The middle years were mostly represented by Vidyasagar as the principal figure of reform and epistemological reworking. Undoubtedly, these were some of the most prominent figures who consistently intervened within the model of colonial modernity – adjusted, questioned, and reframed the contours of the evolution of a modern Bengali subject. However, figures such as Akshay Dutta or Bhudeb Mukhopadhyay, who mostly worked through the middle years of the century, have, I presume, not received adequate critical attention in terms of their significant interventions into and sometimes a radical critique of the cultural polemic of an evolving modernity.

Although Akshay never finished his formal education, while a student at Gourmohan Auddy's Oriental Seminary he was trained in the mornings and evenings by Hardman Jeffrey (a teacher at Oriental Seminary) in Greek, Latin, Hebrew, and German.[6] He was also trained, according to his biographer Nakurchandra Biswas, in physics, geography, geometry, algebra, trigonometry, higher mathematics, psychology, English literature, and the works of Homer and Virgil.[7] All this reading and training are adequately reflected in his works and speak of the range of his influences. However, Akshay was also deeply invested in indigenous texts, initially as a Brahmo ideologue and later on as someone with a keen interest in minor religious sects. As a rationalist he would sometimes argue with some tenets, but he was a keen and careful reader. His opinions reflected in his writings were thus an eclectic mix of cultural and intellectual influences of a connected and comparatist nature that was peculiar of the way in which the influence of modernity and indigeneity was absorbed by a section of the educated intelligentsia during the period. Akshay's professional life was brief compared to most of his contemporaries. The most productive period of his career was between 1843 and 1855, when he was the editor of the *Tattwabodhini Patrika*, the organ of the Brahmo Samaj. He had also written school textbooks in the vernacular. Most of them were in the form of short pieces on varied subjects ranging from astrology to geography, morality to general knowledge. His discourses in the *Tattwabodhini Patrika* were often such essays on science or morality, but also on religious practice, minor religious sects, the glory of an ancient Hindu past, or a critique of colonial modernity and its effects on the indigenous population. His more voluminous works such as *Dharmaniti* or *Bhayabastur Sahit Manabprakritir Sammandha Vichar* or the two volumes of *Bharatvarshiya Upashak Sampraday* were complex works on ethics, cultural and religious histories, and the relationship between man and the universe, and grappled with questions that were meant to frame a debate around the epistemic fabric of race (*jati*) or society (*samaj*). Akshay Dutta's works demand careful and focused reading not only to make sense of the varied nature of his influences, but also to understand the internal contradictions that were inevitably intrinsic to his works. How did he assimilate what he read? What were the parameters that led him to pick and choose texts that belonged not only to the known ideological patterns of colonial modernity, but beyond, connected both synchronically and diachronically to varied influences and ideologies? What was the nature of his intervention, and how was it similar to or different from his peers and contemporaries? Who were his target audience? These are some of the questions that I would want to address in this book.

It is possible that one of the reasons for the general neglect of Akshay Dutta's works is the apparent lack of a direct political intent. The political intent of an argument is more or less immediately apparent or conspicuous for most other foundational figures of nineteenth-century Bengal – be it a Rammohun or a Vidyasagar, a Bankim or a Rabindranath. For Akshay, on the other hand, this becomes a difficult exercise for the reader. One comes across in Akshay a certain clear desire to underplay politics. Most of his works have a quiet structure of empirical analysis that moves towards a conclusion like a scientific experiment. With few exceptions, most of his works display an equanimity that is apparently apolitical and whose intent is to educate the common, literate person in ways of leading a worthwhile existence. However, read between the lines, there is in much of what Akshay writes a radical alterity, a subversion that is not immediately apparent, and a consolidation of values that is singularly original. Although somewhat sceptical in using this term, I feel that there is in Akshay's writing strategy a deconstructive method in place. His writing is not immediately subversive, neither is it a direct counter-narrative to the general narrative flow of the policies and strategic manoeuvres of the colonial government. He would go with the flow, as if consolidating the general rubric of colonial modernity and its associated tropes of education and governance. However, in the course of his argument he would strategically place a point of view quite incommensurate with the general flow, thereby dismantling the larger rubric he had begun with. To take an example, Akshay translated George Combe's famous treatise on phrenology, *The Constitution of Man*,[8] into Bengali. Reading the translation, one gets the impression that Akshay was in complete agreement with the general course of the argument on racial superiority that Combe elaborated in his book. However, a careful reading reveals that Akshay's translation was selective, not only due to the fact that he was writing for a native readership who would not be able to contextualize European examples (as he claims in his introduction), but also because he was deliberately omitting certain examples by Combe that could have been quite germane to his argument. While Combe, for example, puts forth the argument of the racial superiority of the brahmins in 'Hindostan', Akshay quietly avoids this section in his translation.[9] Such an emendation, for example, gives Akshay's argument a different spin, although not categorically underlined, but evidently pointed out by the absence. In my close reading of his works, I intend to emphasize this particular aspect of his strategy. Such a strategy both sets him apart from the dominant political agency of his milieu and has perhaps led to a certain erasure of his contribution to the dominant rubric of reactive politics that has generally been under the scrutiny of the historians of South Asia.

Choosing an Analytic Framework

Akshay's intervention as an intellectual was arguably less political in its intent than most of his renowned predecessors, contemporaries, and successors. In her book *Elementary Aspects of the Political*, Prathama Banerjee posits an important argument in this regard. She argues that since anti-colonial struggle in India needed to mobilize all sections of the population, its primary focus was on the idea of democracy and not on the other aspects of modernity, namely education, modernization, or the governmentalization of the society.[10] The modernity that emerged in India, therefore, due to the contingencies of historical need was primarily political in nature. In order both to talk about the political and to distance herself from its immediate and causal agency, Banerjee evolves her own strategy of analysis:

> As I see it, this book belongs to [the] deterritorial intellectual domain where, despite geopolitical obstructions, scholars find each other struggling to move on from the moment of (postcolonial/ decolonial) critique and undertake the positive and experimental task of reassembling diverse philosophies and experiences of struggle from across the world. So when I ask, What is the political?, I ask it from a crossroads that is no one's country but only a modest meeting place, where we share our philosophies and histories with each other.[11]

As I began to think about Akshay Dutta's location, Banerjee's argument began to take on new and multiple meanings. I was urged to consider if Akshay was adopting an almost similar strategy in his way of intervening into the political in nineteenth-century Bengal. In the first place, it was easier now to place Akshay within the discourse of the political in nineteenth-century Bengal without having to invest in him a necessary and pronounced political stance as it were. Second, it was easier now to put one's finger on Akshay's specific and different role as an intellectual within his milieu. As both an object and agent of history, he was one of those rare examples who was standing on the crossroads and trying to reassemble influences and effects through both a rational and an affective analysis. He was capable of seeing colonial modernity in its totality – in terms of both its sophisticated constitutive parts and the immediate needs of colonial rule and governmentality. There was in Akshay a constant attempt to search for or formulate epistemologies of both reform and resistance. As a player within the inner circle of the reformists, he was conscious of the varied influences that were contained within any idiom of articulating representation. He was standing at a distance, and Banerjee's notion of reassembling is a good fit to Akshay's intentions. The various genres of writing that he tried out were symptomatic of such a confluence of ideas and ideologies. He was aware that colonial modernity was a machine, and that the indigenous population, varied as it were in too many senses, also lacked a consolidated counter-narrative to articulate anti-colonial resistance. By reviving the past in its *samajik* or social form, and consistently investing it with the newer and acquired articulations of modernity, Akshay was trying to see if a tentative epistemology would evolve, not necessarily as a counter-narrative to colonial modernity, but as a collated narrative with abrasive potential. Akshay Dutta had never travelled abroad in his lifetime. He was neither collaborating nor trying to garner support from the varied epistemologies. He was only connecting them, putting together narratives of past collaborations, the present realpolitikal, and the vision of an emerging Bharatvarsha in the future with an epistemic composure. Akshay was never waging a war; he was only resisting ideological impositions through a subtle strategy of reviving a narrative from a different cultural or epistemic system and positing it alongside the dominant master narrative merely as a means of unsettling it ever so slightly. He was also expanding his readership, or the stakeholders, by deliberately moving beyond his immediate *bhadralok* milieu and reaching out to the hitherto unrepresented.

The methodology that Akshay was assuming in his works, therefore, was both global and local. On the one hand, he was reaching out to both British and non-British systems of representation and ideological apparatus while, on the other, he was reaching into those esoteric pockets of the native population whose existence was rarely acknowledged and never written about within the domain of the elite *bhadralok* population. It was a complex ideological position that Akshay had carved out for himself. The crucial question that I encountered therefore was to look for an analytic framework where I could possibly place Akshay in order to bring out his peculiar importance within the scope of anti-colonial or post-colonial writings.

In a series of lectures on an Indian historiography of India, Ranajit Guha raises and answers a crucial question on education in the context of colonialism. While speaking of the plan of dissemination of knowledge in India by the British rulers, Guha makes the following astute observation:

Did education have nothing other than intellectual exertion and advancement of knowledge as its content? Was it simply the code of an alternative culture? Although colonialism and the many-sided thrust of liberal politics made it out to be so, there was more to education than was thus conceived. It stood not only for enlightenment but also authority – a fact which it has been the function of ideology in all its forms, including historiography, to hide both from the educators and the educated. In other words, it was an ideological effect that made both the propagators and the beneficiaries of education regard the latter as a purely cultural transaction and ignore that aspect of it which related directly to power.[12]

Against such authority and power Guha posits the figures of Rammohun Roy, the Derozians, and Iswarchandra Vidyasagar as the initial detractors who were looking to articulate an alternative historiography, while the rest were 'a sprawling mediocrity given to boast its uncritical imitation of the West as a cultural achievement'.[13] Subsequently, Guha reads the rise of nationalism as the 'other' of such domination and servitude and unsurprisingly brings up the figure of Bankimchandra. He sees in the figure of Bankim the polemicist who would try to recover from the past a native historiography that could immediately be placed against the machinations of colonial modernity and its usurpation of the narrative of the colonized. Guha writes about Bankim's project: 'For he had already endowed the past with the sanctity of an ancestral time … where *purbamahatmya* (former glory) was assimilated to *amadiger purbapurushdiger gourob* (the glory of our forefathers) and the recovery of the past as history prescribed as a filial duty to redeem the family name.'[14] One wonders why, in the course of these three lengthy lectures on the formulation of an Indian historiography in the nineteenth century, Guha never for once mentions the name of Akshay Dutta while focusing entirely on Bengal. I would not say that Guha had considered Akshay as part of the 'sprawling mediocrity', but very specifically, I suppose, he was looking for counter-narratives. This elision, which I have mentioned earlier and will point out many times in the course of my argument in this book, is the very crux of my interest in Akshay. Why is it difficult to place him within a framework of understanding intellectual dissent during colonialism? In the fourth chapter of this book I will argue how Akshay preceded Bankim on the questions of a native historiography and representations of Bengali selfhood and that it was quite possible that the latter was influenced by some of the writings of the former. Nevertheless, it was possibly the heuristic and tentative nature of Akshay's training that gave him a certain manner of argumentation which could not be immediately placed as a template within a binary.

In a fascinating study on the 'entangled' nature of transnational connections, Kris Manjapra talks about the relationship between German and Indian intellectuals over the early to middle years of the twentieth century.[15] He focuses on the political recognition between these two otherwise disparate geographical spaces, due to scientific and scholarly encounters that went beyond national and colonial boundaries. Manjapra clarifies at the beginning of the book the reason for his study of such entanglements between disparate geopolitical spaces: 'How do groups use trans-societal interactions and linkages to satisfy their own specific local political interests?'[16] No doubt Manjapra's use of the notion of 'entanglement' opens up a nuanced version of engagement underlying disparate political friendships, whereby it is possible for individuals from nations or states with widely different power dynamics to assemble on a common platform of interaction and exchange – and to reframe the questions about colonial politics and representation. However, I realized quickly that using this frame of entanglement as the analytic model for studying the works of Akshay Dutta was not tenable for a number of reasons. In the first place, the political space that Manjapra is talking about in his work is the post-enlightenment world, already much more evolved in terms of connections and networks than mid-nineteenth-century India was. Manjapra clearly insists that by post-enlightenment he means 'the sea change in scientific and scholarly production that began at the end of the nineteenth century and continued into the mid-twentieth century, marked by widening communication networks among white and colored thinkers across world regions'.[17] The master-episteme of European enlightenment as the torchbearer of progress was already suspect and tentative with the two wars and the emergence of newer epistemic systems that questioned 'the great signifiers of nineteenth-century Western universalism: Europe, Enlightenment, and Empire'.[18] The world that Akshay Dutta inhabited, on the other hand, still considered the enlightenment as the prime mover within the domain of intellectual progress. If Akshay and his contemporaries were reading German, French, Greek, or Sanskrit texts, those were, more often than not, secondary material that helped either consolidate or critique the claims of colonial modernity. The latter was a given, and networks for intellectual exchange with the non-British epistemic systems across the globe were generally, even if available, rare. Akshay had never left India, and his access to non-British material was mostly incidental or accidental, and not part of a system that had the purposiveness of a counter-narrative. Second, as I will argue at length in the second chapter, Akshay was a science-worker and not a scientist, writing vernacular textbooks for young adults or the uninitiated, introducing them to the scientific developments of the time. He would not exactly fit the scope of Manjapra's project of 'scholarly and scientific encounters'[19] that happened in different parts of the globe, often determining the political positions of the participating nations. Whereas his geographical imagination would take him to places that would help imagine a possible historical narrative that unsettles the claims of a hegemonic master-narrative of the colonizer, the symptoms of such movements or manoeuvres were localized. Akshay was indeed talking about the cultural geography of an ancient India, its connections (or entanglements) with other parts of the globe, but as an agent of history his own participation in the network or the process was limited to occasional correspondences and not regular encounters. The scale within which Manjapra has imagined the entangled encounters is of a different intellectual and political world, quite far removed from Akshay Dutta's almost imperceptive interventions into the enlightenment episteme. However, there is another observation that Manjapra offers which is quite germane to the world that Akshay inhabited – that of discourse practised as dialogue where there is always a possibility of dissent even within the most humble intellectual practice, say, translating a book from English to Bengali, or talking about the *samaj*, rather than the nation, as a model of historical narrative. This is what Manjapra calls 'differentiated articulations of intellectual politics',[20] a phrase that can be very aptly used for Akshay's interventions.

However, the analytic category that helped me the most in thinking about the nature of intervention that Akshay was making through his works was perhaps global intellectual history. In their introduction to the edited volume on the subject, Samuel Moyn and Andrew Sartori talk about the global as an actor's category (among others) and have urged their readers to think in terms of 'intermediaries, translation, or networks'.[21] They make a crucial point about training the discipline of history to treat the 'local' in terms of the 'global' in the way that categories of analyses may be opened up to the contingent nature of any master-narrative, and how variedly it may be interpreted across geopolitical landscapes. The emphasis of the editors on the 'eternal localism of globalism'[22] adds the necessary impetus to the possibility of the continuous conception of meta-narratives that reframe the ideological inflections of the grand-narratives, particularly in the context of colonial praxis. By insisting on the importance of 'global consciousness as a native category', the editors of the volume opened up avenues for me to critically engage with the global in terms of the complex vernacular milieu that Akshay inhabited and represented, in spite of an implicit universalism that has been apparent in much of his work. That such a universal vision could be read with an un-Hegelian lens, piecemeal, breaking each argument up into smaller parts that engaged in a dialogue with the Eurocentric colonial register in its peculiar way, is a strategy that was suggested to me by this collection. In the course of my argument in the book, I will posit the idea of a 'hyperreal Bengal' that emerged through the works of Akshay Dutta and Bhudeb Mukhopadhyay which subtly interpolated its logic into the more powerful one of 'hyperreal Europe',[23] thereby disconcerting, ever so slightly, the historiographical agency of the colonizer. Along with the emphasis on the local, the global history framework also opened up for me the possibility of exploring what Sartori and Moyn have described as 'the connectedness of disparate sites or emphasize the disjunctures that interrupt the continuity between disparate sites'.[24] I will explore how, situated within the constricting domain of a colonized space, Akshay was foregrounding an argument about his notion of historicality and the representation of the native subject through a cosmopolitan lens that engaged races, and time periods, and ideologies in a manner that not only connected the history of human civilization across space, time, and categories, but also pointed out the disjunctures between what constituted the liberal spirit of modernity at the centre (read England) and its aberrations in the practice of colonial modernity. Of course, I have my own differences with the model of global history as Moyn and Sartori have read it, and I will take that up for a brief discussion in the book. However, the way the category of the global has been opened up in terms of intellectual history has only facilitated to address the works of someone like Akshay Dutta who has been more or less neglected otherwise in the way colonial Bengal and its intellectuals have been discussed within the rubric of South Asian and colonial histories. Akshay was pushing at the contours of the local, expanding its boundaries, perhaps one of the earliest Bengali intellectuals trying to comprehend the local as a category. He was emphasizing the importance of the vernacular as language, the minor sects in terms of religion, the indigenous *samaj* as a category of the social, and the voyage of ancient Hindus across the seas with the history of capital. He was connecting such attempts to similar movements across continents. He was also placing the non-*bhadralok* colonial subject within the debates on representation, thereby eliciting a forced space for them within the larger debates on colonialism and modernity. The local was being enmeshed in the global, each qualifying the other, and Akshay as a tentative representative of the liberal *bhadralok* fold was deliberately positing traditional knowledge alongside the universalist claims of western enlightenment, thereby raising questions that had epistemic implications. He brought the global to the local, and vice versa, and this is where I have found Moyn and Sartori's volume as a necessary tool to articulate some of my thoughts.

The Plan of the Book

The book has been planned across six chapters. The first chapter introduces Akshay Dutta as part of his milieu in nineteenth-century Bengal. It traces the trajectory of his initial ideological training through the works of Rammohun Roy, the influence of Debendranath Tagore, his conversion to Brahmoism, and being involved in the workings of an elite Calcutta *bhadralok* society that was suitably marked by its many influences and an eclecticism that was instrumental in the evolution of the civil society. The chapter also focuses on Akshay's lengthy debate with Debendranath about the nature of the Vedas, determining the tenets of Brahmo worship, and discussions around the setting of the template of the Tattwabodhini Sabha and the *Tattwabodhini Patrika*. It also discusses the crucial companionship between Akshay Dutta and Iswarchandra Vidyasagar, whom I have called 'bhadralok allies', who both explored the tenets of a rationalist modernity and a revival of indigenous intellectual traditions that would shape Bengali selfhood.

In the second chapter I will discuss Akshay's engagement with the science practice of the period. Akshay was not a scientist, but his keen interest led him to visit the Calcutta Medical College often to study botany and chemistry, and one might say that he mostly led a life of the sciences. He wrote textbooks on science, taught science for a brief period, and most of the latter part of his life was spent in the empirical pursuit of the various sciences at his home 'Sovonodyan' in Bally, Howrah. In this book I have called him a 'science worker'. This chapter explores the tenets of western scientific practice within the colonized space, and its implications for the educated *bhadralok* milieu who were variously affected by the way the colonial master class was using science as both epistemology and praxis. The chapter argues how Akshay was instrumental in carrying this new-fangled science education to the doorstep of the common yet literate householder through attempting a new idiom for writing science in the vernacular. Akshay was literally inventing a new scientific language to make such education accessible to the commoner. He also regularly published articles on science in the pages of the *Tattwabodhini Patrika*, in spite of the fact that it was meant to be an organ for the Brahmo Samaj. The chapter locates Akshay at the cusp of tradition and modernity, a faith in the traditional systems of moral practice complemented by the curiosity of empirical science practice. It argues how Akshay's scientific spirit was born out of an eclecticism that was defined by his complex location within an equally fraught milieu. The first two chapters would thus place Akshay Dutta within a kind of analytical framework informed by the society around him and how it embraced or critiqued colonial cultural and scientific practices.

In the third chapter I shall broach the discussion on the self-fashioning of the Bengali *bhadralok* subject in terms of the various influences, from across the globe, that were being churned within the intellectual milieu of nineteenth-century Bengal. Here, I will try to closely read some of the essays in the *Tattwabodhini Patrika* under the editorship of Akshay Dutta, trying to see how the universal or the global was being imagined and discussed vis-à-vis the interface between indigenous practices and colonial governmentality. I will use Akshay's conception of *viswa rup mul grantha* (or the elementary book of the universe) as a pivot to read how he was connecting strands of thought from Rammohun Roy to George Combe to establish a moral-philosophical order for the native subject, and subsequently moving on to the historical conception of an idea of Bharatvarsha. In this chapter I will also broach and try to answer the crucial question, 'How global was Akshay Dutta?' I will also attempt an analysis here of a question that Moyn and Sartori had asked in their book – 'Is a premodern global history possible?'[25] – by contextualizing how Akshay was connecting the notions of Bharatvarsha and *bhumandal* (the universe) in an essay on trade relations between ancient Indians and other geographical spaces.[26] Subsequently, although I will talk about the possibilities of the 'global' in the ways Akshay delineates a particularist understanding of the history of Bharatvarsha, I will also point out the traces of the universalist in his writings. In short, I will argue that the historiographic position that Akshay was assuming in terms of Bharatvarsha as a space was complex and contingent, and could not be immediately marked by any theoretical closure.

In the fourth chapter I will focus primarily on the idea of historiography and attempts among the nineteenth-century Bengali intellectuals to trace and categorically formalize a past for the race. I will specifically focus on and read closely the writings of Akshay Dutta and Bankimchandra Chattopadhyay, trying to trace the differences and commonalities in their attempts to foreground an idea of history of the Bengali race. In this context, I will emphasize how, in spite of the many common threads in their writings and Akshay anticipating Bankim in a number of ways, Akshay's role has largely been marginalized and often forgotten by historians and theorists alike. With the notion of *dharma* as the fulcrum, this chapter will try to read the idea of the indigenous *samaj* in the context of a consolidation of selfhood in nineteenth-century Bengal.

In the fifth chapter I will talk about Akshay Dutta's engagement with the modelling of the public sphere and how he approaches the question of the *janasamaj* in terms of the affective. For Akshay, quite averse to any direct confrontation with officialdom, the affective was a singularly apt strategy to interrogate the civic machinations of colonial governance. I will use the idea of 'disaffection' to explore how Akshay was strategically dismantling the supposedly benevolent façade of 'modernity' and its implications within the colonized space. I will also closelyread, in this context, Akshay's significant essay on the plight of country folk in the hands of a bureaucracy fed by the ruling class, and how he sees this as symptomatic of bad governance.[27] Dissent and dissatisfaction are expressed firmly yet strategically by Akshay, a ploy that was interestingly effective in the years just before the mutiny of the sepoys.

In the sixth and final chapter I will revisit the idea of Bharatvarsha once again and attempt to address the questions of identity, history, and nationhood in terms of their global epistemologies, and how Akshay's writings suitably intervene into the idea of *viswa* (world) through its possible local manifestations. I will also explore the notion of imagined history developed as a template for selfhood and identity, and compare such dream narratives written by Akshay Dutta and Bhudeb Mukhopadhyay. I will also explore the idea of race or *jati* and how Akshay connects it to the *jagat* or the world, thereby situating the local in the global and vice versa. Finally, I will argue how Akshay brings together in his writings the notions of *samaj* (society), *jati* (race), and *itihas* (history) that would posit a hermeneutic proto-narrative to be placed alongside the larger narratives of modernity and progress, thereby anticipating the future reframing of the templates of the enlightenment, or the movement towards post-enlightenment.

I hope this book will help claim for Akshay Kumar Dutta his rightful place in the narrative of native intervention into the space of colonial intellectual hegemony. His was a small but significant voice that both borrowed from and anticipated the more discussed voices of dissent or disruption of the imperial logic. Even though he may not have been instrumental in formulating any epistemic violence on the method and logic of colonial practices, he deconstructively unsettled the system through his insistence on particularisms, his avowed vernacularism, and his faith in the heuristic insight of the *swadesh* and its *samaj*.

Notes

1. See Swapan Basu (ed.), *Akshaykumar Dutta Rachana Sangraha*, vol. 1 (Kolkata: Paschimbanga Bangla Academy, 2008), p. 3.

2. Akshay Dutta, 'Palligramastha Prajader Durabastha Barnan', in *Akshaykumar Dutta Rachana Sangraha*, ed. Swapan Basu, vol. 1 (Kolkata: Paschimbanga Bangla Academy, 2008), pp. 586–606.

3. See Asitkumar Bhattacharya, *Akshaykumar Dutta ebang Unish Sataker Banglay Dharma o Samajchinta* (Kolkata: K. P. Bagchi and Co., 2007), pp. 128–129.

4. See Ashish Lahiri, *Akshaykumar Dutta: Andhar Rater Ekla Pathik* (Kolkata: Dey's Publishing, 2019), p. 153.

5. See, for example, *Dwisatajanmabarshe Akshaykumar Dutta*, ed. Tapas Bhowmik, *Korok Sahitya Patrika*, Kolkata, 2020; Pijushkanti Sarkar, *Bismrita Abismrita Akshaykumar Dutta*, vol. 1 (Kolkata: Kabitika, 2020); Dwijendra Bhowmik (ed.), *Akshaykumar o Vidyasagar, Swarantar* (Kolkata: January, 2021).

6. Nakurchandra Biswas, *Akshay-Charit* (Calcutta: Adi Brahmosamaj Press, 1891), p. 10.

7. Ibid.

8. George Combe, *The Constitution of Man Considered in Relation to External Objects* (Cambridge: Cambridge University Press, 1828/2009). This was translated as *Bahyabastur Sahit Manab Prakritir Sammandha Vichar*, vols. 1–2, in *Akshaykumar Dutta Rachana Sangraha*, vol. 1, ed. Swapan Basu (Kolkata: Paschimbanga Bangla Academy, 2008), pp.113–316.

9. Combe, *The Constitution of Man*, p. 144.

10. Prathama Banerjee, *Elementary Aspects of the Political* (Durham and London: Duke University Press, 2020), p. 2.

11. Ibid., p. 3.

12. Ranajit Guha, *An Indian Historiography of India: A Nineteenth-Century Agenda and Its Implications* (Calcutta: K. P. Bagchi, 1988), p. 15.

13. Ibid., p. 17.

14. Ibid., p. 58.

15. Kris Manjapra, *Age of Entanglement: German and Indian Intellectuals across Empire* (Cambridge, MA: Harvard University Press, 2014).

16. Ibid., p. 6.

17. Ibid., p. 9.

18. Ibid.

19. Ibid., p. 2.

20. Ibid., p. 7.

21. Samuel Moyn and Andrew Sartori (eds.), *Global Intellectual History* (New York: Columbia University Press, 2013), p. 17.

22. Ibid., p. 18.

23. See Dipesh Chakrabarty, 'Postcoloniality and the Artifice of History', in *Provincializing Europe* (Princeton, NJ: Princeton University Press, 2000), pp. 27–46.

24. Ibid., p. 14.

25. Ibid., p. 5.

26. See Akshay Dutta, 'Bharatvarsher Sahit Ananya Desher Purbakalin Banijya Bibaran' (parts 1 and 2), *Tattwabodhini Patrika* 3, no. 78, Magh, 1771 Saka, pp. 153–166, and 4, no. 85, Bhadra, 1772 Saka, pp. 68–76.

27. Akshay Dutta, 'Palligramastha Prajader Durabastha', *Tattwabodhini Patrika* 4, no. 81, Baisakh issue (pp. 5–12) 4, no. 84, Sraban issue (pp. 49–55), and 4, no. 88, Agrahayan issue (pp. 115–121), 1772 Saka or 1850.

1

The Discontents of Eclecticism

The Milieu of Akshay Kumar Dutta

In order to know and understand the world of Akshay Dutta, it is imperative to comprehend the complex social and cultural milieu that he inhabited. Many and various discourses had come together in an uneasy confluence to delineate both the quotidian and the intellectual lives of Calcutta in the nineteenth century. As David Kopf writes:

> ... varieties of Western ideas seemed to flow easily into the port of Calcutta, which was the capital of British India and a veritable laboratory of intercivilizational encounter between the East and the West. Radical ideas that challenged the bases of the traditional world order in Europe and America were a form of intellectual cargo unloaded on the docks of the great metropolis, along with other industrial and commercial products.[1]

To attempt to write about Akshay Dutta's milieu is to first try and understand, at least in a broad and general way, some of the major strands of intellectual influence that marked the mind of the thinking person in nineteenth-century Calcutta. Between the beginning and the middle of the century, Calcutta had culturally and intellectually become almost as busy as London with the proliferation of printing and publishing establishments, the abundance of western scientific, philosophical, and literary matter, public libraries, English and vernacular newspapers, and cultural, literary, and social associations of various nature and inclination. Contained within the colonial logic itself was a culture of debate and discussion that involved both the ruler and the ruled in a way that was curiously set aside from the general narrative of colonial administration and its major decision-making processes.[2] This is not to say, however, that these debates and discussions had little or no impact on the administrative policies of the colony. The mechanism of colonization was in many ways a symbiotic process, an 'intercivilizational encounter', as Kopf would put it. Therefore, there would be frequent interfaces, subtle adjustments, and careful tweaking of policy decisions keeping in mind the cultural, educational, and religious preferences of the native subject, so that the larger structure of colonial governance could remain intact. With the proliferation of printing presses, the increased circulation of newspapers, the general spread of enlightenment education beginning with the primary school,[3] and the coming together of many and different ideological paradigms, the *bhadralok*[4] class of the city was suitably busy forming and disseminating opinions about every matter of lived experience.

Akshay Kumar Dutta, the protagonist of this book, discovered himself in the middle of such churning quite early in his life. He was all of nineteen years of age in 1839 when his friend, the poet Iswarchandra Gupta, took him to meet Debendranath Tagore, the founder of the Tattwabodhini Sabha.[5] Debendranath was already familiar with the writings of Dutta in the columns of the *Sangbad Prabhakar*, a newspaper run by Iswarchandra Gupta, and had asked after him.[6] He liked the young man, and like a true patrician employed Dutta as a teacher of physics and geography at the Tattwabodhini Pathshala that he founded next year. I will return to this subject of the Tattwabodhini Sabha, the *Tattwabodhini Patrika*, and the role of Akshay Dutta in both of these in some detail in Chapter 3. What I am suggesting here is that this event of Akshay Dutta meeting Debendranath Tagore was a crucial moment not only in the lives of either of them, but also in the development of the cultural history of the Bengali race in many ways. Akshay and Debendranath were the unlikeliest of friends or colleagues. They came from very different milieus, had radically different backgrounds, were divided by the obvious village–city binary, and then there was the gaping class divide. However, the fact that they became colleagues of a sort, who intimately worked with each other for more than a decade in spite of such major differences, is crucial in understanding the intellectual climate of Calcutta during the first half of the nineteenth century. The one important commonality, however, was the fact that both of them were identified as *bhadralok*. The disposition of the *bhadralok*, as I have already mentioned, has been discussed by almost all historians and commentators on nineteenth- and twentieth-century Bengal. Joya Chatterji is of the opinion that the *bhadralok* 'were essentially products of the system of property relations created by the Permanent Settlement'.[7] As a category it was heterogeneous and tiered, and as Tithi Bhattacharya notes, 'the *social* composition of the bhadralok ... occupied two *class* positions united by the common ideology of education'.[8] Bhattacharya is referring to the two positions of the comfortable middle class and the lower rung of the *bhadralok* while also keeping in mind a figure such as Pearychand Mitra, who hailed from a rich *banian* family and belonged to neither of these categories but was still very much a representative of the *bhadralok* identity.[9] In the case of the Akshay–Debendranath relationship, the former belonged to the 'poor but bhadra'[10] category; the latter was a representative of the rich *banian*s and businessmen who also possessed considerable cultural capital. This coming together of Akshay Dutta and Debendranath Tagore was fraught in multiple ways, and I will discuss the complex dynamic of the relationship in the course of this chapter and later as well. To begin with, however, the possibility of such a relationship needs to be considered carefully to comprehend the nature of the cultural politics that would make Akshay Dutta such a representative figure of the so-called Bengal renaissance. Also, it is perhaps a closer and nuanced look at this relationship and its various manifestations that will help us understand why an intellectual of such magnitude as Dutta has been generally neglected in most studies of nineteenth-century Bengal. Born in the same year, and his contemporary and comrade for a considerable period of time, Iswarchandra Vidyasagar has been studied carefully by scholars and historians. Likewise, the entire family of the Tagores have been the source of much research and writing, analysis, and commentary, even to this day. In this book I intend to explore the crucial, complex, yet almost forgotten impact of the life, work, and philosophy of Akshay Dutta on the intellectual, moral, and cultural history of the Bengali people. But, to begin at the beginning, it is imperative to talk about Raja Rammohun Roy.

Rammohun Roy, Atmiya Sabha, and Unitarianism: The Cultural Politics of Confluence

It will possibly be easier to understand the ilk of Debendranath, Akshay Dutta, Iswarchandra Vidyasagar, and their colleagues, and how, in spite of their many differences, they could work together, if we trace this narrative of intellectual history back to Rammohun Roy. It was perhaps Rammohun Roy, like no other, who formalized the debates around religion, god, western versus eastern forms of education, or the philosophy of daily living, and initiated the debates around those structural referents of existence in the early years of the nineteenth century that were to become the vortex of intellectual engagement in the succeeding years. As I have already mentioned, personalities such as Debendranath, Akshay Dutta, or Vidyasagar were schooled within discursive systems that were formatively different and sometimes even contradictory. They came together as the result of a pull that was irresistible in terms of its intellectual content. This content cannot be defined simply in terms of their endorsement of a particular mode of education, the content of textbooks, the various rubrics of religiosity within the domestic sphere, or even by the larger contexts of nationalism or colonial politics. What brought them together could perhaps be philosophically understood in terms of a common belief in a *system* of thought whose general principles were precious to all of them. This is not to suggest that there were no contradictions within the system itself. In fact, there were many and major contradictions, and there was a continuous churning of these contradictions in each of their writings, lectures, or debates. But the faith in the system was largely consistent, at least till the middle of the nineteenth century, and this is where the influence of Rammohun was profound and instrumental.

The core of Rammohun's idea of religion and religious practice was defined less by their foundation in belief and antiquity, and more by enlightenment rationalism and utility. Although he was considerably drawn towards the tenets of Christianity, it will be a misreading to assess Rammohun's religious inclinations on the basis of his training in western schools of thought. The Atmiya Sabha, which he founded in 1815, for the study of Hindu scriptures and explorations of Theism, was a first of its kind and accommodated in its fold a curious mix of people. Along with the obvious presence of his *bhadralok* acquaintances such as Dwarkanath Tagore, Brajamohun Mazumdar, Nanda Kisore Bose, or Rajnarayan Sen, who were representatives of a particular class identity, there were also such peripheral tantric practitioners as Hariharananda Tirthaswami or representatives of the ruling colonial class such as David Hare. In later years, it was Hariharananda's brother, Ramchandra Vidyabagish, who played a pivotal role in the Brahmo Sabha, and later on in the Brahmo Samaj, and went on to become the *acharya* of the Samaj and a preacher of the Brahmo Dharma. He was also someone who had worked closely with both Rammohun and Debendranath. If the discussions of the Atmiya Sabha were generally restricted to its small coterie of members, Rammohun was at the same time engaged in translating and publishing the *Kena Upanishad* and *Abridgement of the Vedant*.[11] He writes in a letter to John Digby, who published these translations in London the next year, about the reason why he chose to translate these texts: '...to convince them [the Hindus] that the unity of God, and absurdity of idolatry, are evidently pointed out by their own scriptures'.[12] A number of important narratives are opening up through these events. What apparently seems to be a matter of religion and subsequent debates about the ways of practising one's faith is actually a significant part of a larger narrative of race, rationalism, and cultural politics. In Rammohun's mind, his idea of religious practice was laced with a notion of modernity, and he was attempting to rescue Hinduism from its many dogmas and sanctions to a new world order that invested value not only on the presence of a singular god or *brahma*, but also his manifest functionality in the material world through benevolent human subjects. As his many debates with Christian missionaries, particularly with the Trinitarians, will show, Rammohun was not an ardent votary of all things 'Christian'. It was not a simple advocacy of the religion of the white master as many of his Hindu critics would argue.[13] Even in his choice and celebration of Unitarianism there was an implicit radical politics, and this was one of the reasons behind his considerable popularity in the intellectual circles of contemporary England. As Lynn Zastoupil writes: 'The Unitarians were in the forefront of the intellectual and political radicalism that led to the undoing of the British establishment in the early-nineteenth century.'[14] Rammohun's faith in enlightenment rationalism had little conflict with his religious inclination. He was looking for a simple, faithful practice of religion for the householder, a faith that could be invested with practical intent and rational judgement. The motley character of the Atmiya Sabha was a proof of an attempted or imagined confluence of rational and practicable religious practice, yet one that had its roots in Hindusim and the Vedanta. Evidently, Zastoupil argues, Rammohun had kept his mind open for different religious dispositions in order to find a median path of religious practice for the common practitioner:

> Rammohun's religious development led him toward a universal theism
> that owed something to Islamic rationalist, Hindu vedanta, and radical
> Christian traditions. The extent of his debt to these distinct traditions
> is still debated, since Rammohun's views changed over time and he

crafted his religious ideas in different languages for his various reading audience.[15]

This is an important remark from Zastoupil. Rammohun wrote regularly in English, Bengali, and Persian, and revisionism was an intrinsic part of his critical disposition. What many of the later enthusiasts of Vedantic forms of thinking either inherited from Rammohun's legacy or naturally possessed was this thirst for knowledge, affinity towards revisionism, and questioning the set principles of the discursive boundaries created either from within their religious or cultural communities or from the outside by the colonial master. Ramchandra Vidyabagish, Iswarchandra Vidyasagar, or Akshay Dutta were all part of such a narrative of revisionist scepticism and thus fitted into the milieu that grew in later years around the *Tattwabodhini Patrika*. No wonder, years later, Protap Chandra Mozoomdar described Rammohun as the one 'who lighted the holy lamp of eclectic theism'.[16] The word 'eclectic' is significantly complex, and I shall come back to it later in the chapter.

Expectedly, Rammohun was attacked by traditionalist Hindus such as Mrityunjay Vidyalankar, the head pundit of the Fort William College, and Radhakanta Deb, who later went on to form the Dharma Sabha in 1829 as a response to the Atmiya Sabha. There was a long discourse that followed between Rammohun and Mrityunjay, Rammohun replying in detail to every accusation of deviance from Hinduism that Mrityunjay levelled against him. This debate is contained in the two books *Vedanta Chandrika* (1817), by Mrityunjay Vidyalankar, and *A Second Defence of the Monotheistical System of the Veds* (1817), by Rammohun Roy.[17] Calling him the 'learned Brahmun', Rammohun retorts in his treatise thus:

It is very much to be feared that, from the perusal of this treatise, called the lunar light of the vedant, but filled up with satirical fables, abusive expressions, and contradictory assertions, sometimes admitting monotheism, but at the same time blending with it and defending polytheism, those foreign gentleman, as well as those natives of this country who are not acquainted with the real tenets of the Vedant, might on a superficial view, form a very unfavourable opinion of that theology, which however treats with perfect consistency of the unity and universality of the Supreme Being, and forbids positively, treating with contempt or behaving ill towards any creature whatsoever.[18]

Contrary to the popular Hindu traditionalist rhetoric, Rammohun's defence of monotheism or Unitarianism in the Vedanta was not meant to please the colonial master. As I have already mentioned, there was a radical intent in his embracing of Christian Unitarianism. This radicalism was also part of his intention in his reply and critique of Mrityunjay Vidyalankar's invective against him, a complex attempt at reformism and modernity to rescue the native indigenous population from the constrictive apparatus of Hindu religious practices. We will discover in Akshay Dutta a similar pattern of radical politics, at once equanimous and firm. Ranajit Guha has discovered in Rammohun's approach to religion and theology not only a close reading of the *shastra*s, or a faith in the rational, but also an abiding compassion mingled in worldly knowledge.[19] In a way, this is where one would discover Rammohun's radicalism. Not only is he well read in the *shastra*s, Guha writes, but he also respects the *shastra*s. But he uses them to consolidate rationalism.[20] And when everything is discounted by the unreason of dogma, Rammohun appeals to the compassion or *daya* of the human heart, its capacity to see beyond the structure of organized religion.[21]

Rammohun's tryst with Christianity in India was not any less complicated. An early record in the 'Periodical Account' of 1816 of the Baptist Mission at Serampore describes him as '... a simple theist, admires Jesus Christ, but knows not his *need* of the atonement'.[22] As staunch Calvinists, however, both William Carey and Joshua Marshman of Serampore were critical of Rammohun's *Precepts of Jesus* (1820), which admonished Trinitarian Christianity and upheld Unitarianism, and Marshman called him a heathen. What ensued was a long and protracted debate beyond the scope of the book. However, it was at the same Baptist Mission at Serampore where Rammohun befriended Reverend William Adam a few years later, and through a series of conversations, Reverend Adam began to see, if not be convinced by, Rammohun's Unitarian rationale. In a lecture delivered much later on the life of Rammohun, Adam recollected:

Love of freedom was perhaps the strongest passion of his soul, – freedom not of action merely, but of thought.... This tenacity of personal independence, this sensitive jealousy of the slightest approach to an encroachment on his mental freedom was accompanied with a very nice perception of the equal rights of others, even of those who differed most widely from him.[23]

The *Samachar Darpan*, a periodical issued from the Serampore Mission Press, continued a sustained invective against Rammohun's Unitarian beliefs, and in his *Brahmanical Magazine* Rammohun pseudonymously defended his faith against Trinitarian Christianity sometimes as Shivaprasad Sharma, sometimes as Ram Doss, and sometimes in the name of his friend Prosunno Coomar Tagore. In a letter to a certain gentleman of Baltimore, Rammohun wrote that his view of Christianity was that 'in representing all mankind as the children of one eternal Father, it enjoins them to love one another, without making any distinction of country, caste, colour, or creed'.[24] In the same manner as he had berated the orthodox representatives of Hinduism, he criticizes the Christian Trinitarians and lays down for them the Vedantic principle of the 'one being', which is the regulating principle of the universe. He writes:

> The divine homage which we offer consists solely in the practice of *Daya*, or benevolence towards each other, and not in a fanciful faith, or in certain motions of the feet, arms, head, tongue, or other bodily organs, in a pulpit or before a temple.[25]

There is a direct systemic link between this Rammohun and some of his later followers such as Akshay Dutta. In his speech, William Adam has given us important markers to understand this link. Apparently, most of the debates that were happening around Rammohun at this time were theological or religious in nature. It was about understanding the *shastra*s or about the various tenets of Christianity. Be it about Unitarianism versus Trinitarianism, or about ways of being a good Hindu, or about searching for a median path of everyday practice in the Atmiya Sabha, all of these would form a kind of context within which we may place Adam's speech. He emphasizes 'freedom of thought', 'personal independence', and 'equal rights' as the principal concerns of Rammohun's philosophy. No doubt each one of these has its own contextual relevance and is open to present-day critique. However, in the context of Rammohun's society and location, these expressions call for a closer reading that would perhaps be able to explain his influence on the generation of Akshay Dutta. The various repressive dynamics of a colonial system need not be overemphasized. On the other hand, there was a considerable hegemonic influence of the traditional Hindu supremacists who vouched on the inviolability of the *shastra*s and *sanatan dharma* and demanded a certain natural allegiance from the common householder or the *grihastha*. Naturally, such notions as 'freedom' or 'independence' or 'equal rights' were alien to the native subject, even within the contemporary personal space.[26] By eliciting the rationalist from the Puranic, and locating the sacred within the secular, Rammohun was initiating a new form of religious historiography that would attract such liberal intellectuals as Akshay Dutta, Iswarchandra Gupta, Iswarchandra Vidyasagar, and their likes in later years. It was not the irascibility of the Young Bengal[27] but a reasoned reinterpretation of the *shastric* through a close reading of the Vedanta that instilled a new confidence in these young men. As David Kopf writes: 'Rammohun was compelled to think comparatively, with the result that his vision sharpened in a refreshingly expansive manner, leaving a narrow sectarian view of the universe behind forever.'[28] His Brahmo Sabha was therefore opening up a space for cultural and historiographic representations that invested colonial modernity with an emancipatory past that was in agreement with the liberalist cosmopolitanism of the western-educated youth who followed in his footsteps.

Akshay Dutta and Iswarchandra Vidyasagar were among the earliest Bengali intellectuals who championed the cause of the vernacular as a means of education, particularly in the sciences. They wanted the common person to read western science in the native language, and accordingly produced textbooks in Bengali. I will discuss this in detail in a later chapter. Even in this, however, they found a precursor in Rammohun. In the first place, he was instrumental in running a Bengali newspaper called the *Sambad Kaumudi* and a Persian newspaper called the *Mirat-al-Akhbar*, both of which dealt with religious, moral, and political matters. Rammohun also wrote a tract in Persian called the *Tuhfat-al-Muwahhidin*, in praise of Deism, and translated into Bengali the relevant tracts of the Vedanta and the Bible that consolidated monotheism.[29] His biographer Sophia Collet compares him to Wycliffe in England and Luther in Germany because of his contributions to the Bengali language. She writes how through Rammohun 'the despised dialect of the common people was made the vehicle of the highest ideas and became thereby permanently elevated. Reformation in religion has often proved ennoblement in language.'[30] No doubt there was a significant motive in this. The emphasis on the vernacular was not only a move towards the enlightenment of a population that did not read Sanskrit but also a significant move towards modernity – a modernity that would embrace enlightenment through western modes of scientific education. In his much-quoted letter to Lord Amherst in 1823, Rammohun writes how 'the Sanskrit system of education would be the best calculated to keep this country in darkness' and he would rather that 'a more liberal and enlightened system of instruction, embracing mathematics, natural philosophy, chemistry, anatomy, with other useful sciences'.[31] As I have said before, Akshay Dutta came into the fold of the Brahmo movement quite accidentally through his friend Iswarchandra Gupta. For a single-minded and determined votary of western education, scientific empiricism, and vernacular means of education, a precursor such as Rammohun had already prepared a narrative. It will perhaps not be an overstatement to suggest that through the often fraught guidance of Debendranath, Akshay Dutta slid naturally into the shoes left behind by Rammmohun. Ranajit Guha discusses how many of the initial beneficiaries of western education imbibed 'a superficial Anglicism'[32] that led to the mere mimicry of the liberalism of metropolitan England, in the form of the Derozians. He sets them clearly apart from 'the far more momentous, far more difficult, and indeed qualitatively different struggles and achievements of Rammohun Roy and Iswarchandra Vidyasagar'.[33] One of the reasons for writing this book is to suggest that it is almost imperative to mention Akshay Dutta with the other two and discuss his role and contribution at this very crucial moment of the history of the Bengali people. Guha makes another important point which needs to be understood in this context. He talks about the movement of language from signality to semioticity. An English education for the native youth could suitably work as a hegemonic instrument for ideological manoeuvres, and the English language would be used for the task of 'committing the colonized to the notion of colonialism as a historically necessary and beneficial development'.[34] This is where the roles of Rammohun earlier and the likes of Akshay Dutta and Vidyasagar a little later were so crucial. Their liberalism was suitably excited by enlightenment philosophy, western sciences, and principles laid down by Bacon or Locke. However, they were not imitators, mimic men, or docile subjects. In fact, in one of his essays, Ramkrishna Bhattacharya emphatically claims that 'Rammohun's rationalism was *not* derived from the West'.[35] In fact, Bhattacharya claims, when Rammohun was writing his tracts on rationalism in Persian, he did not have enough training in the English language, or any other western language for that matter: 'His mindset apparently had already been made up before he learnt English. What Western education (learnt privately, not in any academic institution) taught him only reinforced his conviction in the power of reason.'[36] The subject position of the colonial intellectual was redefined through this emphasis on vernacular education, and the development of the spoken language of the commoner into an academic instrument.

The Foundations of Eclecticism: Akshay Dutta and Brahmo Philosophy

There is, undoubtedly, a sense of collation in Rammohun's idea of monotheism. Evidently, he was influenced by the principle of a single god in Judaism, Christianity, and Islam. He went back to the ancient shastric texts and deliberately revived those portions from the *shastra*s that spoke about the *advaita* (or non-dual) idea of a Supreme Being. The emergence of the Brahmo Sabha as a universalist theistic society in 1828 was foundationally dependent on influences that had manifold origins – in terms of both culture and cartography. Kopf has argued how this radical approach to religion and society 'emerged out of the changing conditions of the nineteenth-century world. It challenged many of the religious presuppositions of the traditional societies of Eurasian civilizations.'[37] What Rammohun and, later on, his followers such as Debendranath or Akshay Dutta were looking for was perhaps a new identity for the colonized subject trained on principles of rationality, yet a narrative that would not easily succumb to the accusations of blind imitation of the colonial ethic of enlightenment or worship. While they associated the irrational with idolatry, their idea of the Supreme Being was invested with a faith that was culled directly from ancient Hindu texts. This was not a very easy problem to face. On the one hand, enlightenment education had clearly put their rationalism in the way of a blind faith in contemporary religious practice endorsed by such associations as the Dharma Sabha. On the other hand, Rammohun's tryst with Christianity and its Trinitarian practitioners had made him wary of the many traps of western essentialism. However, theirs was not exactly a median path between the colonizer's religion and that of the colonized; neither was it the compromise of a Hinduism invested with a flavour of colonial modernity. It was in fact a complex cultural construction invested with a heterogeneity that was instrumental in bringing intellectuals of various dispositions together.

It is in this context that Brian Hatcher has discussed the crucial difference between syncretism and eclecticism.[38] Roughly defined, syncretism may be understood as the cultural construction of religion where there is a combination of various religious forms, a collation of sorts, that 'blends', 'synthesizes', or 'harmonizes' the various religious constructions into a kind of singularity.[39] There is a certain historical narrativization involved in the process of syncretism, the marking of a process of change. Eclecticism, on the other hand, is a much more delicate and subtle process, a hermeneutics of sort. As Hatcher writes, it does not denote

> patterns and processes of historical change, but a particular method of change – a method based on conscious selection – and the systems of criteria and classification that may (or may not) guide this method. To follow this distinction, syncretism names a historical process, while eclecticism names a method of interpretation and appropriation.[40]

Hatcher goes on to talk about individual guidance and 'intention and purpose'[41] involved in the methodology of eclecticism. With this important distinction Hatcher is probably talking about a smaller scale and a greater intensity. In fact, if one were to study the history of the Brahmo movement, the presence of strong individual leaders is immediately discernible. At the same time, the intellectual history of the Samaj shows us a methodological variety, not only in the diverse nature of the Atmiya Sabha, but also in the various debates between Debendranath and Akshay Dutta in later years, or the presence of Iswarchandra Vidyasagar as an ardent outsider invested in the publication and dissemination of the *Tattwabodhini Patrika*. Most of the major stakeholders were also trained in western rationalist traditions. They had read their Bacon, Hume, and Locke and were critically engaged with the colonizer on issues of religious and cultural representation. There was an aura of modernity around Brahmoism, debate, and discussion, and Hindu religious identity, however radical, was for the first time in the nineteenth century being invested with a spirit of democracy. As Hatcher writes, 'the democratic eclecticism of the Brahmos may be seen to reflect the peculiar context of religious reform in early-nineteenth-century Calcutta'.[42] Hatcher also problematizes this further by bringing in the idea of scepticism. Radical reactions to Hindu orthodoxy would manifest itself in either the eclecticism of the Brahmo movement or the scepticism of the Young Bengal. However, eclecticism and scepticism were not necessarily exclusive in their identities. Many sceptics who questioned traditional religious practice would not radicalize themselves in the manner of the Derozians and start eating beef, or convert to Christianity, or relinquish all ties with their Hindu identity. Instead, they would choose the eclectic way of selective appropriation, which would both problematize the discursive framework of Hindu identitarianism and yet not be immediately essentialized by the tropes of colonial modernity.

> How closely skepticism and eclecticism were intertwined in colonial Calcutta can be seen when examining the biographies of the many young Bengali men for whom an English education served to undercut their allegiance to Hindu norms but failed to guide them into the Christian fold. One thinks of men like Tarachand Chuckerbutty, Ramtanu Lahiri, Rajnarain Bose, and Akshay Kumar Dutt. These were men who found themselves caught in a tug-of-war between rationalistic skepticism and the theological eclecticism of groups like the Brahmo Samaj.[43]

Most of them, however, and chiefly Akshay Dutta, could strike a fine balance between scepticism and eclecticism, at least during their initial years of association with the Brahmo Samaj. There were major differences between Debendranath and Akshay on the nature of the Supreme Being and/or the universe as such, and Debendranath's deep faith in revelation was consistently undercut by Akshay's firm belief in natural theology. This is where, perhaps, Akshay was closer to Rammohun than Debendranath. As Ramkrishna Bhattacharya has pointed out, Rammohun 'speaks neither of liberation (*mukti*) nor of realizing God as the end of life. He does not believe in the virtue of prayer as a means of getting rid of troubles (*durgati*) or cure from diseases. He has no faith in any revealed text.'[44]

The important thing to understand here is that there was a certain contingent notion of religiosity, worship, faith, and practice within Brahmoism in spite of its close association with Hinduism. There was a space for interpretation, for a hermeneutics that could be the site for rationality and scientism. There was a possibility of co-existence in spite of major differences in the conception of god or exegetical analyses. As Hatcher writes, 'by opening up the world to exegesis, the Brahmos effectively admitted the possibility of deriving truths from the evidence that might be found in the record of humanity's religious experience'.[45] It was, therefore, a rational, choice-based, hermeneutical, and intentional world of religious thought that Akshay Dutta stepped into while still in his teens, and contributed to its intellectual flourishing in the next couple of decades.

Akshay Dutta and Debendranath Tagore: A Fraught Friendship

In order to understand Akshay Dutta's milieu and his influence on contemporary society in nineteenth-century Calcutta, we need to specifically understand his relationship with the most important figure of the Brahmo Samaj after Rammohun, Debendranath Tagore. The first reference to Akshay Dutta in Sivanath Sastri's *History of the Brahmo Samaj* (1911) is with reference to the theological school called the Tattwabodhini Pathshala that Debendranath founded in 1840 to 'train up a number of young men in the principles of the new faith'.[46] Sastri writes: 'A youthful and enthusiastic scholar and writer, named Akshay Kumar Dutta, was appointed a teacher of this institution. He subsequently took an important part in moulding the theology of the Samaj.[47]

It is in the context of this 'moulding' that Sastri refers to here that we need to contextualize the location of Akshay Dutta within the rubric of the Samaj. There is a certain beatific narrative that associates Debendranath with the Brahmo Sabha movement, and his becoming the torchbearer a few years after Rammohun's departure and death. Sastri calls this 'providence' and his conversion from the daily worship of Kali or Parvati as 'miraculous'.[48] There is also the other popular narrative of Debendranath, having already given up idolatry completely, chancing upon a 'page from some Sanskrit book flutter past me'.[49] When Shyamacharan Bhattacharya (the son of the Tagore family pundit Kamalakanta Chudamani) was unable to explain the meaning of the Sanskrit words on the page, Ramchandra Vidyabagish was requested to explain the contents to Debendranath. Ramchandra discovered this to be a page from the *Isha Upanishad* (one of the twelve *shruti*, or revelation texts) and unpacked the meaning for Debendranath.[50] He was deeply moved by this verse from the Upanishad that spoke about the entire universe being the manifestation of god through nature and the message of the renunciation of worldly pleasure. He writes in his autobiography:

> … when the divine voice declared that I should renounce all desire of worldly pleasure and take my delight in God alone, I obtained what I had wished for, and was utterly flooded with joy. It was not the dictum of my own poor intellect, it was the word of God Himself…. My faith in God took deep root; in lieu of worldly pleasure I tasted divine joy.[51]

With the help of Ramchandra Vidyabagish he started reading the *Isha*, *Kena*, *Katha*, *Mundaka*, and *Mandukya Upanishads*, and subsequently on the day of *krishna chaturdashi* (fourteenth day of the dark half of the moon) he founded the Tattwaranjini Sabha, whose object was 'the diffusion of the deep truth of all our *shastra*s and the knowledge of Brahma as inculcated in the Vedanta'.[52] In the second meeting of the Sabha, Ramchandra Vidyabagish was ordained as the *acharya*. He renamed it the Tattwabodhini Sabha, and thus on 6 October 1839 the Sabha was formally founded.

Clearly, the dialectic between faith and reason was foundationally present within the working of the Brahmo Samaj. The manifestation of god in the phenomenal world, which was the crux of the verse from the Upanishad that was responsible for Debendranath's epiphany, was simultaneously accompanied by his idea of the Vedanta as revelation and therefore *apaurusheya* or not composed by man. This is where Akshay's rationalism and his belief in the works of Bacon and Comte intervened. This is a complex space and needs to be unpacked with caution. Anyone reading on Akshay Dutta is familiar with the often-referred episode of his explanation to some students of the Hindu College about the importance of prayer. Akshay's equation in discounting the role of prayer in human life was simple:

Labour = Crops
Labour + Prayer = Crops
∴ Prayer = 0[53]

However, I believe that the importance of this equation need not be overemphasized. Many discussions on the religious vision of Akshay Dutta are predicated on the somewhat simplistic assumption that this equation holds the key to his rejection of the necessity of prayer through rationalism. Even Ramkrishna Bhattacharya accords it a value it perhaps does not deserve. In his essay, Bhattacharya is keen to establish Akshay's atheism: 'He began his career as an Adi Brahmo Samaj activist (he was one of the editors of the *Tattwabodhini Patrika*) but proceeded slowly but steadily first towards agnosticism and then to uncompromising atheism.'[54] Bhattacharya uses this equation to consolidate his argument. Ashish Lahiri, one of the important discussants on Akshay Dutta among the present-day Bengali intelligentsia, also uses this equation as one of the means of establishing Akshay's atheism.[55] In my opinion, however, such attempts are clear simplifications of a complex and nuanced mind, pulled into myriad directions by the spirit of the times. Prayer has many forms and multiple intentions. In this case, Akshay was talking about a particular kind of prayer – the prayer that asks for some material benefit from god. This, according to Akshay's perspective on the idea of an immanent god, was not a possibility. Crops in this case, as well as the entire material world, were a manifestation of god's design and will, and no amount of prayer could change this. But that does not go on to suggest that Akshay discounted the value of prayer as such. As he writes in the *Tattwabodhini Patrika*:

> The One who has established rules of nature for the welfare of mankind, the One who has given in abundance water, air and light so that mankind does not have to pay for it … is it not our duty to be grateful towards Him? Is it not proper to bestow upon Him our heartfelt respect? [56]

It will be difficult to logically establish Akshay's atheism in this context, at least during the period when he wrote this equation. There was a complex mix of theism and positivism in Akshay's ethic. In his own way, Akshay was trying to evolve a methodology of worship or faith – an eclectic hermeneutics of practising his own *dharma*. In my opinion, in trying to label Akshay as an atheist, critics such as Ramkrishna Bhattacharya and Ashish Lahiri were missing the nuances of a complex mind, and possibly trying to lead the readers towards a specific and narrow politics of understanding. In this context I would also like to mention Saradacharan Mitra's essay 'Akshaykumarke Jemon Dekhechhi' (As I Have Seen Akshaykumar), in which he recounts his personal interactions with Akshay.[57] As a close associate and an executor of Akshay's will, Saradacharan had seen him from close quarters during his last days. He writes how Akshay's bedroom had paintings of Newton and Darwin. He also gives us an interesting piece of information. The draft of Akshay's will, prepared by one of Saradacharan's assistants, began with the invocation 'Sri Sri Hari'. When Saradacharan took it to Akshay, he enquired if it was mandatory to invoke god at the beginning of the will, and if it was possible to replace it with the word 'Viswaveej' – literally translated as the 'cause of the universe'.[58] Saradacharan concludes that such an observation from Akshay was symptomatic of the revolution that was happening within him in terms of his religious faith. However, I emphatically insist, this does not suggest, as some of his biographers have observed, that Akshay had become an atheist in his later life.

No doubt there were obvious and unbridgeable differences between Debendranath and Akshay Dutta as there were between the other members of the early Tattwabodhini Sabha – Iswarchandra Gupta, Iswarchandra Vidyasagar, Ramgopal Ghosh, Rajendralal Mitra, and Ramaprasad Ray. Their commonality lay less in their individual conceptions of Brahma and more in their zeal for social and cultural reform. As Hatcher writes:

> Readers familiar with the history of nineteenth-century Bengal will recognize in this roster some of the most vocal and industrious men active in educated society before the middle of the century. Even this simple list serves to reveal a range of strikingly divergent family backgrounds, ranging from rural Brahmin (Isvarchandra) to urban progressive (Ramaprasada), as well as a gamut of attitudinal dispositions that runs from cautious scholarship (Rajendralal) to savvy business acumen (Ramgopal).[59]

One can imagine that there were smaller coteries among this group of men, like-minded individuals veering towards each other, and as Hatcher puts it succinctly, 'there was complexity at the very start'.[60] The most fraught among these relationships was perhaps the one between Debendranath and Akshay. Akshay was personally handpicked by Debendranath, and when the latter decided to publish the *Tattwabodhini Patrika* in 1843, he asked several members to submit essays so that he could pick an editor from among them for the journal. He liked Akshay's essay the most and selected him as the editor, although the differences between the two were already apparent:

> In his essay there appeared to me to be good points as well as bad. The good points were that his style was very charming and graceful. The fault that I found with it was that he had sung the praises of the matted-haired, ash-begrimed *sannyasi* living under a tree; but I was not in favour of the symbolism of outward renunciation. I thought, however, that if I was careful about the opinions expressed, I could certainly utilise him as an editor....[61]

Incidentally, it was in the same year that Akshay Dutta, along with twenty other members of the Sabha, formally embraced the Brahmo Dharma promulgated by Debendranath. In a few days' time, Akshay was also helping Debendranath to write the sacred book of Brahmo Dharma.[62] If one were to go by the arguments of atheism put forward by the likes of Ramkrishna Bhattacharya or Ashish Lahiri, it would be to divest Akshay Dutta of any agency as an intellectual or a thinker. It would seem as if it was merely to keep his job at the *Tattwabodhini Patrika* on a salary of 8 rupees a month that Akshay accepted a change of religion and meekly submitted to the will of his master. As we shall see in the course of this book, Akshay Dutta went through multiple phases of doubt and belief. He was struggling, as any intellectual would, with his belief and ideology all his life. He would have serious doubts about faith in god or belief systems which led him to write, towards the end of his life, perhaps the most serious work of his life, *Bharatvarshiya Upashak Sampraday*, in two volumes, where he explores in great detail and with empirical precision the questions of faith and religiosity. But to insist, along the lines of Ramakrishna Bhattacharya, that he was an 'uncompromising atheist' is to discount the complexity of one of the finest minds of nineteenth-century Bengal.

Debendranath brought the Brahmo Samaj and the Tattwabodhini Sabha together,[63] and the meetings of the Sabha were merged with those of the Samaj. Akshay was an intrinsic part of both. His faith in the Brahma was part of his faith in natural theology, and was always accompanied by the scepticism of the rational mind. He would question the means and the methodology, which led to protracted debates with Debendranath. But he would rarely doubt the presence of the Brahma. Incidentally, Debendranath's insistence on the divinely revelatory (or *apaurusheya*) nature of the Vedas was opposed not only by Akshay, but also by other members of the Samaj, such as Ramgopal Ghosh and Ramtanu Lahiri.[64] It is important to understand that this was an intellectual debate on the question of methodology and germane to the climate of curiosity and reformism of the time. Debendranath participated actively in the debate as both a mentor and an adversary. It will only be a narrow logic to assume that Debendranath was trying to establish his opinion by force, although there is little doubt that he fervently believed in the position he was defending. In order to consolidate his position, Debendranath sent four students, Ananda Chandra Bhattacharya, Ramanath Bhattacharya, Baneshwar Bhattacharya, and Taranath Bhattacharya, to Kashi (present-day Varanasi) to study the Vedas. Later he himself travelled to Kashi, and in 1849 returned with Ananda Chandra Vedantabagish to continue the debate. Kshitindranath Tagore, the last editor of the *Tattwabodhini Patrika*, writes in the Jaisthya, Saka 1839 (1917), issue of the *Patrika* on the debate:

> ... around this time there was a debate between Debendranath and Akshay Kumar Dutta.... Debendranath himself travelled to Kashidham

to discuss the *Vedas* and the *Vedantas*, and returned in *Saka 1769* with
Anandachandra Vedantabagish. It was due to this discussion that in
the beginning of the same year the Brahmo Samaj was freed from the
notion of the infallibility of the *Vedas*.... It is difficult to imagine now
what immense mental strength was needed to arrive at this decision ... a
great spiritual revolution happened without bloodshed.... Debendranath
never denied that he was helped in this by Akshaykumar.[65]

Read between the lines, the above piece does not ascribe any agency to
Debendranath. Rather, it reflects on how Debendranath had to swallow a
bitter pill in spite of being the driving force behind the Samaj. No doubt this
was one of the most foundationally crucial events within the Brahmo Samaj
and had its impact across all spaces of religious practice in contemporary
society. It was an ideological battle fought with dignity and mutual respect on
either side. Of course, it was an important defeat for Debendranath, the leader
of the Samaj. However, I do not think that this incident can be used to create
an easy binary between the intellectual worlds of Debendranath and Akshay.
They were literally founding a new religion, and the zeitgeist of the milieu
they inhabited was one of debate and discussion. Too many influences were
working at the same time: Hinduism, and the debates around it, in the larger
part of the society; Christianity, its branches, and questions of conversion
of natives;[66] the subtle differences between enlightenment modernity
and colonial modernity, and its manifestations in *bhadralok* society;[67] the
comparatism practised by the colonial master in reading the present time
against a more philosophically and spiritually evolved past, among many
others. It was a complex web of influences and counter-influences, a careful
methodological selection and rejection through which the philosophy of
the Samaj was emerging. Considering its impact on contemporary society,
it would perhaps be unfair to think of either the Brahmo Samaj or the
Tattwabodhini Sabha as being run on the whims of Debendranath Tagore,
as critics such as Ashish Lahiri have done. Motley intellectuals had come
together to consider the evolution of a communitarian religious ethic invested
in modernity, and distinctly different from either contemporary Hinduism or
the borrowed Christianity of the colonial master. Whether such 'bourgeois
Hinduism' of the *bhadralok* succeeded or not is another question, discussed
by Brian Hatcher in his work *Bourgeois Hinduism* and beyond the scope of my
concern in this book.

It is not that Debendranath did not express his disappointment with the way his intention of moulding Akshay to the editorial needs of the paper did not succeed. Neither is it that he subscribed to Akshay's views just because he lost the debate on the infallibility of the Vedas. In his autobiography he regrets how in the Friends' Society, a group started by Akshay, 'the nature of God was decided upon by a show of hands'.[68] He regretted that he did not see signs of religious feeling or piety in those who surrounded him, and that 'each only pitted his own intellect and power against the other'.[69] In a letter to Rajnarayan Basu he even expressed his disgust at how the paper committee of the *Tattwabodhini Patrika* (responsible for selecting essays to be published in it) was run by some *nastik*s (atheists), in all probability hinting at Akshay Dutta and Iswarchandra Vidyasagar.[70] Still, in the introduction to Debendranath's autobiography, his son Satyendranath Tagore calls Akshay Dutta the 'intellectual leader' of the Samaj and Debendranath its 'spiritual head': 'At a general meeting of the Brahmos, it was agreed that the Vedas, Upanishads, and other ancient writings were not to be accepted as infallible guides, that Reason and Conscience were to be the supreme authority....'[71] Even in the years after the Akshay–Debendranath debate, speculations about whether Akshay Dutta was a theist, agnostic, or atheist continued within the Samaj and outside. Rajnarayan Basu called him an agnostic, and Dwijendranath Tagore, a later editor of the *Tattwabodhini Patrika*, tried to devalue Akshay's contributions to the Samaj on similar grounds.[72] Much later, as late as 1887, while writing in *Bangla Bhasa o Sahitya Bishayak Prastab*, Ramgati Nyayratna was surprised at how Akshay had peppered the primer called *Charupath* (first published in 1852) with references to the Supreme Being. In exasperation he writes:

> God is a good thing, and it is our duty to remember him all the time, but if at the fall of the palm fruit – at the movement of the leaf – at the flight of the bird – that is if at every event one is reminded of God, then I think such instruction is never successful.[73]

What I am trying to suggest is that it is not easy to come to a definitive conclusion about whether Akshay Dutta was a theist, agnostic, or atheist. In fact, for a mind as curious and open as his, and for the milieu of continuous debate and discussion to which he belonged, it is rather simplistic to draw such a conclusion. The abstract idea of a *parameshwar* or Supreme Being could have different manifestations in his mind during different times in his life or, in fact, at the same time. There are always fine lines between theism, agnosticism, and atheism – and Akshay Dutta's mind was quite capable of such intermittent vacillations. Likewise, it will only be idle speculation to try and determine whether Debendranath threw Akshay Dutta out of the *Tattwabodhini Patrika* or he left on his own. There were major ideological differences between them, but also considerable mutual respect. I find it difficult, therefore, to agree with Ashish Lahiri's analysis of the relationship. Lahiri has reduced it to a relationship between the employer and the employed. He finds in Debendranath a regressive classist, a man prone to consistent self-contradiction, and completely averse to independent thinking.[74] Lahiri writes:

> If someone would oppose him rightfully, he would not tolerate that person, he did not have the necessary democratic temper. The same thing happened with Akshay Kumar. He would not tolerate a salaried editor to go against his ideology. He did not know the meaning of pluralism.[75]

This is indeed a harsh critique of Debendranath, and somewhat simplistic and skewed. In the above discussion, I have tried to counter such reductionism. Contradictions and ideological differences were part of the spirit of the times, as were the multiple ways of looking at both the phenomenal and the existential worlds. Akshay Dutta was an intellectual and a thinker in his own right. It is perhaps unnecessary to posit him against a villainously classist adversary to prove the point. I would rather agree with David Kopf than Lahiri in my assessment of the relationship between Debendranath and Akshay:

> It is a credit to Debendranath's broad sympathies as a leader of the reformation movement that he could recognize and support a young intellectual whose openly proclaimed rationalism, deism, and scientism were so alien to his own highly mystical and intimate theistic faith.[76]

Through the pages of the *Tattwabodhini Patrika*, Akshay Dutta was trying to train a reading public in a modernity and scientific spirit that had its foundations within a traditional ethic along with the capacity to think beyond the dogmas of *sanatan dharma* (the absolute set of duties or practices incumbent upon all Hindus). I shall come back to this in more detail in the next two chapters.

Akshay Dutta and Iswarchandra Vidyasagar: *Bhadralok* Allies

Between Akshay Dutta and Iswarchandra Vidyasagar, the latter is undoubtedly the more discussed figure within the framework of the cultural history of Bengal in the nineteenth century. There is enough evidence of their coming in close contact with each other and working together for a common cause, although none of the major biographers of either of them, particularly in the vernacular, has written much on the subject. They were probably not friends in the narrow sense of the word, but it is possible to surmise that among the earliest members of the Tattwabodhini Sabha, their class identities were the closest. Both of them had roots in the village, and having come to Calcutta, both of them were beginning to make a mark in the intellectual circles by virtue of their merit. Also, in the debate between Akshay and Debendranath, the former would easily find an ally in Vidyasagar. It was perhaps their abiding inclination towards scientism and rationalism that brought them together within what was largely a space of religious reform. Vidyasagar was a Hindu brahmin while Akshay, a *kayastha*, had converted to Brahmoism. However, throughout their lives both of them maintained a sceptical debate with religion and religiosity alive. Both of them championed the cause of vernacular education, and within it emphasized the singular importance of scientific rationalism and principles of morality through the writing of primers and school textbooks for children. There was a certain contingency in their approach to the question of faith. This is perhaps the reason why both of them have often engaged with the question of God and yet been termed atheists by critics and commentators. It will possibly not be off the mark to call them ethical determinists who made stringent demands on society in terms of moral responsibility towards one's fellow being and the importance of *paropakar* or doing good to one's neighbour. Akshay was clearly a deist, and Vidyasagar's essay in an early edition of the *Tattwabodhini Patrika* (which was actually a reprint of his lecture in the Tattwabodhini Sabha)[77] clearly refers to an 'all powerful God' (*sarbba shaktiman parameshwar*).[78] However, one might say that they always maintained a kind of reverential distance from god as deity. They were rather more inclined to an empirical exploration of means for the common man to lead morally principled lives based on an awareness of the world around them and a sense of duty for the fellow being. Also, Kopf's remark on Vidyasagar's reverence for western systems of knowledge will hold equally true for Akshay Dutta, and it might be said that they 'favored the modern learning of the West not because it was Western, but because the West had broken away from an uncritical, unthinking reverence for tradition'.[79]

In their own ways, the likes of Akshay and Vidyasagar were shaping the discursive contours of the milieu of the bourgeois *bhadralok*, the most significant generic figure of nineteenth-century Bengal. Beginning within the category of 'poor but bhadra',[80] they derived agency due to their education and managed to acquire positions of influence within the emergent intelligentsia. While print culture, native educational institutions, or societies and *sabhas* were still run with the money of the rentier class, it was this middle rung of the *bhadralok* population that gradually infiltrated into the intellectual or ideological moorings of such places. English education, a familiarity with the scientific and philosophical texts from the western world, and, most importantly, an implicit spirit of reform made the educated *bhadralok* the central figure of the 'renaissance'. Thus, if Debendranath were to successfully run a society or a periodical, in spite of his economic agency, he had to depend on the Akshays and the Vidyasagars to lend the necessary intellectual agency to his project. Brian Hatcher has put this succinctly:

> As advocates of an 'improved' Indian society men like Dutta and Vidyasagar held rather bourgeois notions about respectability, propriety, hard work and social responsibility. Both men were also part of a particularly influential subset of bhadralok society made up of reform-minded intellectuals associated with such progressive organisations as the Brahmo Samaj (est. 1828) and the Tattvabodhini Sabha (est. 1839). [81]

Thus, on the one hand, they were the 'new' voice of reform that someone like Debendranath would require to promote whatever his theological philosophy was; on the other hand, however, by emphasizing the bourgeois qualities of respectability, propriety, hard work, and social responsibility, these men were creating structures of influence or setting up standards for the common householder to follow or emulate. The newly emergent middle class was considerably influenced by the mores of colonial modernity. Intellectuals such as Akshay or Vidyasagar were complicating this trope by a careful collation of the western with the eastern, and promoting a practical form of indigenous religiosity invested less in *bhakti* and forms of worship and more in rationality and the daily practice of morality. It was a two-pronged way of imagining the native society through a lens of radical alterity. By forcing Debendranath to recede on his argument about the infallibility of the Vedas, they were attempting a reform from within traditional narratives of a Hindu religious ethic; at the same time, by their insistence on vernacular education, a sustained critique of imperial strategies of dominance, and bringing theory and praxis closer to each other within the domain of religion through an insistence on positivist methodologies, they were problematizing the tropes of hegemonic colonial modernity. This was the new intellectual, located within an uneasy space between the rentier class and the common householder, and through a newly acquired agency, eliciting mostly favourable responses from both sides of the divide. In this book I shall try to analyse how Akshay Dutta, through his various works, unsettled the contemporary native discourse through such strategic incursions into the cultural politics of nineteenth-century Bengal.

Impact of the Milieu: The Cultural Imaginary of Emancipation

I will conclude this chapter with a brief discussion on whether these incursions that Akshay Dutta and his ilk attempted into the lived life of the contemporary Calcutta society did really have its desired effect. This is a complex question and cannot be easily answered. Hatcher writes how the colonial middle class 'played a major part in codifying the norms of industry, domestic life, moral responsibility, religion, and worldly success that eventually became essential to modern Hindu identity'.[82] There are a few important things that need to be addressed before we subscribe to this claim. In the first place, one must remember that in spite of the efforts of Rammohun and his followers, the number of people who ultimately subscribed to the Brahmo religion were a miniscule part of the larger population. There was a certain class identity attached to the Brahmo faith. In spite of its apparent eclecticism, a confluence of people from motley backgrounds, there was a certain gentrification easily associated in popular imagination with the Brahmo faith. It was an elite space generally meant for the western-educated Bengali *bhadralok*. There was at the same time a corresponding, if not parallel, narrative of nationalism that had garnered considerable agency by the middle of the nineteenth century. The impact of the nationalists on the society of Calcutta (and Bengal) was more immediate than the more sophisticated appeal of the rationalists of the Brahmo Samaj or the Tattwabodhini Sabha. Incidentally, in spite of their strong sentiments in the matter of indigenous culture and language, Rammohun, or those who came after him, such as Debendranath, Akshay, or Vidyasagar, did not have strong nationalist sentiments. They were more reformists than nationalists, focusing on the immediate reality of educating or modernizing the population than leading an armed rebellion against the colonial power. Also, nationalism found easy iconography from within Hinduism, and the politics of binarism – Hindu–Christian, colonized–colonizer, native–*sahib* – was easier to grasp than the more sophisticated diffusion of western modernity with eastern models of daily living. More popular was the easily distinguishable model of understanding the western code as one invested in materiality and the eastern as invested in spirituality.[83]

Set in the 1880s, Rabindranath Tagore's novel *Gora* (1909) addresses this problematic of reception of western modes of thinking as evidenced through liberal Brahmo practice seen through the lens of conservative Hinduism. Early in the novel, Gora, the protagonist, visits Paresh Bhattacharya's house for the first time. At this point in the novel, Gora is a staunchly conservative Hindu who refuses to have tea at the Brahmo household of Pareshbabu. There is a brief altercation between him and Baradasundari, Pareshbabu's wife, when Gora refuses food or tea at their place:

Barada: Will you not have any of these?
Gora replied, 'No'.
Barada: Why? Will you lose your *jat*?
Gora said, 'Yes'.
Barada: You follow the diktats of *jat*?
Gora: Is the idea of *jat* my creation that I'll discount it? If I abide by the rules laid down by the society (*samaj*), I also abide by the diktats of *jat*.
Barada: Does one have to go by everything laid down by the *samaj*?
Gora: If not then one is breaking the rules.
Barada: What is the harm?
Gora: What is the harm in sawing the branch of the tree on which all of us are sitting? [84]

Soon, on the same occasion Gora is involved in another altercation with the Brahmo schoolmaster Haranchandra Nag when the latter refers to and critiques certain rituals of the Bengali people. Gora quips: 'What you refer to as regressive rituals are things you know nothing of, but only a result of mugging up English books. Speak of these when you can dismiss the regressive rituals of the English in the same way.' [85] Clearly, therefore, there was a narrative of rejection, trained on ideas of nativism and nationalism that were equally relevant in the context of colonial modernity.

It is also crucial to understand that figures such as Akshay Dutta or Vidyasagar were not typically invested in the dissemination of the Brahmo Dharma. Vidyasagar was not even a Brahmo. As I have already discussed, they came together within the rubric of the Tattwabodhini Sabha as votaries of eclecticism, but the question of God, even if important, was not central to their ethic. Religious reform for the likes of Akshay Dutta was incidental to the larger canvas of dissemination of scientific or philosophical knowledge and rationalism, and to determine a narrative of a modern life-world for the society at large. Therefore, contrary to Debendranath's wish, the *Tattwabodhini Patrika*, under the editorship of Akshay, became more of an organ for discussing scientific, philosophical, historical, and social issues rather than one for preaching the Brahmo Dharma. Mahendranath Ray writes: '... that instead of being a purely religious organ *Tattwabodhini* became a receptacle for many other lively and informative subjects such as literature, science, history, biography, philosophy etcetera was due to the enthusiasm, sincere effort and relentless industry of Akshaybabu'.[86] For Akshay, god was not a mystical or metaphysical presence, but a strict guardian of moral principles and ethical values, and manifest in the phenomenal everyday world. Under his aegis, the *Tattwabodhini Patrika* became thus an organ for celebrating the presence of god through educating the masses about the world around them. He insisted in private conversations on the value of the *Tattwabodhini* as being 'beneficial for the masses'.[87]

In conclusion, in order to comprehend or assess Akshay Dutta's impact on the social and cultural history of an emergent Bengali modernity in the nineteenth century, it is crucial to understand his peculiar location within the larger framework of his milieu and beyond. His religious and moral philosophy were entrenched in a study of the universe manifest as the elementary text (*viswarup mul grantha*), and every order that determined the workings of human life was to be culled from this self-evident textbook of natural theology. As he writes in the 1773 Saka, Phalgun issue of the *Tattwabodhini Patrika*: 'Whoever from whichever part of the world will diligently read and comprehend the core meaning of this profound elementary text (the universe) will be able to allay the delusions of another. There is no other way of acquiring true knowledge, no second way of inculcating religious education.'[88] His insistence on the necessity of training in the English language, or reading the philosophical and scientific texts of the western world such as Newton or

Laplace or Bacon or Comte did not come in the way of his reverence for the works of Bhaskaracharya or Aryabhatta or Gautama or Kanad.[89] It is possible that his scientism was mostly a result of his reading of continental scientific texts, but his rational rigour, similar in so many ways to Rammohun's, did not prevent him from questioning the tenets of western religiosity. As he writes: 'Faith in Hinduism is being dissipated due to scientific knowledge. It is due to the influence of science that the foundations of Christianity have been consistently shaken.'[90] Evidently, he carried this idea of the fallibility of religious ideologies as he became instrumental in the foundation of the new faith of Brahmo Dharma. Without foregrounding the question of his faith in god as such, it is possible to unpack his misgivings about religious practice. His debate with Debendranath was less about the question of the manifestation of god and more about the cultural and social implications of the moral universe that Brahmoism was going to open up for its followers. Idol worship was not Akshay Dutta's concern. He was already beyond that. For him, the new faith meant a celebration of a code of living that followed a narrative of rationality invested in the moral psyche of the people. To call it 'liberal' is to simplify the matter. In a sense it was more complicated than the mere induction of a set of people into a new faith – a faith that had supposedly culled the best of many religions, divested itself of dogma, and was instrumental, in certain ways, in the spread of modernity. For him, Brahmoism was a way of life more than a religious movement. And he was one of the key figures instrumental in its founding and dissemination. In much of his writings during that time, and till many years after, he was trying to establish rules for a righteous and moral life for the common man. In his introduction to the second volume of *Bahyabastur Sahit Manab Prakritir Sammandha Vichar*, he insists on how the best way to serve god was to follow the set of rules that He has laid down for the world. To be mindful of these sets of rules and follow them with happiness was the true *dharma* of the believer: 'What are the rules that have been set so far, and how to learn and follow these rules have been laid down as far as possible in this book. Thus, this book is useful for the religious education of the Brahmos.'[91] A careful scrutiny will reveal that Akshay is more keen here on a positivist exercise rather than any religious fervour. His idea of a mind inclined to religious practice was one that followed a set category of rules for personal and social harmony. Mahendranath Ray writes how, for Akshay, the ways of a religious life were to show kindness to living beings, a spirit of friendliness, use of chaste language, and a propensity for charity.[92] Also, Ray writes that, for Akshay, to follow rules was *dharma* and to ignore them was *adharma*.[93] He goes on to suggest that while by founding the Brahmo Samaj Rammohun had paved the way for religious reform, it was left to people like Akshay to make it acceptable to the educated class.[94] It might thus be said that Akshay's interventions invested a kind of cosmopolitan modernity to the Brahmo Samaj and moulded it suitably for the use of the *bhadralok*. In the next few chapters I shall attempt a close reading of some of Akshay Dutta's works to understand his influences and the basis of his scientific and philosophical training. There were significant breaks in and continuous revisions of his ideas that shaped the trajectory and intention of what he wrote and why he wrote. I shall try to read these changes into the larger debates on religion and modernity, nationalism and colonial modernity, and the shaping of the cultural and intellectual life of nineteenth-century Bengal. In the chapter that immediately follows this I will examine the role of Akshay Dutta as a 'science worker' within a rather complex dynamic of scientific training and education in nineteenth-century colonial India.

Notes

1. David Kopf, *The Brahmo Samaj and the Shaping of the Modern Indian Mind* (Princeton: Princeton University Press, 1979), p. 42.

2. Previously, I have distinguished between the two forms of modernity that were manifested within the colonial space of Calcutta – one that had a direct bearing on administrative decisions and forms of governmentality and invested in the running of the system of colonialism, while the other was brought in through intellectual and epistemic shifts and was more directly informed by the logic of enlightenment and catered primarily to the upper and middle classes in terms of their intellectual pursuits. The former I have termed 'managerial modernity'. See Sumit Chakrabarti, *The Calcutta Kerani and the London Clerk in the Nineteenth Century* (London: Routledge, 2021), p. 8.

3. In his biography of Akshay Dutta, Mahendranath Ray has pointed out how in his zeal for learning, Dutta had admitted himself to a free missionary school in Khidirpur soon after he came to Calcutta from his native village. His relatives, particularly his local guardian in Calcutta, Haramohan Dutta, disapproved of Akshay going to a school run by Christian missionaries. Subsequently, noticing his intense desire for learning, Haramohan admitted him to the Oriental Seminary run by

the native patriarch Gourmohan Auddy. From the biography we know how Dutta, while still in Auddy's school, was already reading Homer and Virgil, geography, and physics, and had already started to question his Puranic beliefs and the tenets of Hinduism. See Mahendranath Ray, *Srijukta Babu Akshay Kumar Dutter Jiban-brittanta* (Calcutta: Sanskrit Jantrer Pustakalaya, 1885), pp. 13–21.

4. The category of the *bhadralok* has been much discussed by the historians and social commentators on nineteenth-century Bengal. See Bhabanicharan Bandopadhyay, *Kalikata Kamalalaya* (Calcutta: Ranjan Publishing House, 1936); Sumit Sarkar, *Writing Social History* (Delhi: Oxford University Press, 1998); Partha Chatterjee, *The Nation and Its Fragments* (Princeton: Princeton University Press, 1993); Sumanta Banerjee, *The Parlour and the Street* (Calcutta: Seagull, 1989); Dipesh Chakrabarty, *Provincializing Europe* (Princeton: Princeton University Press, 2000); Tithi Bhattacharya, *The Sentinels of Culture: Class, Education, and the Colonial Intellectual in Bengal (1848–85)* (Delhi: Oxford University Press, 2005).

5. Ray, *Srijukta Babu Akshay Kumar Dutter Jiban-brittanta*, p. 44.

6. Ibid., p. 41.

7. Joya Chatterji, *Bengal Divided: Hindu Communalism and Partition, 1932–1947* (Cambridge: Cambridge University Press, 1994/2002), p. 5.

8. Bhattacharya, *The Sentinels of Culture*, p. 52.

9. For a comprehensive discussion on this, see ibid., pp. 35–67.

10. Ibid., p. 51.

11. For a brief discussion on Rammohun Roy's translation of the Upanishads, see Ramkrishna Bhattacharya, 'Rammohun Roy as Translator of the *Upanishads*' (Kolkata: Conference on Nineteenth-Century Bengal, 2006), https://www.researchgate.net/publication/308777209 (accessed on 11 August 2020).

12. Quoted in Sophia Dosbson Collet, *The Life and Letters of Raja Rammohun Roy* (Calcutta: A.C. Sarkar, 1914), p. 37.

13. For discussions on this, see Bruce Robertson, *Raja Rammohan Ray: The Father of Modern India* (New Delhi: Oxford University Press, 1999). See, especially, chapter 1, 'Rammohan Ray: An Outline Sketch of His Life and Times', pp. 32–35, and chapter 7, 'Public Controversy *Vedantacandrika* versus *Bhattacarya Sahit Bicar*'. Also see Dermot Killingley, 'Rammohun Roy's Controversies with Hindu Opponents', in *Perspectives on Indian Religion: Papers in Honour of Karel Werner*, ed. Peter Connolly (Delhi: Sri Satguru, 1986), pp. 145–159.

14. Lynn Zastoupil, 'Defining Christians, Making Britons: Rammohun Roy and the Unitarians', *Victorian Studies* 44, no. 2 (2002): 215–243, 220.

15. Ibid., p. 220.

16. Protap Chandra Mozoomdar, *The Faith and Progress of the Brahmo Somaj* (Calcutta: Calcutta Central Press, 1882), p. 1.

17. After Rammohun's death, all his responses were serially reprinted in the early issues of the *Tattwabodhini Patrika*.

18. Rammohun Roy, *A Second Defence of the Monotheistical System of the Veds: In Reply to an Apology for the Present State of Hindoo Worship* (Calcutta, 1817), pp. 1–2.

19. Ranajit Guha, *Daya: Rammohon Ray o Amader Adhunikata* (Kolkata: Talpata, 2012), p. 47.

20. Ibid., p. 17.

21. Ranajit Guha discusses these qualities of Rammohun in the context of his long and protracted battle with contemporary pundits on the subject of *satidaha* or *suttee*. For a detailed discussion on this, see Guha, *Daya*.

22. Quoted in Collet, *The Life and Letters of Raja Rammohun Roy*, p. 60.

23. Ibid., p. 71.

24. Ibid., p. 76.

25. Ibid., pp. 82–83.

26. For a nuanced understanding of Rammohun's ideas of rights, property, and indigenous subjecthood, see Milinda Banerjee, '"All This Is Indeed Brahman": Rammohun Roy and a "Global" History of the Rights-Bearing Self', *Asian Review of World Histories* 3, no. 1 (2015): 81–112.

27. The Young Bengal were a group of rebellious youth, students of the Hindu College and followers of Henry Derozio. They were known to subvert social and moral codes, upset social hierarchies, and be counter-discursive. They were also known as Derozians. Some eminent members of the Young Bengal were Krishnamohan Banerjee, Pearychand Mitra, Radhanath Sikdar, and Ramtanu Lahiri. For more details, see Sivanath Sastri, *Ramtanu Lahiri o Tatkalin Bangosamaj* (Kolkata: New Age, 2009).

28. Kopf, *The Brahmo Samaj and the Shaping of the Modern Indian Mind*, p. 13.

29. See Rammohun Roy, *Tuhfat-al-Muwahhidin or A Gift to Deists* (Calcutta: Adi Brahmo Samaj, 1889). Also see Girishchandra Sen, *Ekeshwarbadider Upahar* (Calcutta: Dharmatattva, 1899).

30. Quoted in Collet, *The Life and Letters of Raja Rammohun Roy*, pp. 112–113.

31. Ibid., p. 108.

32. Ranajit Guha, *Dominance without Hegemony: History and Power in Colonial India* (Cambridge, MA: Harvard University Press, 1997), p. 167.

33. Ibid., p. 168.

34. Ibid., p. 174.

35. Ramkrishna Bhattacharya, 'Rationalism in Bengal: An Overview', *Psyche and Society* 10, no. 1 (2012): 43–51, 46.

36. Ibid., p. 46.

37. Kopf, *The Brahmo Samaj and the Shaping of the Modern Indian Mind,* p. 3.

38. Brian Hatcher, *Eclecticism and Modern Hindu Discourse* (Oxford: Oxford University Press, 1999).

39. Ibid., p. 8.

40. Ibid.

41. Ibid., p. 9.

42. Ibid., p. 97.

43. Ibid., pp. 101–102.

44. Bhattacharya, 'Rationalism in Bengal', p. 44.

45. Hatcher, *Eclecticism and Modern Hindu Discourse*, p. 105.

46. Shibnath Sastri, *History of the Brahmo Samaj* (Calcutta: R. Chatterji, 1911), p. 8.

47. Ibid.

48. Ibid., p. 83. For a detailed critical discussion on this 'miraculous' conversion of Debendranath after the death of his grandmother in Kashi, see Brian Hatcher, *Bourgeois Hinduism, or the Faith of the Modern Vedantists: Rare Discourses from Early Colonial Bengal* (Oxford: Oxford University Press, 2008), pp. 35–38.

49. Debendranath Tagore, *The Autobiography of Maharshi Devendranath Tagore* (London: Macmillan and Co. Limited, 1914), p. 56.

50. The original verse from the *Isha Upanishad* reads:

     īśā vāsyamidaṁ sarvaṁ yatkiñca jagatyāṁ jagat |
     tena tyaktena bhuñjithā mā gṛdhaḥ kasyasviddhanam ||

The verse means: 'All this is for habitation by the Lord, whatsoever is individual universe of movement in the universal motion. By that renounced thou shouldst enjoy; lust not after any man's possession.' For this translation, see Sri Aurobindo, *Isha Upanishad, The Complete Works of Sri Aurobindo*, vol. 17 (Pondicherry: Sri Aurobindo Ashram Press, 2003), p. 5. Another translation by Patrick Olivelle reads: 'This whole world is to be dwelt in by the Lord, whatever living being there is in the world. So you should eat what has been abandoned; and do not covet anyone's wealth.' See Patrick Olivelle, *The Early Upanishads: Annotated Text and Translation* (Oxford: Oxford University Press, 1998), p. 407. For a detailed discussion on the *shloka*, also see Atul Chandra Sen, Sitanath Tattvabhushan, and Mahes Chandra Ghosh (eds.), *Upanishad: Akhanda Sangskaran* (Calcutta: Haraf Prakashani, 1980), pp. 7–8.

51. Tagore, *The Autobiography of Maharshi Debendranath Tagore*, p. 59.

52. Ibid., p. 62.

53. For a discussion on this, see Ray, *Srijukta Babu Akshay Kumar Dutter Jiban-brittanta*, pp. 92–94. This incident is mentioned in almost every critical work on Akshay Kumar Dutta and has become the easiest example of his rational spirit.

54. Bhattacharya, 'Rationalism in Bengal', p. 46.

55. See, Ashish Lahiri, *Akshaykumar Dutta: Andhar Rate Ekla Pathik* (Kolkata: Dey's Publishing, 2019), p. 60.

56. Prasad Sengupta, 'Akshaykumar Dutter Dharmabodh', in *Dwisatajanmabarshe Akshaykumar Dutta*, ed. Tapas Bhowmik, *Korok Sahitya Patrika*, January–April 2020, pp. 72–89.

57. See Saradacharan Mitra, 'Akshaykumarke Jemon Dekhechhi', in *Dwisatajanmabarshe Akshaykumar Dutta*, ed. Tapas Bhowmik, *Korok Sahitya Patrika*, Kolkata, 2020, pp. 265–270.

58. *Viswaveej*, a compound word, consists of *viswa* (world or universe) and *veej*. The word *veej* etymologically comes from the root *jan*, or to be born. In the Vedas, Puranas, Smritishastras, Tantras, and ancient medicinal treatises, and even ancient Indian mathematics, the word *veej* has been associated with *adi*, that is, origin, or *karan*, that is, cause. In Indian imagination, *veej* is often integrally used in various theories of creation. For example, it is mentioned in the eighteenth verse of the ninth chapter of the *Gita*. In *Chandi*, verse 5 of chapter 11 mentions *viswaveej*, where Mahamaya is described as the cause (*veej*) of the universe. The *Mahabharata* has several instances of envisioning the world as manifest in the form of a tree and a seed, or *veej*, as its source. Further examples may be cited from the *dhyanamantra* of Shiva in the *Ganesha Purana*, where Shiva is referred to as the *viswaveej*. In Bengali, the word *viswaveej* was also used by Rameshwar Bhattacharya in *Shibayan* as epithets of Shiva in multiple instances. See, for instance, Swami Jagadananda (ed.), *Gita*, trans. Swami Jagadiswarananda (Calcutta: Udbodhan Karyalaya, 1961), p. 210; Swami Jagadiswarananda (ed. and trans.), *Sri Sri Chandi* (Calcutta: Udbodhan Karyalaya, 1962),

p. 301; Rameshwar Bhattacharya, *Shibayan* (Calcutta: Sutabihari Ray, 1903), pp. 11, 44, 62.

59. Hatcher, *Bourgeois Hinduism*, p. 52.
60. Ibid.
61. Tagore, *The Autobiography of Maharshi Debendranath Tagore*, p. 71.
62. Ibid., pp. 167–168.
63. Ibid., pp. 66–68.
64. Sengupta, 'Akshaykumar Dutter Dharmabodh', p. 88.
65. *Tattwabodhini Patrika* 3, no. 886, Jaisthya, Saka 1839, Kalpa 19, pp. 25–26.
66. See, for example, the incident where Rajendranath Sarkar complains to Debendranath about his brother Umeschandra and his wife being converted to Christianity at Alexander Duff's house. The matter went to the Supreme Court. See Tagore, *The Autobiography of Maharshi Debendranath Tagore*, pp. 98–101.
67. For a brief discussion on this and the varied manifestations of *bhadralok* society within the rubric of colonialism, see Chakrabarti, *The Calcutta Kerani and the London Clerk in the Nineteenth Century*
68. Tagore, *The Autobiography of Maharshi Debendranath Tagore*, pp. 203–204.
69. Ibid., p. 204.
70. Lahiri, *Akshaykumar Dutta*, p. 64.
71. Tagore, *The Autobiography of Maharshi Debendranath Tagore*, p. 5.
72. The reactions of Dwijendranath Tagore and Rajnarayan Basu have been discussed in detail in Sengupta, 'Akshaykumar Dutter Dharmabodh', pp. 81–86. Sengupta quotes Rajnarayan as writing about Akshay Dutta: 'The Babu long ago abjured his belief in Brahmoism and turned an agnostic....' (p. 84).
73. Quoted in Sengupta, 'Akshaykumar Dutter Dharmabodh', p. 86.
74. Lahiri, *Akshaykumar Dutta*, p. 68.
75. Ibid.
76. Kopf, *The Brahmo Samaj and the Shaping of the Modern Indian Mind*, p. 49.
77. In the early period of the Tattwabodhini Sabha, the members would give lectures, generally to a private audience. These lectures, delivered by such members as Debendranath Tagore, Ramchandra Vidyabagish, Iswarchandra Vidyasagar, Akshay Kumar Dutta, Ramaprasad Roy, and others, were later published in a volume titled *Sabhyadiger Baktrita* in 1841. Some of these lectures were later printed in the early issues of the *Tattwabodhini Patrika*. For a detailed discussion on the problems of

authorship, the content of the lectures, and the analysis of the discourses by the members, see Hatcher, *Bourgeois Hinduism*.

78. See *Tattwabodhini Patrika*, no. 7, Phalgun, Saka 1765, p. 56.

79. Kopf, *The Brahmo Samaj and the Shaping of the Modern Indian Mind*, p. 56.

80. Bhattacharya, *The Sentinels of Culture*, p. 51

81. Brian Hatcher, *Vidyasagar: The Life and After-life of an Eminent Indian* (New Delhi: Routledge, 2014), p. 32.

82. Hatcher, *Bourgeois Hinduism*, p. 70.

83. For a detailed discussion on this, see Partha Chatterjee, *Nationalist Thought and the Colonial World; A Derivative Discourse* (London: Zed Books, 1993), pp. 54–84.

84. Rabindranath Tagore, *Gora*, in *Upanyas* Samagra, vol. 2 (Kolkata: Sahityam, 2003), p. 39.

85. Ibid., p. 41.

86. Ray, *Srijukta Babu Akshay Kumar Dutter Jiban-brittanta*, p. 50.

87. 'Sarvasadharaner hitakari', as quoted in ibid., p. 53.

88. Quoted in ibid., p.88.

89. See the discussion (and footnote) on this in ibid., p. 95.

90. Quoted in ibid., p. 100.

91. Akshaykumar Dutta, *Bahyavastur Sahit Manab Prakritir Sammandha Vichar*, vols. 1–2, in *Akshaykumar Dutta Rachana Sangraha*, vol. 1 (Kolkata: Paschimbanga Bangla Academy, 2008), p. 220.

92. See Ray, *Srijukta Babu Akshay Kumar Dutter Jiban-brittanta*, p. 103.

93. Ibid., p. 104.

94. Ibid., p. 108.

2

The New World of Science

Akshay Kumar Dutta as the 'Science Worker'

In this chapter I plan to read and understand, in a global framework, the scientific milieu that shaped the mind of Akshay Kumar Dutta. As a companion piece to the previous chapter, the present one will help to consolidate the epistemological framework within which the intellectual world of Akshay may be located and read. It will not be off the mark to refer once again to the letter that Rammohun wrote to Lord Amherst in 1823 emphasizing the need for science education in the form of mathematics, natural philosophy, chemistry, anatomy 'with other useful sciences which may be accomplished … by employing a few gentlemen of talents and learning, education in Europe and providing a college furnished with necessary books, instruments, and other apparatus'.[1] This letter could be read as symptomatic of the intellectual climate of Calcutta during the early decades of the nineteenth century. Not due to the consequence of this letter, but due to imperatives of history and their complex colonial manifestations, there was a radical epistemological movement, particularly in the field of the sciences, during the nineteenth century in India. This change or shift was procedurally complex, and the consequences were far-reaching in terms of their impact on the intellectual history of both India as an emerging nation and Bengal as its epicentre. There is little scope here of a sweeping judgement, and generalities need to be carefully interrogated before they may be assigned axiomatic veracity. No wonder, there were major scientific and technological developments during this time in India, and things were happening at a considerably fast pace. Largely, there was a Eurocentric thrust to this development, and with it an obvious and subsuming narrative of colonialism, and the emancipatory logic of modernity. Western-educated natives, conversant with the English language, were often a part of an almost pervasive project of scientific and technological modernity. Also, such a project had complex manifestations within the different disciplinary tributaries of scientific and technological practice, and the participation of the colonized subject was not always homogeneous and consistent within this veritable melting pot of scientific advancement or the narrative of progress. It is important, therefore, to trace a pattern of this culture of science within the colonized space to understand not only the patterns of development of scientific practice in India, but also the emergence of such personalities as Akshay Dutta: equipped with enlightenment education; English educated, with a knowledge of other European languages;[2] an active agent of scientific modernity within the native population; not a 'scientist' himself but deeply engaged in the development of scientific education within his milieu; and a writer of textbooks on science in the vernacular. It is in this sense that I have called Akshay a 'science worker' in the title of this chapter. But before I attempt to formulate the nature of the 'science worker' in nineteenth-century Bengal, and locate Akshay as a representative of such a group, it will be topical to outline, briefly, the pattern of development of this culture of science in British India.

Western Science and Scientific Practice in the Colonized Space

Basalla's Model

In an important article titled 'The Spread of Western Science' published in 1967, George Basalla gives us a diffusionist model of western scientific practice spread across colonized spaces.[3] It will be useful here to attempt a brief reading and analysis of Basalla's model and see if it helps us in formulating a framework for understanding the scientific milieu that Akshay and his peers inhabited within the sphere of science practice in colonial India. Basalla discovers three overlapping phases of scientific development: Phase 1, where the nonscientific society provides a source for European science; Phase 2, which is the period of colonial science; and Phase 3, where an independent scientific tradition or culture is achieved by the native society. Basalla, however, provides an interesting caveat to his use of the word 'nonscientific' about the colonized society: 'The word *nonscientific* refers to the absence of modern Western science and not to a lack of ancient, indigenous scientific thought of the sort to be found in China or India.[4] Thus, at the very foundation of the model of western science practised in the colonial space, Basalla situates the question of modernity and yet invests his model with the possibility of a nuanced understanding of definitions and nomenclature. The word 'science' is therefore narrowed down, in his model, to mean the colonizer's tradition of scientific practice, in this case that of the practice of European sciences in India. In spite of these careful reservations that Basalla proposes, it is perhaps this link with modernity and science that Rammohun was writing about in his letter to Lord Amherst in 1823. The early decades of the nineteenth century, one could say, was a period of late Phase 1 or early Phase 2, or a combination of both, if we are to follow Basalla's model.

In the first phase, the colonizer looks at the newly discovered space with curiosity, and there is little or no possibility of any collaborative effort with the indigenous population. The discovery or domination of the new land excites the scientific explorer, and both the earth sciences (botany, zoology, geology) and the geographical sciences (topography, cartography, hydrography, meteorology) make rapid progress as the novelty of the new discovery opens up newer possibilities of exploration and research. These are followed closely by anthropology, ethnology, and archaeology – a reason for which is not difficult to imagine. Both the professional scientist and the amateur (such as the explorer, traveller, missionary, diplomat, physician, merchant, missionary, military or naval man, artist, or adventurer) are engaged in their own peculiar ways in these explorations. However, as Basalla writes: 'What is important is the fact that the observer is a product of a scientific culture that values the systematic exploration of nature.'[5] Interestingly, in this context of the exploration of the New World, Basalla mentions the importance of the advice of Francis Bacon,[6] a man who had a profound influence on Akshay Dutta. I will discuss this later in the chapter. What Basalla tries to establish is that the colonizer tries to understand and explore the new space from within the set framework of scientific understanding that has been discursively mapped within the European observer through a celebration of rationalism and a consequent negation of the mystical: 'He is the heir to the Scientific Revolution, that unique series of events that taught Western man the physical universe was to be understood and subdued not through unbridled speculation and mystical contemplation but through a direct, active confrontation of natural phenomena.'[7] There is, no doubt, a striking similarity between Basalla's depiction of the vision of the European scientist and Akshay Dutta's engagement with the physical world around him. Of course, Akshay's world was more complex in the way he had to assimilate this 'modern' scientific temper that was easily associated with the colonizer, with his indigenous pull towards a culture that had its own traditions of faith and rationalism, along with a critique of both the eastern and the western cultural mores that did not resonate with his idea of the universe based on the designs of the *parameshwar* and predicated on a rational system of moral values. The second phase, which Basalla calls 'colonial science', is more of a collaborative effort where the native scientist, trained in European traditions of enquiry, begins scientific practice within the colonized space and participates in the project of scientific modernity laid down by the colonizer's epistemic preferences. This is the phase when institutions are set up, a structured pattern of native scientific culture (albeit in the model laid down by the colonizer) begins to emerge, and there is the possibility of an exchange of ideas. Once again, Basalla gives us a caveat here. Although colonial science is 'dependent science', the term he says is not pejorative in its import: 'It does not imply the existence of some sort of scientific imperialism whereby science in the non-European nation is suppressed or maintained in a servile state by an imperial power.'[8] He sees this as a process whereby the second phase leads to the third when, with the expansion of scientific practices and the opening of more institutions that come together with nationalist zeal, 'both political and cultural',[9] it was time to begin thinking of independent scientific practice and the creation of a new, modern scientific tradition: 'Although the colonial scientist looks for external support, he does begin to create institutions and traditions which will eventually provide the basis for an independent scientific culture.'[10]

There is some amount of simplification that is immediately discernible in the almost linear logic of the growth and flourishing of western sciences in the colonial context.[11] It is not difficult to imagine that the complex social milieu I have discussed in the previous chapter will have its own dynamic of exchange with this intervention of scientific modernity. If one were to take Basalla's claims at face value, it would seem that the diffusion was almost seamless and there was minimum intervention from the perspective of colonial political logic in such dissemination of a scientific epistemology that was being passed on to the colonized space. Obviously, scientific and technological interventions within the colonized space had its own deterministic framework, and there were fine lines that connected the narrative of progress and civilization with those of control and domination. From cartography to geology, from medicine to botany, from ethnography to mathematics – every sphere of epistemic manoeuvre quite naturally had its own political intent. From mapmaking to road construction, from the botanical gardens to the railways, from the establishment of medical colleges to the trigonometrical surveys, each had its specific extra-scientific political purpose. Richard Drayton makes an important point in *The Oxford History of the British Empire* (1999). He notices an ideological symbiosis between the scientific and imperial motives that undercuts the naiveté of Basalla's analysis:

> The laws of mechanics and geometry, political arithmetic and anatomy, provided a perspective on Man's place in nature which celebrated the power of informed authority to intervene. With Newton's laws, visible in the transit of cannonballs and stars, nature seemed to have shared her secrets with the British ... this universal knowledge appeared to equip Britain to undertake the cosmopolitan responsibility of 'improving' exotic lands and peoples. Science and technics came to supplement Christianity as justification for imperial outreach. By the late nineteenth century Comtean Positivism and Social Darwinism gave formal expression to older assumptions about Britain's rung on the ladder of Creation.[12]

Drayton is opening up a whole new narrative here. Interestingly, it foregrounds the narrative of science and technology against religion, as a strategy for a secularized and modernized dominance. If in the previous chapter we have seen Brahmoism trying to carve out a separate niche identity for itself that is separate from either traditional Hinduism or the various tenets of Christianity, so also the impact of Darwin or Comte was profoundly felt by the likes of Akshay Dutta. Even if we accept Drayton's understanding of a scientific hegemony that tried to replace a religious hegemony as the logic of empire, for Akshay Dutta and his milieu it was perhaps historically contingent to embrace the former as a more acceptable form of modernity. At that moment in history, it was perhaps not possible for a significant part of the English-educated intelligentsia to comprehend the full impact of Drayton's logic that could only be constructed from within a post-colonial understanding of imperial history. Within the discursive framework available at that moment, the positivism of a Comte or the scientism of a Darwin was simply more emancipatory and rational than perhaps a conversion to the colonizer's religion.

This trope of European modernity is what Gyan Prakash calls 'an uncanny double'[13] that was practised in the colonized space in the garb of universal reason. Despotism in terms of rule and dominance went hand in hand with the modernist narratives of freedom and enlightenment, and there was no way 'to close the deep internal rift in their discourses'.[14] Prakash sees the appropriation of the enlightened native intelligentsia as symptomatic of the strategy that the colonizer employed in order to play out their scheme of scientific modernity. It entailed a dislocation of European modernity, a translation, and re-contextualization of it in terms of their mechanism of control and domination. The native intellectual fell into the trap quite easily and let the colonizer appropriate his agency through the trope of reason:

> Enchanted by science, they saw reason as a syntax of reform, a map for the rearrangement of culture, a vision for producing Indians as a people with scientific traditions of their own. The elite produced biting critiques of 'irrational' religious and social practices, and acted with an acute sense of the novelty of their mission.[15]

Whereas this logic could have been picked up around the middle of the nineteenth century by the nationalists who developed out of this a unique form of Indian modernity laced with Hindu practices of science and technology, an attempt at rediscovering the past through reason rather than religion, there were interstitial locations within such attempts as well, those that could not be easily addressed by such a past–present or western–eastern binary. Someone like Akshay Dutta would, in a sense, refuse to read the political within the scientific and refuse to discover in himself either the oriental despot or the 'white but not quite' representative of the native intelligentsia. For someone born and bred for a large part of his childhood in a remote village, the journey to Calcutta itself was a veritable cartographic shift. The rest, exposure to western education and mores of scientific thought, was a natural corollary that shaped his intellectual constitution without him investing it with an immediate political intent. Neither in his milieu at the Brahmo Samaj, nor in his editorial work for the *Tattwabodhini Patrika*, nor in his writing of school textbooks on science in the vernacular was there a direct political intention or attempt at a deliberate subversion of the metanarratives of either imperialism or nationalism. Often enough there was a protracted critique of imperial intention and misrule, or that of the inability of the colonized to train himself in the extant, but almost forgotten, traditions of knowledge and governance, but a disruptive political intent was absent in Akshay's writings. It was only on rare occasions that he would venture into the political and write an essay invested in direct political concerns of his time.[16] His was a separate breed of the western-educated intellectual whose subject-position could not be subsumed immediately into one of the categories of the colonized or mapped into set narratives of interpretive communities. It is in this that he was distinctly different from Vidyasagar, who was always in the middle of raging social or political debates. Akshay's reformism was quieter in tone, almost like an undercurrent that flowed quietly over the pebbles of dissent, never directly confrontational with the major political debates of his time. In this sense, Akshay was perhaps not a typical representative of the 'nationalist' *bhadralok* either. His reformism was neither vociferous nor forced. It was more of a resilient ascetic who by sheer perseverance and logic would establish his opinion within a debate. His lived life was an example of such continuous distancing from his milieu as well – religious, scientific, or social – finally becoming a recluse in the suburbs of Calcutta, in Bally, where he grew plants and trees and led his quiet life. By divesting Akshay of the political, however, I do not intend to take away either his individual agency or the claim that Prakash makes about the likes of Akshay becoming an implicit instrument of the civilizing mission. Akshay fought for his ideological beliefs, as we know from his prolonged debates with Debendranath, the establishment of the Atmiya Sabha in 1852, or his insistence on publishing scientific articles in the pages of the *Tattwabodhini*. Likewise, it is quite possible that for the common man and the ruling class alike, someone like Akshay would automatically stand for the generic representative of the bourgeois, Hindu or Brahmo, upper-caste *bhadralok* who would uphold the narrative of modernity as seen through the lenses of enlightenment and liberal education.

Science Education, Governance, and Colonial Modernity

I should emphasize at this point of my argument that Akshay Dutta's place within the larger scheme of scientific development of the colonial world was peculiar. Akshay Dutta was not a scientist. He was not one of those practitioners of colonial science who would engage either in abstract research of the physical or chemical sciences or in practical explorations like the geologist or the geographer. Neither was he an assistant to a *sahib* scientist culling practical knowledge of the sciences by observing the European methodology of science research. V. V. Krishna, in his analysis of the colonial model of science practice and the emergence of national science in India, talks about three categories of the colonial scientist: (*a*) the 'gate-keepers' who helped to keep science dependent; (*b*) the 'scientific-soldiers' who merely executed their occupational roles; and (*c*) 'national' scientists who struggled to cultivate modern science in the framework of emerging nationalism.[17] Evidently, Akshay Dutta belonged to none of these three categories. There was a separate community of intellectuals not associated directly with the practice of science within the colonial space but deeply entrenched within this epistemic category. Often they were those who would write textbooks for the native population, sometimes in the vernacular, and open up for the masses the fruits of scientific enlightenment. They were not at the forefront of the systemic change that was happening around, but in the background. However, they were also a bridge between the ideological narrative of modernity and its execution at the level of the general public within a colonized space. I think that someone like Akshay Dutta, who wrote important textbooks on science, particularly in the vernacular, sometimes translating the English-language texts in a language accessible by the common person, becomes the pivot around whom there germinated the possibility of a scientific turn in culture. As the editor of the *Tattwabodhini Patrika*, an organ specifically meant for the dissemination and popularization of Brahmoism, Akshay consistently wrote and published articles on science and technology in his attempt to establish a culture of scientific thinking in the popular imagination. As I have already said, Drayton's post-colonial logic of dominance and hegemony practised through European science by the colonizer was perhaps not immediately relevant to Akshay Dutta, Iswarchandra Vidyasagar, and their contemporaries. For them, science education, particularly those that trickled in from Europe, was a necessary tool for modernizing the society around them in a way that was both novel and important. This was a window to a new order of things, and civilizational debates on racial superiority, political dominance, or cultural hegemony were less important than establishing rationalism or scientism as a way of lived life.

It is crucial to understand an important disconnect in this context. The colonial project of science practice in India also needs to be understood, at least cursorily, to better comprehend the location of an Akshay Dutta within it. The imperial project was primarily a political and economic one, invested in the narratives of exploration, surveillance, and control geared towards both governance and profit. Thus, the applied sciences and technology were more important markers of scientific development in the colonial context, rather than abstract or philosophical models of engagement. As Deepak Kumar has rightly pointed out:

> The state involvement made colonial science more 'utility-oriented'. In Britain itself there had occurred a gradual shift from science-as-a vocation to science-as-enterprise. In the wake of the industrial revolution there had developed ... an entrepreneurial ideology of science. Bacon and Bentham both coalesce on the point that the men who mattered began to look for utility or result-oriented science.[18]

It is quite beyond debate that the imperial project was not one of benevolence and philanthropy. Understandably, therefore, the 'entrepreneurial ideology' rather than the spread of science education in India was foremost in the mind of the imperialist government. Science, and primarily technology-oriented education, was, in a sense, beneficial for culling revenue and profit that is expected of a colonial government. The Charter of 1813 suggested a

> sum of not less than one lakh of rupees (£10000) in each year shall be set apart and applied to the revival and improvement of literature and the encouragement of the learned natives of India, and for the introduction and promotion of a knowledge of the sciences among the inhabitants of the British territories of India.[19]

Subsequently, the first educational dispatch in June 1814, which allowed the disbursal of the said amount, was interestingly careful in its emphasis on oriental forms of scientific knowledge. Not only did it speak about the rich heritage of plants and drugs in India, but also emphasized the need to tap into the Sanskritic traditions of astronomy, geometry, and algebra for those working in the observatories or the engineering departments.[20] But this entailed the learning of Sanskrit, and given the general mood of immediate economic gain, this idea was quickly replaced by the more practical solution of making the natives learn English. Also, delving into the Persian and Sanskritic traditions entailed a kind of labour that the generally contemptuous attitude of the likes of Macaulay did not encourage. In fact, Macaulay was not even keen to make the native population aware of the western sciences either, emphasizing more on the importance of basic literary and accounting education that would produce clerks and accountants rather than scientists or thinkers. In fact, in 1835 the 'General Committee of Public Instruction even recommended the abolition of the existing science professorship at the Hindu College and discontinued the instruction of chemistry there'.[21] In its stead, geology, mathematics, and such other practical sciences gained importance within the sphere of colonial science education in a bid to assist the European engineer, architect, surveyor, or mechanist. As Kumar writes:

> ... a need was certainly felt to have a class of apothecaries, hospital assistants, surveyors and mechanics to serve the fast-growing medical, survey and public works departments. Training local youths was obviously much cheaper than getting technical personnel from abroad. So there opened, in 1822, a medical school, and in 1843, an engineering class at the Hindu College.[22]

In spite of this general motif of profiteering and empire that was intrinsically linked to the project of science education in the early years of the nineteenth century in India, there were other parallel narratives of scientific thought and practice that evolved as part of the social process of assimilating the mores of colonial dominance. With the setting up of such institutions as the Asiatic Society of Bengal in 1784 or the Botanical Garden at Calcutta in 1787, the process of dissemination of a culture of science had already been initiated.[23] Although controlled almost completely by the colonial rulers, these institutions were instrumental in setting a template for a methodological pursuit of the sciences among the native intelligentsia. Likewise, in spite of the utilitarian approach to science education and practice, one could not discount the presence of a class of *bhadralok* practitioners of the sciences who either out of individual agency or as chance by-products of institutional systems emerged as native scientific minds capable of doing science and deconstructing racial myths. In Bengal itself, Radhanath Sikdar in 1852 was the first to compute and find out the highest point on earth; as one of the founding members of the Agricultural and Horticultural Society of India, Radhakanta Deb showed remarkable knowledge about the chemical elements in the Indian soil; Deb, Ramcomul Sen, Madhusudan Gupta, and Raja Kalikrishna Bahadur were elected members of the Medical and Physical Society of Calcutta and contributed fruitfully to its scientific programme. *Bhadralok* entrepreneurs and the landed gentry were also making fruitful economic contributions in the system of science practice. Kumar writes: 'From among the multitude of Indians who ignorantly worshipped the steamers, came Mutty Lal Seal who immediately recognized its importance, invested in shipping and ran a very profitable business.'[24] Likewise, with the establishment of the Calcutta Medical College in 1835, Ramgopal Ghosh presented nineteen volumes of new medical works, and Dwarkanath Tagore offered scholarships.[25] And all of this was happening during the first half of the nineteenth century when radical nationalist politics was still not a major player within the rhetoric of colonial scientific practice. In fact, colonial science could be seen as a crucial metaphor to understand the techniques of dominance and hegemony on the one hand and its many subversions on the other: through native participation as a player in the process; through undercutting the economic intent by excelling, as a native, in the epistemic; through economic participation by the native subject; through the revival of narratives of past excellence and engendering a narrative of traditional knowledge systems. This is what Roy McLeod describes as the idea of the 'moving metropolis' where the colonized space assumes an autonomy of its own within a set framework of imperial dominance.[26] That is to say, within the set framework of a kind of techno-based, survey-heavy utilitarian form of science practice intended by the master class, there were always possibilities of subversion while remaining within the framework. Akshay's attempts at writing science textbooks in the vernacular, based on his enlightenment scientific education, while insisting on a moral code that had an indigenous import was, in a way, a counter-narrative that would speak against the grain of the pervasive narrative of dominance without being directly confrontational or subversive.

Science and the Question of Education

What most of the historians writing on the British empire in India agree upon is the fact that the colonial state was not in any way a welfare state, and that the education meted out to the native population was primarily meant to be utilitarian in import rather than emancipatory. Moreover, since science education was on the one hand expensive and on the other not meant to produce as many low-rung native workers (in terms of clerks, accountants, pleaders, and so on) as a basic language and calculation skills would, there was more emphasis on the latter than the former. A gradual realization of the deeply ingrained nature of the religious ethic among the native population also led to less emphasis on religious matters, at least at the level of governmentality. It was easier to promote a secular humanities education, at the basic level, to create a group of workers and Company and government servants the colonizer needed to run the system of administration smoothly and yet with a certain democratic perception of opportunity and participation on the part of the colonized. However, in the matter of the dissemination of education as such, there was a discernible class bias in terms of 'who to teach' and 'what to teach'. In her book Gauri Viswanathan has argued how the native subject was reduced to a conceptual category, 'an object emptied of all personal identity to accommodate the knowledge already established and being circulated about the "native Indian"'.[27] The foundation of education for the British ruler, according to Viswanathan, was merely an instrument of 'discipline and management'.[28] Thus, even with general humanities education, there was clearly a sifting done in terms of reasonability and/or usability of the imparted knowledge. It is interesting, in this context, to read the note on public education in India written in 1823 by Holt Mackenzie, Secretary to the Governor-General-in-Council in the Territorial Department. In one part of the note Mackenzie writes:

> … the educated and influential classes should be the more immediate objects of the care of the Government than the support and the establishment of elementary schools for the masses…. Further, the natural course of things in all countries seems to be that knowledge introduced from abroad should descend from the higher, or educated classes and gradually spread through their example.[29]

The intention of the government is quite apparent here. It also meant that the resources were to be used on the basis of class identity and in a limited manner. The implicit assumption is that the upper and therefore educated class would eventually be responsible for the spread of education to the lower and the less privileged classes. Likewise, English education, which went beyond mere rote learning, was also meant for the native population who had a specific class and caste identity – namely the *bhadralok*. Obviously, science education, which was expensive and scarce, was reserved for an even smaller section of the *bhadralok* population.

It is in this context that I want to locate the role of Akshay Dutta as a science-worker. In a way, he was consolidating the claim that Mackenzie makes in his note about the upper or *bhadralok* class spreading education to the lower classes. However, what I intend to argue is that even if Akshay was consolidating such a claim, it may not be read as part of the colonial logic that Mackenzie claims it to be. In many ways Akshay Dutta deviated from the class identity that would club him naturally with his *bhadralok* contemporaries. In the previous chapter I have located him within the framework of a *bhadralok* identity. Generally speaking, Akshay would belong to this category. However, the empty and homogeneous signifier, according to Viswanathan, that the *bhadralok* identity (or for that matter any other native identity) represented to the colonial ruler is perhaps inadequate to represent Akshay, who was a deviant in many senses. The nineteenth-century Bengali society to which Akshay belonged was deeply invested in the caste question. In fact, the *bhadralok* identity was more often than not represented by and predicated upon the upper-caste members of the society. Caste difference was crucial to the creation and maintenance of the social fabric in the city and the country alike. Akshay was an exception. There are at least two apocryphal stories that consolidate this claim. One of them narrates how once Akshay, while on a trip to Damdama, would smoke *hookah* from a person of low caste (of Paundra origin). Subsequently, when he asked for the *hookah* from an upper-caste person, he was flatly refused on the ground that he had lost his *jat* as he had smoked from the same *hookah* as the lower-caste person. It is said that Akshay replied, 'I don't believe in the caste system.'[30] The second incident was narrated by one Ambikacharan Chattopadhyay, who was travelling with Akshay in 1883. This was around the time when Akshay was finishing the second volume of *Bharatvarshiya Upasak Sampraday*. Suddenly, Akshay alighted from the car and began speaking to a man of Dhangar caste and started discussing their forms of ritual and religious practice. When Ambikacharan tried to participate in the discussion, the Dhangar flatly refused and pointing at Akshay said, 'He has gone to our place, he has killed our differences.'[31] If these incidents are true, Akshay's presence within the Calcutta *bhadralok* society of the nineteenth century was rather iconoclastic. Thus, the easy dynamic of a utilitarian diffusion of education that the colonizer had envisioned, faulty as it was in its conception, which could possibly be true in the general sense, would not be applicable to the subject-position of someone like Akshay. For him, the belief system was less modelled on his awareness of colonial education and its political implications, and more on his unique and individual use of his self-taught awareness of the enlightenment and how it moulded his vision of the world around him. It was also invested in his own experience of community lives around him, and the deep disparities that the class and caste constructions entailed within the native society. In a peculiar sense, it was much less political than for many others belonging to his class. His perception of the world was marked by his immediate response to an event, qualified by his enlightenment education, and asserted by a moral fabric born less out of discursive training and more out of a philosophical engagement with the question of being and the phenomenal universe around him. This is not to say that it was not political if read through a post-colonial lens of representation. What I argue is that his responses were not born out of the typical *bhadralok* framework implicated by a proto-colonialism and consolidated by the 'favourable' treatment of his particular class by the colonial master.

Likewise, that he wrote in the vernacular also had its own logic that may not be explained away by its simple correspondence with nationalism and anti-colonial sentiments. In fact, in the entire oeuvre of Akshay Dutta, it will be difficult to find tracts where he directly opposes the colonial government politically or expresses strong sentiments in favour of nationalism. Therefore, it may perhaps be claimed that Akshay's choice of the Bengali language as the medium for writing about science was predicated less upon any political contingency and more upon his genuine concern of disseminating science education among the natives. In this sense, we could look upon Akshay as a teacher, an educator, and a revolutionary who was merely interested in popularizing science education among the common people and thus pushing them gently towards a narrative of modernity. It will be unfair to invest it with a deliberate political intent. In fact, the only political intent that may be read into such an act would be to notice how Akshay stepped out of the comfort zone of his by-now elite *bhadralok* identity in trying to bring science education to the doorsteps of the literate common householder. It may well be said that the esoteric and elitist principles on which the spread of western scientific practice in colonial India was predicated were undercut by Akshay's efforts to popularize science education in a Bengali that was easily accessible by the general mass of literate people. Reverend John Anderson is known to have said to his students at the General Assemblies Institution in praise of Akshay Dutta: 'Akshaykumar is Indianising European science.'[32] Mahendranath Ray goes on to write how Akshay had moulded European sciences and philosophy to fit the context of his milieu, and set it within a firm moral framework.[33]

The other interesting aspect that needs to be pointed out here is the somewhat arbitrary manner in which Akshay wrote about science. It is difficult to trace a set narrative of development or any focus on a rounded training programme in the basic sciences that Akshay had attempted in his books. He writes tracts on geography and physics, and very often also writes on technology and technological innovations. The topics on science that he chose to write about in the three volumes of *Charupath* (1853–1859) were likewise eclectic in nature and haphazard. For example, he writes on volcanoes, on walruses, on the birth of plants and trees, on the movements of the earth, on glaciers, on the solar system, on the size of the universe, and on various other topics that are not necessarily related to each other by a logical compass of association. Nor were they meant to be instrumental in forming a system of science learning that would provide a framework for the uninitiated. Evidently, the choice of a subject was related to his general idea about what his readers would benefit from knowing, and also perhaps on what he was reading or thinking of at that moment. The topics do not seem to emerge from a larger plan on developing a curriculum of science for the reading public and were possibly intended more for general knowledge imparted in the vernacular than anything else. In a sense, it is perhaps not difficult to guess the reason for such an arbitrary dissemination of knowledge practised by Akshay. His own training in institutions was also somewhat sketchy, haphazard, and incomplete. His initial years were spent at his native village learning Sanskrit with Gopinath Tarkalankar and Persian with Munshi Aminuddin; staying with an elder cousin in Calcutta he picked up the English language; it was at Gourmohan Auddy's Oriental Seminary that he first got the taste of formal education, learning Greek, Latin, Hebrew, and French, reading Homer and Virgil, and beginning with a foundational science education through physics, geography, geometry, and algebra.[34] Subsequently, due to his father's death he had to discontinue his formal education and start looking for means of sustenance. Through a series of events and a few friends, the gates of the Sobhabazar Rajbari library opened for him, and here at a mature age he studied trigonometry, conic section, and differential calculus along with some astronomy.[35] Even as he was editing the *Tattwabodhini Patrika*, Akshay would visit the Calcutta Medical College and attend classes on chemistry and botany. Mahendranath Ray claims that there was a growing feeling in Akshay about how the Hindu race was ignorant of its scientific and cultural history. Ray writes how during his time as the editor of the *Tattwabodhini*, Akshay 'read more than thousand books'[36] in order to find out all that had been written about the development of the Hindu race. He even trained himself in French and German in order to read up on what the west had written about the Hindu past, as well as to know about scientific developments in the west. In a footnote in his book, Mahendranath Ray recounts how a Sitanath Chattopadhyay, who owned a bookshop that Akshay used to frequent, had once discovered a German book in his shop with scribblings in the hand of Akshay Dutta. When asked about whether he understood the language, Akshay is believed to have replied: 'I have always had the determination to be engaged in the practice of science all my life. However, whatever I practice it is imperative to learn English, French and German.'[37] What I am suggesting is that there was an arbitrariness about the training that Akshay received, and much of it was self-taught. Therefore, perhaps, there was an identical lack of any discursive design in the way Akshay wrote about science. I would argue that it is this contingent nature of engagement with the teaching–learning process that made Akshay stand out as an exception within the larger rubric of colonial science practice in India. While there was a firm economic and utilitarian principle that defined the mode and manner of dissemination of scientific knowledge that the colonizer was importing from the west, Akshay's methods of both learning and teaching would only undercut that attempt in a curious way. It was definitely not an opposition, but it was also not a blind imitation. Akshay's method, or lack of it, neither put forward a nationalist narrative nor endorsed the larger colonial plan of exploiting the native for its own scientific purpose. Interestingly, though, Akshay was training himself, and his reading public, largely in western traditions of scientific learning, and the curious mix of science and morality in his textbooks could be construed as a curious mix of Francis Bacon and Auguste Comte. I will discuss the influence of Bacon and Comte on Akshay Dutta later in this chapter, and the influence of George Combe in the chapter where I discuss *Bahyavastu* in some detail.

A Brief Genealogy of Science Textbooks: Akshay's Milieu

I have already mentioned in the previous chapter that by the second decade of the nineteenth century the printing press was already playing a major role in the dissemination of knowledge across Bengal. The printing presses and their publications, in both English and Bengali, were competing with each other to gain the attention of the reading public. However, Deepak Kumar makes an interesting statistical observation regarding the proliferation of such publications: 'The number of publications was many. In 1857, 571670 copies of 322 books were issued in Bengali from 46 printing presses. But this included only 9 works on natural science, of which 12,250 copies were printed.'[38] Such statistics would tell the reader a number of things: first, the sciences were not a priority for the reading public who were more interested in other forms of literature; second, in terms of preference, natural sciences were more of a priority than technical or utilitarian sciences; third, even during the middle of the nineteenth century something like a culture of science learning had not yet emerged in a milieu that was considerably engaged within a narrative of modernity. The only book on engineering, Kumar says, was Durga Charan Chakravorti's *Vishwakarma*, published much later in 1886.[39] Also, Kumar mentions that most of the Bengali writers who wrote on science, such as Akshay Dutta, Ramendrasundar Trivedi, or Bankimchandra Chattopadhyay, would generally focus more on the natural sciences rather than engineering or mechanics. Trivedi even went on to write in *Mayapuri* (1910): '... science for the sake of knowledge and nothing else. Telegraph, telephone, dynamo, motor, electricity, steamships are very small, lowly and negligible in comparison with the sublime ecstasy which a truth seeker derives from pure science.'[40] Such a perspective will already open up a strain of analysis that at once consolidates and complicates my argument. On the one hand, it seems quite evident that a class of the bourgeois *bhadralok* had systematically deconstructed the utilitarian project of science practice (in terms of the prioritization of technical- and skill-based knowledge) by veering towards a study of the pure and abstract sciences, in spite of minimum government support for such pursuit and being mostly dependent on individual enterprise and privately run presses. However, this emphasis on pure science also reeks of a certain privileged class identity of a section of the *bhadralok* who preferred abstract, armchair thinking rather than a direct engagement with the practical aspects of technical education. Also, in a caste- and class-based hierarchized society, labour in any form (the practice of utilitarian sciences such as geology, botany, engineering, statistical, or trigonometrical surveys involved considerable amount of physical labour) was considered to be generally suitable for classes below the *bhadralok* or for that rung of the *bhadralok* who were economically weak. Thus, in a way, the larger project of colonial science promoted by the ruling class was already being read against the grain by a section of the upper-class *bhadralok*, albeit in a way that was curiously not oppositional, but culturally determined. On the other hand, however, I am uneasy in the way Kumar clubs Akshay Dutta with Ramendrasundar and Bankim. Akshay, Bankim, and Ramendrasundar belonged to three different generations of Bengali intellectuals, and the rapidly changing nature of the civil society in nineteenth-century

Bengal would automatically locate their discourses in separate planes of comprehension and praxis. Also, I would argue that in terms of agency both Bankim and Ramendrasundar were more powerful representatives of their class than Akshay. Also, Akshay was less politically relevant than either of them within their respective milieus and was rarely read as a person who was making a nationalist intervention through his work. In his own self-effacing way, Akshay was a quiet science worker, writing textbooks first under the aegis of the Brahmo Samaj as a teacher at the Tattwabodhini Pathshala and then as a private enterprise. He was never in the middle of nationalist politics, categorically opposing the colonial educational enterprise, nor championing the cause of the utilitarian techno-scientific model put forward by the colonial master class. Writing in the vernacular, developing a new idiom for writing about science in Bangla, mixing basic natural science education with some knowledge of technology, and setting the entire enterprise within a rational–moral framework – this is what Akshay was doing in an almost imperceptible manner during his working life within the intellectual milieu of nineteenth-century Bengal.

Buddhadeb Bhattacharya has written an important book on the spread of science education in Bengal, *Bangasahitye Bijnan* (1960), which gives us, if not a well-argued thesis, an inventory of science books published in Bengali during the nineteenth century. Interestingly, in what he calls the 'age of construction' (*gathan jug*) of science education in Bengal, he puts Akshay Dutta as the central figure of the enterprise. He begins his discussion on this age of construction in the following manner:

> Scientific discussion in the Bengali language was begun by Europeans.
> However, their use of the language was mostly artificial and complex.
> It was Akshay Dutta who suitably dressed western science in the native
> language by overcoming this artificial idiom.[41]

No doubt there were other *bhadralok* intellectuals who contributed, in their own way, to the development of science education in Bengal around the same time. Notable among them were the likes of Reverend Krishnamohan Banerjee, Rajendralal Mitra, Bhudeb Mukhopadhyay, Bankimchandra Chattopadhyay, and Ramendrasundar Trivedi. However, it might perhaps be said that Akshay was a pioneer in this, being one of the earliest to write about science in a Bengali that was easily accessible to the common speakers of the language.

As I have already mentioned, the colonial government was not very keen on the dissemination of scientific knowledge among the common people. It was left mostly to private enterprise, and the establishment of the Calcutta School-Book Society (CSBS) in 1817 went a long way in laying the foundations of such knowledge.[42] Interestingly, though, some of the earliest books on science written in Bangla were by Europeans who had acquired the language in the early part of the project of colonialism when the colonizer envisioned a blueprint of rule primarily through the acquirement of the native language. Thus, one of the earliest books on mathematics written in Bangla was *May Ganit* (also known in Bengali as *Angkapustakang*) by Robert May, an inspector of schools, in 1817, published by the CSBS. Likewise, Reverend John Harle, a missionary working in the Chinsurah region, published his tract on mathematics, *Ganitanka*, in 1819. Incidentally, Harle's book carefully followed the eastern traditions of accountancy and could be considered as one of the earliest orientalist science textbooks to be published. In the years that followed, several other science textbooks were written by Europeans in Bangla and published by the CSBS in collaboration with either the Mission Press in Serampore or the School Press in Chinsurah. Among them were John Marshman's *Jyotish ebang Goladhyay* (1819), a book on astronomy and geography; *Bhugol Brittanta* (1819) by W. H. Pearce; and J. D. Pearson's *Bhugol ebang Jyotish Ityadi Bishaye Kathapakathan* (1824) on the same subjects of geography and astronomy. Some of them tried to teach scientific truths through elementary rhymes and short verses, while others tried catechism or dialogue. If we are to look at the sales figures of some of them, they may be considered to have been moderately successful.[43] However, for most of them, the use of the Bengali language was considerably mechanical. Felix Carey's *Bidyaharabali* was perhaps the first encyclopaedic work on the sciences in Bangla, printed at the Mission Press in Serampore, and its first volume was published by the CSBS in 1819. These were translations of certain foundational European scientific texts. Carey was helped in his translations by his father, William Carey, and in the vernacular turn of scientific terms and the use of language by Srikanta Vidyalankar and Kabichandra Tarkachudamani.[44] John Lawson's *Pasvabali*, a pictorial depiction of animals and their habits and habitat, was published serially from 1822, till the CSBS published the collected edition in 1828. Bhattacharya is of the opinion that although the use of language was lucid, the book was primarily of the storytelling sort with 'severe dearth of scientific facts'.[45] Another important book written in a dialogic form was William Yates's *Padarthabidyasar* (1824).

However, as Bhattacharya has argued, there was little of physics in it, and the book was mostly a discussion on astronomy, geography, geology, biology, and botany. Moreover, the scientific arguments in the book were often clouded by religious faith, written as it was by a Baptist missionary.[46] The Scottish missionary John Mack, a professor at the Serampore College, wrote the first vernacular book on chemistry. *Kimiyabidyar Sar or Principles in Chemistry*, published by the Serampore Mission Press in 1834, was an assortment of his class notes prepared on the basis of his study in the European methods of chemistry, and appeared in both English and Bengali. The *Calcutta Christian Observer* wrote on Mack's use of Bengali:

> Of the Bengali version in general, we have small observation to make: there is little in it of any very peculiar character; it is faithful certainly, and as a composition as fair as most of the productions of European foreigners that have hitherto appeared in the language of the Bengal province; not altogether free from those exotic peculiarities which have often been remarked upon, yet certainly freer from striking violations of native idiom and phraseology, than many of them have exhibited. If we find not much to call for encomium, there is at the same time little that asks for the severity of critical censure.[47]

It will not be relevant to continue adding to this catalogue. It will suffice to say that there was already a considerable body of work written mostly by Europeans in Bangla promoting scientific knowledge before Akshay Dutta started to write on science in the vernacular.

What is noteworthy, however, is that there was clearly some kind of a collaborative enterprise between the enlightened native subjects and a certain section of the colonial master class that was responsible for the evolution of a modern teaching–learning process for the dissemination of the sciences in nineteenth-century Bengal. There might have been several complicated reasons for such a collaboration. On the one hand, the native *bhadralok* was keen to be part of the cosmopolitan enterprise of modernity, and scientific and technological advancement was part of the deal. Being part of societies and committees that promoted an advancement of the masses was also a strategy of liberalism that would give them both social leverage and presence. There was also the genuine intention of trying to think past a dogmatic or a pre-modern past, or revisiting the past through the lens of emancipatory modernity. For a section of the master class, there was also the zeal for philanthropy mingled with both a sense of guilt and the admiration for their own epistemic system that they wanted the world to acquire. Plain orientalism or a missionary zeal for religious conversion was perhaps not the reason for so many Europeans coming forward to write books on science in the vernacular. In fact, one of the rules set down by the CSBS in its manifesto clearly mentions:

> That it forms no part of the design of the Institution, to furnish religious books – a restriction, however, very far from being meant to preclude the supply of moral tracts, or books of a moral tendency, which without interfering with the religious sentiments of any person, may be calculated to enlarge the understanding, and improve the character.[48]

It is crucial to notice how religion and morality have been carefully separated. This may be read as an intelligent attempt to sift between the missionary intention of conversion and the orientalist one of a superior system of training the native mind towards a better (western) way of life. I would presume that most of the native *bhadralok* intellectuals, whether liberal like Rammohun Roy or conservative like Radhakanta Deb, were satisfied by such an areligious yet moral turn of the project of education. It would seem that Akshay Dutta also subscribed to identical views. In fact, in most of his written work, be it in the *Tattwabodhini Patrika* or *Bahyavastu* or *Charupath*, while his rationalism always pulled him away from a traditional religious ethic based on blind faith or unreason or superstition, his tracts on the sciences were always complemented by tracts on moral education and the need for training in a life invested in being virtuous. It is possible that his lifelong faith in the works of Francis Bacon was influenced by this milieu of intellectuals who, through the publications of the CSBS and myriad other means, provided for Akshay a framework of reason and morality coalesced into an epistemic system. In fact, interestingly, the third report of the CSBS carried a suggestion 'that a translation of some of Lord Bacon's works (as his Novum Organum & etc) which has been the groundwork of much of the Science cultivated in England would offer much interesting matter for publication'.[49] I would presume that even in the apparent lack of a structural design in Akshay's project of education, there was a moral–rational pattern that he had partly borrowed from Francis Bacon.

The discussion on Akshay's scientific milieu will remain incomplete without a brief discussion of the science magazines and journals that gained a life of their own during the period. It may be said that the establishment of the Mission Press in Serampore in 1800, the mentorship of the CSBS, and the steady proliferation of printing presses in the city led to the increasing publication of books, journals, and newspapers in the vernacular and the consequent socialization of reading matter among the general public.[50] However, among the myriad matters that were being printed during this time, there was no consolidated effort to popularize modern science till at least the middle of the century. Although many journals and periodicals such as the *Digdarshan* (1818), the *Samachar Darpan* (1818), the *Bangadoot* (1829), the *Sangbad Prabhakar* (1831), and the *Sangbad Purnachandroday* (1835) were intermittently publishing scientific matter, it was not until the publication of the *Bidyadarshan* (1842) that a consolidated effort to publish and promote scientific knowledge in a popular and comprehensible language was undertaken. Published under the aegis of Prosunno Coomar Ghose of Taki, most of the scientific articles in this monthly periodical were written by Akshay Dutta. However, as Bhattacharya writes, Akshay's intention was to dispel all kinds of false beliefs and superstitions and engage the public in matters of science and reason.[51] But there were not many takers for his articles at that time as 'people were more entertained by such ribald periodicals as *Mahanabami* or *Rasaraj* … *Bidyadarshan* could not keep itself afloat for more than six months'.[52] It may be said that it was only after the publication of the *Tattwabodhini Patrika*, under Akshay Dutta's editorship, that a consistent culture of printing and reading of scientific articles emerged in Bengal. Akshay was discerning enough as an editor to realize that a paradigm shift of cultural praxes had to be achieved gradually. It was perhaps the popularity, albeit short-lived, of the Brahmo Samaj and its insistence on a somewhat rational and modern outlook that helped Akshay in his endeavour. As a representative of the Brahmo Samaj, the *Tattwabodhini Patrika* would engage in debates and discussions with the belief system of traditional Hindu religious practice and try to act as an intellectual organ that was interested in an enlightened version of both religious and cultural practice. However, interestingly, the *Tattwabodhini* did not begin to publish articles on science instantly. The first twenty-five issues of the *Patrika* did not carry any scientific article. From the twenty-fifth to the forty-sixth issue there were some basic science articles on nature and biology. It was only from the forty-seventh issue (Asad, 1769 Saka) that a serious engagement with the sciences was undertaken.[53] No wonder most of these articles were written by Akshay himself, and many of these were later published as independent volumes. By this time Akshay had also found a language to articulate scientific arguments in the vernacular, an idiom that was more accessible to the native speaker than the convoluted vernacular that was used by Akshay's European predecessors. In the pages of the *Tattwabodhini*, Akshay published articles on astronomy, mathematics, physical sciences, geology, geography, and the life sciences. For a periodical that was considerably popular among the reading public, this proliferation of scientific articles was symptomatic of a shift, or at least a movement, in the cultural and intellectual life of the community. It is in this sense that I would use the term 'science worker' for Akshay. There was an implicit canniness in his enterprise of science education. On the one hand, there was rarely any nationalist or subversive rhetoric in his discussion, but an undercurrent of a purposive revival of a Hindu past and its scientific achievements.[54] Neither was there a challenge of modernity that Akshay was throwing at his readers, only hinting at the possibility of a comparatist model to past scientific endeavours and technological skills. Most of his essays or articles were objective documents on aspects of science, merely meant to inform and educate, and rarely ever passing a judgement on aspects of culture. The entire ethical battle, whether the *Tattwabodhini Patrika* would remain merely an organ for preaching the ideals of the Brahmo Samaj or become a periodical for the rational or scientific training of the reading public, was fought within the Samaj itself. Unlike a Rammohun or a Debendranath or a Vidyasagar, Akshay would generally remain behind the scene, and his reformism took the form of an objective pursuit and dissemination of knowledge as modernity, without raising a voice that could be easily subsumed into either politics or rhetoric. He was foregrounding a cultural shift in terms of scientific thinking and there was a foundational moral framework within which he functioned, but neither of these was expressed through any overt political intent or the individual charisma of the public intellectual. It was a labour-intensive process, a quiet but determined application of a training acquired almost through individual enterprise, accompanied by a restraint culled from the moral discourse that he preached through his work. About the articles on science published in the pages of the *Tattwabodhini Patrika*, Bhattacharya writes: 'The practice of writing scientific essays that were simple and comprehensible initiated by the *Tattwabodhini* was followed by other contemporary and later day periodicals. Also, the *Tattwabodhini* played an important role in dispelling the contempt with which the general public would look at the Bengali language.'[55] Thus, in the years to follow, many periodicals such as *Pokkhir Bibaran* (1844), *Satya Pradip* (1850), *Satyarnab* (1850), *Bibidharthyasangraha* (1851), and *Bangyabidya Prakashika* (1855) would become popular organs for the dissemination of scientific knowledge. It may be said that Akshay Dutta was largely responsible for the proliferation or popularization of a scientific culture among the native reading public in the middle years of the nineteenth century.

The Influence of Francis Bacon and Auguste Comte

As someone who did not finish his formal education or did not adhere to a set epistemic framework of academic learning, it is a little problematic to trace a definite narrative of intellectual influence for Akshay Dutta. If one were to read his body of work or critical texts written on him, it is, however, possible to elicit the names of a few intellectuals and thinkers he seems to have read or whose works seem to have had an influence on him. Francis Bacon and Auguste Comte seem to be the foremost among them. Although, due to the scattered nature of his education, it is difficult to put one's finger on the exact period when Akshay was reading either Bacon or Comte, or the exact texts that he might have read that influenced his view of the world around him, there is little doubt that he was considerably influenced by both of them. As he writes much later in *Bharatvarshiya Upashak Sampraday*:

> That Europe has produced two invaluable gems at two different periods of time has not been emulated ever again anywhere in the world. Bacon and Comte are like two suns on two landmasses [England and France]. These two sacred and luminous words are the very definition of knowledge.[56]

It will not be a digression, therefore, to briefly talk about the influence of these two thinkers on Akshay, and to try and understand how they might have been instrumental in determining his science worker self.[57]

Francis Bacon

It was in one of Akshay Dutta's later works, in the introduction to the second volume of *Bharatvarshiya Upashak Sampraday*, that we find a direct reference to Francis Bacon. In this particular context, Akshay was discussing the various interpretations of nihilism, logic (*nyayavada*), and the *Vedantasutra*s that have been practised within the eastern systems of religio-moral thinking from Vyasa to Sankaracharya to Brahmananda Saraswati.[58] In his opinion, many of these philosophers and interpreters were born with a natural intelligence, and it was only the lack of a pure 'scientific path' towards establishing a truth or a fact (Akshay was thinking of the question of epistemology here, and I will take this up for detailed discussion later in the book) that had prevented India from being equal to Europe. Akshay regrets that instead of trying to determine the natural rules of the universe, many of these eastern thinkers have merely engaged in collating a few established ideas with certain imagined ideas, thereby engendering an inaccurate system of understanding: 'They lacked a guide. They needed one Bacon – one Bacon – one Bacon.'[59]

As I have already said, it is difficult to determine either the exact moment in his life when Akshay read Bacon or even the specific texts that he was engaging with. However, it is evident from the writings of Rammohun, Vidyasagar, and their contemporaries that the works of Francis Bacon were quite popular among the English-educated intelligentsia in nineteenth-century Bengal.[60] Texts such as *The New Organon* and *The Advancement of Learning* seem to have been available to the reading public in Bengal during the nineteenth century. Therefore, Bacon's idea of the 'Great Instauration', which was his comprehensive plan for the advancement of the sciences and a reform of learning through a fruitful combination of natural philosophy and science, was not totally unknown to the educated Bengali reader. It is, however, imperative to understand Bacon's idea of god in order to comprehend Akshay's faith in and use of Bacon in his understanding of the world. For many of his critics, Akshay's faith in the rational was a direct and definitive proof of his rejection of the god question, or of the fact that he was an atheist. If one were to accept such a contention, it would be rather difficult to argue that Akshay was influenced by Bacon as the quote from the *Bharatvarshiya Upashak Sampraday* seems to suggest. No wonder Bacon's Instauration was a project that invested power and industry in man, and invested him with agency. In a sense, it was a celebration of man's power of choice, the development of a rational system of understanding the natural world through scientific and empirical knowledge, and making informed choices that would lead to a freedom of action. However, this act of free will was part of a larger design:

> From the Genesis narrative of creation Bacon derived principles which were essential to the Instauration. The first principle was that Bacon's God was the God of order who had constructed an orderly and predictable universe … that the universe was so structured that it always operated according to rules which governed the realm of

secondary causes; and practically, it meant that if the human role in the Instauration were to be carried out properly, man must follow the prescriptive hierarchy which was manifested in the order in which all things came to be.[61]

The secondary causes that Matthews refers to here are those that are engendered by human agency, a result of the earthly pursuit of knowledge and always according to the 'prescriptive hierarchy' inherent in the system. The secondary causes are part of a chain of causality, and not independent in nature, whereby they are divested of the charges of atheism. As Bacon writes in *The Advancement of Learning*:

> And as for the conceit that too much knowledge should incline a man to atheism, and that the ignorance of second causes should make a more devout dependence upon God, which is the first cause; first, it is good to ask the question which Job asked of his friends, *Will you lie for God, as one man will do for another to gratify him?* For certain it is that God worketh nothing in nature but by second causes; and if they would have it otherwise believed, it is mere imposture, as it were in favour towards God; and nothing else but to offer the author of truth the unclean sacrifice of a lie.[62]

For Bacon then, the chain of causes creates the necessary space where human beings, as free-willing agents, perform their experiments on the universe and arrive at empirical conclusions about the natural world. However, as the one true agent, the role of God as the grand designer is never discounted in Bacon's work or in his idea of the Instauration. Therefore, for an ardent follower of the Baconian principles, Akshay Dutta would also, likewise, in much of his work, refer to the Supreme Being (or the *parameshwar*) as the grand designer. Also, for Bacon, the intention of natural philosophy was to reveal the manifestation of God in a well-ordered universe:

> As Bacon had interpreted Matthew 22:29 in the *Meditationes Sacrae*, nature and the Scriptures were complementary theological sources, the former revealing God's power, and the latter his will.[63]

Human agency and free will were also central to this design according to which Bacon planned the Instauration. It was the duty of the human subject to observe nature and to formulate, through experiment, the ways and means to gain mastery over the natural order. Method and procedure were thus at the heart of the Baconian principle.

It will be interesting to read the opening lines of Akshay Dutta's *Bahyavastu* in this context. In this volume Akshay is trying to establish the relationship between the external, material world and the nature of man. This is how he begins:

> If one were to observe this phenomenal world it would be clearly evident that all living beings as well as all non-living objects have an intrinsic character, and each has a definite relationship with all the other objects. Any person set on theoretical enquiry would, after deliberating on the relationship of the objects with each other, clearly realize the incomprehensible, unique, eternal, absolute entity of *Parameshwar* at the heart of all this ... that God has created various objects, has determined a relationship between each of them, that is has established principles for governing the world all for the well-being of the universe.[64]

The design of the Baconian Instauration is clearly evident here, as is the realm of secondary causes where man plays the significant agential role in understanding the method of the universe through its inherent causality, and trying to gain control over it through experimentation and understanding. However, although Akshay's understanding of the world and its mechanism was informed considerably by the works of Francis Bacon, it will perhaps be important to remember that there were many other thinkers who influenced him. Not only did he go back to indigenous forms of understanding the universe, there were also other European influences that need to be considered. The entire argument in *Bahyavastu*, for example, follows the works of George Combe. Comte, Darwin, and Newton were also discernible influences in his work.

The reader of Akshay needs to be aware that he was a complex product of his time whose intellectual horizon was as much informed by the enlightenment as it was invested in indigenous forms and methods of understanding the universe. In the manner of any thinking mind, his was mired in confusion, questioning both his discourse and his belief system at various moments in his life. I intend to take up these doubts and confusions in Akshay's intellectual world in the course of discussing his works in more detail in the next few chapters. However, the layered nature of his thinking would resist quick conclusions and simplistic interpretations. Asish Lahiri, for example, has devoted a short chapter in his book *Andhar Rate Ekla Pathik* on the influence of Bacon on Akshay Dutta.[65] In this chapter he rightly discovers a series of self-contradictions in Akshay. However, Lahiri is too quick to conclude how Akshay, as his facility in the physical sciences increased, 'began to realize how the laws of nature were not ordained by God. Instead of determining nature in terms of God, he began to determine God in terms of nature. Soon he started asking if the laws of nature were true, how can one sustain the idea of God?'[66] This will be a direct contradiction of the Baconian principle. Moreover, Lahiri does not point out where in Akshay's work one may find such a definitive conclusion. There is no doubt that Akshay had too many doubts about the nature and form of god or divine presence throughout his life. Time and again his rationalism stood in the way of his faith, as his debate with Debendranath clearly shows. However, that the east needed 'one Bacon' was a claim that Akshay was making in his last published work, almost towards the end of his life. It is possible that he was still holding on to certain Baconian principles and the idea of the Great Instauration. It is also quite possible that along with the empirical principles that Bacon advocated, Akshay also subscribed to the Baconian idea of the systemic faults of atheism. What I am trying to suggest is that in order to foreground Akshay's faith in the rational, critics such as Lahiri have divested him of a complexity that is necessary to comprehend both the mind and the milieu of Akshay. Akshay's intellectual shifts were not complete and final movements from one system of belief to another that could be cleanly divided into separate phases. It was a continuous churning replete with doubts, contradictions, and revisions, as will be evident when I take up his works for close reading in the next few chapters.

Auguste Comte

The intrinsic connection between the scientific and the spiritual was also a central concern in Comte's work and his elaboration of the tenets of positivism. In trying to ascertain the intellectual character of positivism, Comte clearly asserts:

> I have long ago repudiated all philosophical or historical connection between Positivism and what is called Atheism.... Atheism is the

most characteristic symptom of anarchy, is a temper of mind more unfavourable to the organic spirit, which ought by this time to have established its influence, than sincere adhesion to the old forms.[67]

The consistent attempt by many critics or commentators to prove that Akshay was an atheist will thus be challenged by these formative influences on him. Although both Bacon and Comte were advocates of an experimental rationalism, it is important to remember that neither of them proclaimed atheism to be a precondition for a rational mindset. Comte saw positivism as a call for social action, an action born out of a scientific training and one that nurtured neither a false sense of optimism nor metaphysical and theological models of understanding the world. He asserts that 'Positivism ... stimulates us to action, especially to social action, far more energetically than any Theological doctrine.'[68] In fact, for Comte the word 'positive' carries within it the essence of 'reality' and 'usefulness', of 'certainty' and 'precision' which entail, for him, the true philosophic spirit, and by which 'the intellect of modern nations is markedly distinguished from that of antiquity'.[69] It is in this that Comte discovered the 'organic' tendency that involves the human being in social action: 'By speaking of Positivism as organic, we imply that it has a social purpose; the purpose being to supersede Theology in the spiritual direction of the human race.'[70]

This is perhaps where most commentators have misread Akshay's purpose. Both Bacon and Comte have been abiding influences throughout his intellectual life. His faith in utilitarian scientism, in trying to know the universe through its physical manifestations – through a knowledge of geography and physical sciences, earth sciences, and the animal and plant lives – was born out of his desire to discover this 'organic' nature of life on earth through experiment and observation, and to locate such observation within a moral or ethical framework. His affiliation to western modernity was part of his emancipatory project leading towards a social goal. The ethico-moral framework of the society was to be determined by the objective presence of a *parameshwar*, a grand architect, who would rarely intervene in the day-to-day functioning of the phenomenal world. It was man, through his labour, discipline, and application, through his curiosity and spirit of experiment and learning, who would run the system. And this system or order was at the core of a communitarian principle of progress, one that had, as Comte would say, a social purpose. This would perhaps explain the labour and crop equation, where Akshay discounts the importance of prayer. The grand architect, who had set the entire plan in motion, was less interested in prayer than in the application of knowledge for the betterment of the social space. As Comte writes: 'The moral value of Positivism ... can be largely developed, independently of any spiritual discipline, though not so far as to dispense with the necessity for such discipline.'[71] It may be said that God was incidental or even redundant to Akshay's intellectual world. The 'certainty' and 'precision' of science, a world that functioned empirically due to set laws of nature, was more relevant to the narrative of modernity that Akshay imagined for the society around him. In a certain sense, it may perhaps be said that god provided one of the possible moral frameworks for the utilitarian and functional universe that Akshay imagined. I would suggest that for Akshay the idea of god was a metaphor that helped him, in a way, to establish the contours of a scientific universe. However, to brand him as an atheist would be a serious misreading of both his intention and influences.

An important principle of the Comtean system of positivism was the notion of social sympathy and the question of social feeling. The entire ethical framework of positivism was predicated on a communitarian principle in which individual interest or self-love was always subordinated to the grand narrative of the interest or the emancipation of the community. Also, interestingly, the principle of 'feeling' was of utmost importance to Comte: 'The moral education of the Positivist is based both upon Reason and on Feeling, the latter having always the preponderance, in accordance with the primary principle of the system.'[72] The rigorous moral principle that it advocated was based on the rational principle of demonstration or experimentation, but this inherent scientism was, in fact, part of the holistic idea of the generation of social feeling among the people. The notions of *paropakar* and *daya* that I have referred to in the previous chapter in the context of Brahmoism are therefore consistent, in their indigenous forms, with the precepts of Comtean positivism. It is quite possible that this novel approach towards the spiritual, towards the making of the *brahmanistha grihastha* within Brahmoism, the householder who is always aware of his communitarian responsibility, reminded both Akshay and Vidyasagar of their reading of the works of Auguste Comte. It is not difficult to imagine that both of them, Akshay as an insider and Vidyasagar as a sympathetic outsider, would discover within the fold of the Tattwabodhini Sabha and the Brahmo Samaj a practical manifestation of their reading of Comte. Also, for both of these men, the notion of *feeling* was not alien. Vidyasagar was already known as *dayar sagar* (the ocean of compassion), and Akshay, throughout his life, was known for his compassion for the masses, particularly those towards the lower rungs of the social ladder. I will try to demonstrate, as I closely read some of the works of Akshay Dutta in the next few chapters, that this notion of 'feeling' has been consistent with the trajectory of Akshay's intellectual life, in terms of both his moral and scientific tracts. It was as if Akshay were demonstrating Comte's dictum: 'Moral education, even in its more systematic parts, should rest principally upon Feeling....'[73]

The other Comtean notions that Akshay has subscribed to throughout his intellectual life were those of 'order' and 'progress'. The scientific principle that was intrinsic to Akshay's thought process was also, primarily, a result of his faith in certain aspects of western modernity, and the ethic of progress was one of the central concerns of this narrative. Likewise, he wanted to establish order in society on the principles of natural philosophy, something that he mentions almost throughout his oeuvre, and something he seemed to have picked up directly from Comte: 'The Positivist regards artificial Order in Social phenomena, as in all others, as resting necessarily upon the Order of nature, in other words, upon the whole series of natural laws.'[74] Comte views the relationship between order and progress to be one between existence and movement, something that he discovers in the natural world, particularly in the functioning of biology. He writes:

> Finding it in all the lower sciences, we are prepared for its appearance in a still more definite shape in Sociology.... In Sociology the correlation assumes this form: Order is the condition of all Progress; Progress is always the object of Order. Or, to penetrate the question still more deeply, Progress may be regarded simply as the development of Order; for the order of nature necessarily contains within itself the germ of all possible progress.[75]

It will not be difficult to find a reflection of these ideas in many instances across Akshay's body of work. I shall take them up for elaborate discussion in the next few chapters. However, it may be worthwhile to take up one such instance here, which within the course of a few lines captures all the aspects of my discussion in this chapter. This one is from the introduction to the first volume of *Bahyavastu*. Here Akshay reflects how in eastern philosophical systems, there has rarely been any attempt to reconcile our physical and mental characteristics with those of the external world. In fact, he says, both in our world and the Christian world, there was this notion of an ideal world that had gone through phases of progressive degeneration till we have arrived at a stage that is beyond repair. However, Akshay writes, due to the advancement of the sciences in Europe, they have now come to realize how as mankind becomes aware of the 'order' of the world (*jagater niyam*), they acquire prosperity, and there is 'progress' (*unnati*) in their condition and disposition. The Europeans are also aware, he says, that such a relationship between order and progress has already been established by *parameshwar*.[76]

Conclusion

The intellectual world of Akshay Dutta was thus a curious medley of ideas and influences that were qualified both by the east and the west, faith and science, and most of his writings carried in it a moral spirit that he thought was relevant for his community to emerge into a modernity that was marked by the rational and the spiritual alike. As a science worker, he was an empiricist; as a man of his milieu, he was a positivist; and in terms of faith, a spiritualist. He produced a curious variety of works, some of which were quite different from each other, symptomatic of a mind that was going through a continuous process of revision and assessment. What a careful reader of Akshay's works would probably discover is a science worker who would want to elicit from his indigenous community a sociocultural response to enlightenment education. Akshay, unlike a Rammohun or a Vidyasagar, was not looking for revolutionary changes in society. He was looking for smaller cultural shifts engaged in a continuous process of rupture and disruption through a scientific critique of a belief system that was mired in superstition and dogma. Science, for him, was to be a way of life, and without discounting a value system, or replacing the one completely with the other, he wanted to use reason and rationality as tools to unsettle a metaphysics of false signifiers. Science, for Akshay, was a cultural tool with which to dismantle dogma and usher in a modernity that he imagined was more egalitarian and democratic in spirit. This is where, once again, he was like Rammohun, with whom it all began.

If one were to study the entire oeuvre of Akshay Dutta, one would notice that apart from his textbooks on geography and physics that he initially wrote for the Tattwabodhini Pathshala and the short scattered pieces in the three volumes of *Charupath*, he did not go on to write elementary pieces on science as he progressed in years. He moved towards a more complex engagement with the sciences in his more voluminous works such as *Bahyavastur Sahit Manabprakritir Sammandha Vichar* or *Dharmaniti* or *Bharatvarshiya Upashak Sampraday* – all of which I shall engage with in the chapters that follow. Also, if one were to go by Saradacharan Mitra's account, in his final years, with a frail and failing health, Akshay was still deeply engaged in the study of geology, botany, and the life sciences.[77] Shortly before his death, Mitra writes, he had ordered for a geological specimen from Britain for 150 rupees, which arrived only after his death.[78] It was in Akshay a combination of this empirical scientific spirit with the more abiding concern for the establishment of a rational and moral perspective along a global scale for the Bengali people that, in my opinion, led to his later works. In the spirit of what I have called the science worker, Akshay's intention was to weave in the scientific spirit organically into the value system of the Bengali subject. That is to say, rationalism would not remain a mere corollary of science education in schools in terms of individual subjects such as geography or physics, but through social practice it would become a part of the *janasamaj* or the lived life of society as such. The *brahmanistha grihastha*, along with his obvious moral fortitude culled mostly from an indigenous cultural narrative, would be epistemologically trained in a spirit of rationalism and scientism and thus become a global citizen of the modern world. This is what Akshay worked towards as a science worker. I would argue that his pursuit of science gradually became more of an individual enterprise, whereas in the public sphere he was more invested in instilling a rationalism and organic scientific temper within the social and cultural practices of contemporary Bengal. However, this is not to claim in any way that Akshay was an atheist or that his scientific rationalism came in the way of his faith in the presence of a *parameshwar*. In the next few chapters I will try to closely read some of Akshay Dutta's works to understand the mind of a rare intellectual from nineteenth-century Bengal.

Notes

1. Quoted in Sophia Dobson Collet, *The Life and Letters of Raja Rammohun Roy* (Calcutta: A.C. Sarkar, 1914), p. 108.
2. Mahendranath Ray insists that although Akshay started to learn English at the age of ten years and four months, his real education in English began at the age of sixteen when he started attending Gourmohan Auddy's Oriental

Seminary. See Mahendranath Ray, *Srijukta Babu Akshay Kumar Datter Jiban-brittanta* (Calcutta: Sanskrit Jantrer Pustakalaya, 1885), p. 17. Akshay also seems to have had a working knowledge of Greek, Latin, German, and French. Also see Subrata Barua, 'Akshaykumar Datter Bijnanmanaskata', in *Dwisatajanmabarshe Akshaykumar Dutta*, ed. Tapas Bhowmik, *Korok Sahitya Patrika*, Kolkata, 2020, p. 59.

3. See George Basalla, 'The Spread of Western Science', *Science* 156, no. 3775 (1967): 611–622.

4. Ibid., p. 611.

5. Ibid.

6. Ibid., p. 614.

7. Ibid., p. 612.

8. Ibid., p. 613.

9. Ibid., p. 617.

10. Ibid.

11. For a detailed discussion on this and other models of analysis, see Deepak Kumar, *Science and the Raj: A Study of British India* (New Delhi: Oxford University Press, 2006), pp. 1–31.

12. Richard Drayton, 'Science, Medicine, and the British Empire', in *The Oxford History of the British Empire, Volume 5: Historiography*, ed. Robin W. Winks (New York: Oxford University Press, 1999), pp. 264–265.

13. Gyan Prakash, *Another Reason: Science and the Imagination of Modern India.* (Princeton: Princeton University Press, 1999), p. 5.

14. Ibid.

15. Ibid., p. 6

16. See, for example, his essay 'Palligramastha Prajader Durabastha Barnan' that appeared in three parts in the Baisakh issue (pp. 5–12), the Sraban issue (pp. 49–55), and the Agrahayan issue (pp. 115–121) in 1772 Saka or 1850.

17. See Kumar, *Science and the Raj*, p. 9.

18. Ibid., p. 16.

19. Arthur Howell, *Education in British India, prior to 1854, and in 1870–71* (Calcutta: Office of the Superintendent of Government Printing, 1872), p. 5.

20. Ibid., pp. 5–6.

21. Kumar, *Science and the Raj*, p. 49.

22. Ibid., p. 51.

23. For an informed discussion on this, see David Arnold, *Science, Technology and Medicine in Colonial India* (Cambridge: Cambridge University Press, 2000), pp. 19–56.

24. Kumar, *Science and the Raj*, p. 58.

25. Ibid., p. 63.

26. Roy McLeod, 'On Visiting the "Moving Metropolis": Reflections on the Architecture of Imperial Science', in *Scientific Colonialism: A Cross-cultural Comparison*, ed. Nathaniel Reingold and Marc Rothenberg (Washington, DC: Smithsonian Institution Press, 1987), pp. 217–249.

27. Gauri Viswanathan, *Masks of Conquest: Literary Study and British Rule in India* (New Delhi: Oxford University Press, 2004), p. 11.

28. Ibid.

29. Quoted in Amitabha Mukherjee, *Reform and Regeneration in Bengal, 1774–1823* (Calcutta: Rabindra Bharati University, 1968), p. 109.

30. See Ashish Lahiri, *Akshaykumar Dutta: Andhar Rate Ekla Pathik* (Kolkata: Dey's Publishing, 2019), p. 41.

31. Ibid.

32. Ray, *Srijukta Babu Akshay Kumar Datter Jiban-brittanta*, p. 78.

33. Ibid.

34. Lahiri, *Akshaykumar Dutta*, p. 151.

35. Ibid.

36. Ray, *Srijukta Babu Akshay Kumar Datter Jiban-brittanta*, p. 77.

37. Ibid.

38. Kumar, *Science and the Raj*, p. 193.

39. Ibid.

40. Ramendrasundar Trivedi, *Maya-puri* (Calcutta: Sahitya Parishat Mandir, 1910), p. 38.

41. Buddhadeb Bhattacharya, *Bangasahitye Bijnan* (Calcutta: Bangiya Bijnan Parishad, 1960), p. 59.

42. For a detailed discussion on the role of the CSBS in the dissemination of knowledge, see Abhijit Gupta, 'The Calcutta School-Book Society and the Production of Knowledge', *English Studies in Africa* 57, no. 1 (2014): 55–65.

43. The first edition of 500 copies of *May Ganit* was quickly exhausted, and the secretary of the CSBS regretted that they should have printed 5,000 copies. Likewise, the first edition of *Jyotish ebang Goladhyaya* also sold around 500 copies. See Gupta, 'The Calcutta School-Book Society and the Production of Knowledge', pp. 61–62.

44. Bhattacharya, *Bangasahitye Bijnan*, p. 17.

45. Ibid., p. 20.

46. Ibid., p. 22.

47. Christian Ministers of Various Denominations (ed.), *The Calcutta Christian Observer*, vol. III, January–December 1834 (Calcutta: The Baptist Mission Press, 1834), p. 576.

48. Charles Lushington, *The History, Design, and Present State of the Religious, Benevolent and Charitable Institutions Founded by the British in Calcutta and Its Vicinity* (Calcutta: Hindostanee Press, 1824), p. 157.

49. Quoted in Bhattacharya, *Bangasahitye Bijnan*, pp. 37–38.

50. In his 2012 essay 'Popular printing and intellectual property in colonial Bengal' Abhijit Gupta writes:

    > For long, scholars have struggled to put a figure on the exact number of presses active in Calcutta – the benchmark figure in this regard is the 46 presses named by the indefatigable Rev. James Long for the year 1853–4. For the period earlier than 1853–4 there are no figures, other than three incomplete lists in the periodical *Samacar Darpan* in 1825, 1826 and 1831, which provide a list of 21 presses.

    See Abhijit Gupta, 'Popular Printing and Intellectual Property in Colonial Bengal', *Thesis Eleven* 113, no. 1 (2012): 32–44, 36.

51. Bhattacharya, *Bangasahitye Bijnan*, p. 67.

52. Ibid.

53. Ibid., p. 68.

54. See, for example, his essay 'Prachin Hindudiger Samudrayatra', *Tattwabodhini Patrika* 3, no. 71, Asad, 1771 Saka, pp. 44–48.

55. Bhattacharya, *Bangasahitye Bijnan*, p. 68.

56. Akshaykumar Dutta, *Bharatvarshiya Upashak Sampraday*, vol. 2 (Kolkata: Karuna Prakashani, 2013), p. 53.

57. In fact, as Pijushkanti Sarkar claims, Rajendralal Mitra, one of the important figures of the 'Bengal renaissance', adopted the philosophy of Bacon as his own due to the influence of Akshay Dutta. See Pijushkanti Sarkar, *Bismrita Abismrita Akshaykumar Dutta*, vol. 1 (Kolkata: Kabitika, 2020), p. 335.

58. Dutta, *Bharatvarshiya Upashak Sampraday*, vol. 2, p. 52.

59. Ibid.

60. Rammohun Roy refers to Lord Bacon as a harbinger of modernity and scientific education in his letter to Lord Amherst in 1823. See Collet, *The Life and Letters of Raja Rammohun Roy*, p. 107. Likewise, in a letter

to Dr Moyet, a member of the Council of Education, Vidyasagar writes in 1853 of his many reservations of the report of Dr Ballantyne on the Sanskrit College where he mentions the latter's 'excellent edition of the *Novum Organum* in English'. See Indramitra, *Karunasagar Vidyasagar* (Kolkata: Ananda Publishers, 2014), p. 738.

61. Steven Matthews, *Theology and Science in the Thought of Francis Bacon* (Hampshire: Ashgate, 2008), pp. 55–56.

62. Quoted in ibid., p. 56.

63. Ibid., p. 69.

64. Akshaykumar Dutta, *Bahyavastur Sahit Manab Prakritir Sammandha Vichar* (1852), in *Akshaykumar Dutta Rachana Sangraha*, ed. Swapan Basu, vol. 1 (Calcutta: Pashchimbanga Bangla Academy, 2008), pp. 13–316, p. 121.

65. Lahiri, *Akshaykumar Dutta*, p. 92.

66. Ibid.

67. Auguste Comte, *A General View of Positivism* (Cambridge: Cambridge University Press, 2009), p. 58.

68. Ibid.

69. Ibid., p. 60.

70. Ibid., p. 60.

71. Ibid., p. 100.

72. Ibid., p. 105.

73. Ibid., p. 106.

74. Ibid., p. 111.

75. Ibid., pp. 111–112.

76. Dutta, *Bahyavastu*, pp. 126–127.

77. See, Saradacharan Mitra, 'Akshaykumarke Jemon Dekhechhi', in *Dwisatajanmabarshe Akshaykumar Dutta*, ed. Tapas Bhowmik, *Korok Sahitya Patrika*, Kolkata, 2020, pp. 265–270.

78. Ibid., p. 270.

3

The *Tattwabodhini* Period

The Conflicting Contours of Self-Fashioning or Towards a Global History?

In the preceding chapters I have laid out the two major, albeit connected, narratives of religion and science that were instrumental in shaping the intellectual horizon of Akshay Dutta's mind. His milieu was one of debate and discussion, influences that emerged out of a complex network of intellectual practice qualified by colonial modernity and its associated implications of a global labour–capital dynamic working from within a colonizer–colonized binary. It was a space where the principal aim of science education and practice was to develop a utilitarian template leading to motives of profit through governance and vice versa. The questions of religion and individual religious practice, on the other hand, were implicated by complex processes of reform and refashioning that often had their own transnational and global influences and subversive intent. The figure of Akshay Dutta emerges through this web-like narrative as part of the *bhadralok* milieu of nineteenth-century Calcutta through events and articulations that will not be subsumed within an easy and overbearing trope of either colonialism or nationalism, modernity or otherwise, but remain as a symptom of the fraught nature of the intellectual tendencies of the period.

Akshay and Rammohun: Imagining the Universe

Akshay Dutta spent the most crucial and active years of his working life as the editor of the *Tattwabodhini Patrika* between 1843 and 1855. A substantial part of his oeuvre, books or tracts that were subsequently published as individual volumes, germinated in the pages of the *Tattwabodhini*. It may be said that the larger part of Akshay's intervention into the intellectual and social structures of nineteenth-century Bengal was initiated or provoked through either what he wrote or what he, as the editor, published in the pages of the *Tattwabodhini*. It was during this Tattwabodhini period that, one might say, Akshay emerged as a crucial player in the larger canvas of Bengali intellectual history through the way he shaped the debates and discussions around the pages of the periodical. In the first chapter I have referred to his ideological debate with Debendranath Tagore regarding the nature of the Brahman and the infallibility of the Vedanta.[1] Although there remained a clear ideological rift between the two, the pages of the *Tattwabodhini* bear ample testimony to Akshay's considerable independence in choosing the subject matter for the issues of the periodical. While Debendranath's chief aim was to discuss religion and spread Brahmoism through the pages of the *Tattwabodhini*, Akshay's intention was the dissemination of knowledge, primarily scientific, and discussions on principles of social reform. As Prasad Sengupta has noted: 'In spite of much surveillance it seems unlikely that he [Debendranath] was able to control Akshay.'[2] It was under the editorship of Akshay that the *Tattwabodhini Patrika* became an instrument of intended social reform, in terms of not only how the reading public would consider questions on religion and god, but also the possibility of learning about the universe and the world through what one might call an engaged cosmopolitanism. Articles on the sciences, general knowledge, economic conditions of the peasantry, and a motley range of other subjects opened up the scope of the periodical to the acquirement of knowledge that went beyond the narrow logic of the dissemination of Brahmoism. That this was a popular move was indicated by the steadily increasing sales figures of the *Tattwabodhini* under Akshay's editorship. Nakurchandra Biswas writes how under Akshay's leadership the periodical gained a wide and various readership: native or foreigner, Hindu or Muslim, Christian or Brahmo, almost all educated persons subscribed to it. Those with lesser economic means appealed to the management for a reduced rate of subscription.[3] Even Debendranath Tagore wrote: 'At some point the number of subscribers of the *Tattwabodhini Patrika* went up to 700; and this was only due to Akshay-babu. If Akshaykumar Dutta were not the editor of the periodical at that time such improvement of the *Tattwabodhini Patrika* would not have been possible.'[4]

In the context of how Akshay's mind worked as the editor of the *Tattwabodhini*, Amiya Kumar Sen suggests that Akshay was perhaps more inclined to the way Rammohun Roy envisioned the principles of knowledge rather than to Debendranath's vision. In fact, Sen makes a rather crucial point while discussing Akshay's discourses on Rammohun in both the Tattwabodhini Sabha and the pages of the *Tattwabodhini Patrika*:

> He [Akshay] pointed out that Rammohan wanted India to be raised above the miserable condition in which it then was; that all superstitious feelings should be replaced by worship of the One, omniscient and omnipotent being, the creator, preserver and destroyer of the universe. Rammohan wanted that the world should participate in the acceptance of these truths. He strove to spread the idea that true religion is transcribed in everliving letters in the hearts of men and the external world. The universe alone is the infallible scripture, the revelation of God.[5]

The belief in a singular god and the use of words and phrases such as 'universe' and 'external world' would open up a politics of understanding and critique that will assume a formative role in my argument in this book. In the previous chapters I have mentioned, albeit cursorily, Akshay's exposure to both European and Oriental forms of epistemic practice and knowledge systems that were instrumental in his ideological development. His milieu was teeming with peers who had identical and often more structured exposure to ideas from across the globe. That Akshay was perhaps drawn more towards Rammohun than Debendranath could be attributed to the former's informed and intense engagement with forms of philosophical and social understanding that straddled different nations and continents, languages, ideologies, and faiths. In his own way, through the pages of the *Tattwabodhini*, was Akshay also opening up a space for the literate Bengali subject towards a more holistic and inclusive understanding of the phenomenal and the existential worlds they inhabited? An analysis of Akshay's affinity for Rammohun may lead us towards imagining or formulating a framework within which this almost iconoclastic Bengali intellectual from nineteenth-century Bengal may be located.

The Authorship Question: A Brief Digression

An important argument needs to be foregrounded, however, before one begins to closely read the *Tattwabodhini* numbers, and that is regarding the question of signatures and authorship. Largely, the articles that appear in the *Tattwabodhini* have no markers of authorship or signature. Some of the earliest issues have a few articles carrying the initials of the authors, in a manner that is often cryptic. The only method by which one may arrive at an author's name for an article in the periodical is by speculation. Brian Hatcher has painstakingly tried to locate and discuss the question of authorship of some of the essays in the *Tattwabodhini Patrika* in the context of discussing another rare and earlier set of twenty-one discourses of the Tattwabodhini Sabha called *Sabhyadiger Baktrita* (or the lectures of the members of the Tattwabodhini Sabha), some of which appeared later on in the pages of the *Tattwabodhini*.[6] Hatcher asserts that in the 'nineteenth-century English periodicals the use of initials as well as the use of pseudonyms, was commonplace'.[7] But he soon admits that 'for the inconsistency in the system of initials … there was wide variability at this time in the use of initials in Bengali publications'.[8] The internal inconsistencies of using different initials for the same author, or using none at all, has left the readers with no concrete manner of asserting authorship of particular discourses other than by figuring out certain consistencies of 'style and theological concerns'.[9] Subsequently, Hatcher has tried to determine the authorship of various discourses of *Sabhyadiger Baktrita* or in the *Tattwabodhini Patrika* written by Debendranath Tagore, or Akshay Dutta, or Iswarchandra Vidyasagar, or Ramchandra Vidyabagish or others, in terms of the kinds of words or phrases they were known to use, or in terms of styles of address, or ideas they would frequently refer to.[10] My contention from my personal reading of the issues of the *Tattwabodhini* is that there is the possibility that many articles other than the signed ones, or the obvious ones that were later collected and published as individual volumes, such as *Bahyavastur Sahit Manabprakritir Sammandha Vichar*,[11] *Dharmaniti*,[12] and *Bharatvarshiya Upasak Sampraday*,[13] or well-known individual essays such as *Palligramastha Prajader Durabastha Barnan*,[14] were written by Akshay Dutta. In fact, Swapan Basu, the editor of the volume of collected works of Akshay Dutta, has also assigned quite a few of the unsigned *Tattwabodhini* articles and published lectures to him.[15] In his long essay, Prasad Sengupta also suggests that a number of unsigned essays in the *Tattwabodhini* numbers bear the marks of Akshay Dutta.[16] There would be certain others, editorial pieces, lectures of the Brahmo Samaj or the Tattwabodhini Sabha, articles on minor religious sects and Vaishnavism, that may probably be assigned to Akshay in terms of style or content. For example, both the Brahmo Samaj lecture and the article on moral knowledge (*nitijnan*) published almost consecutively in the same Paush 1766 Saka (1844) issue of the *Tattwabodhini* bear clear markers of belonging to Akshay.[17] While the first lecture talks about the perfectly balanced presence of air in the atmosphere being the fine handiwork of *jagadishwar*, the second one talks about the virtues of compassion, forgiveness, gratefulness, and generosity as ways of following the path of *parameshwar*. Likewise, the lecture of the Brahmo Samaj published in the Phalgun 1773 Saka (1851) issue praises Rammohun Roy from within a framework of analysis that is unmistakably typical of Akshay Dutta.[18] It is possible to provide several other instances as speculative pointers to establish Akshay's signature in terms of style or content.

I would rather argue that most of the issues of the *Tattwabodhini Patrika* published under the editorship of Akshay Dutta bear indelible markers of his influence. While the speculative logic of assigning authorship belies certitude of any kind, a sizeable number of the articles published during this period have an over-arching thematic rubric that point towards the editor's direct or indirect involvement. Science and morality, praise of the *parameshwar*, celebration of the Brahmo Dharma as a religion invested in the rational and the communitarian, general knowledge spanning across continents, education for the woman, education in the vernacular, discourses on minor religious sects were all subjects in which Akshay was reasonably invested. Although many of his peers associated with the periodical would be in agreement with these thematic concerns, the general intent of the articles is unmistakably inclined towards Akshay's system of beliefs and trajectory of argumentation. I would contend that Akshay, as the editor, had a considerable influence on the choice of articles for the issues of the periodical. Of course, there were long discourses on the Upanishads, and there were interpretations by the likes of Ramchandra Vidyabagish or Sridhar Nyayratna, debates on questions of religious conversion, or the periodical publication of Debendranath's *Atmatattwavidya*.[19] However, the intellectual influence of Akshay is evident in most of the articles during the period, and many of them were quite certainly written by him as well. For the moment though, instead of continuing to speculate about authorship, it will perhaps suffice to say that the sociopolitical intent of the *Tattwabodhini Patrika* during the period of Akshay Dutta's editorship was largely determined by him or a paper committee that was largely inclined towards him ideologically.[20]

Rammohun, Akshay, and *Viswa Rup Mul Grantha*

David Kopf writes about how on the day of Rammohun's funeral in Bristol in September 1833, the Reverend Lant Carpenter remembered with much feeling and sense of companionship the 'enlightened Brahmin from the British capital of Hindustan'.[21] Kopf tries to understand why the 'enlightened' unitarians across England and the United States were drawn towards someone like Rammohun and comes up with three possible reasons for such affinity: liberal religion, the idea of social reform, and the idea of universal theistic progress.[22] Two key words of considerable theoretical intent are used here by Kopf, 'liberal' and 'universal'. I will take up the first one for detailed analysis in a later chapter. For the time being, I will try and understand the idea of the 'universal' that Kopf foregrounds here. In a provocative essay on Rammohun and the idea of the rights-bearing self, Milinda Banerjee locates Rammohun's writings at the confluence of 'the porous frontiers between the "universalistic", "the world-historical", and the "global"'.[23] Within the fraught dynamics of historical categories and their discursive registers, the 'global' is claimed to have a more inclusive intent in the sense of its eschewal or critique of Eurocentric assumptions about the narratives of world history that make Hegelian claims of universality for European modernity.[24] Later in this chapter I shall take up this idea of the 'global' for an informed discussion in the context of reading Akshay's location. Banerjee begins the essay by staking a claim for Rammohun within the rubric of globality in the way the latter has used comparatist models of analysis in locating his social-reformist critique. Banerjee writes: 'I suggest that Rammohun constructed the vision of a "global" self by creating relationships between multiple Sanskritic, Perso-Islamic, and European models of globality, and thereby also offering a kind of world-historical approach based on comparisons between the cultural mores of different societies".[25] It was by adopting a comparative-historicist approach that Rammohun was undercutting the Hegelian *Weltgeschichte* model of understanding the history of the world, and placing disparate historical periods and societies within a comparative axis in terms of their notions of divinity or rights to property or larger principles of morality or the movement of capital.

A topical question, however, in this context, would be one of rhetoric and terminology. Whether one was envisioning a comparatist model of the 'global' or implicitly critiquing the notion of Eurocentric progress embedded in the 'world-historical', there remained the crucial problematic of finding the language to articulate this notion of the 'individual self' connected to the 'global other' (or other global selves) both synchronically and diachronically through a narrative of nuanced diversity. Banerjee argues that for Rammohun, the idea of the soteriological was located in the self, qualified by a universalist structure of morality and articulated through a language that encompassed all the peoples and societies across time and space: 'Rammohun's understanding of globality was embedded in frequent use of terms such as *vishva*, *jagat*, and *sarva* in Sanskrit and Bengali quotations and writings, and the use of terms such as "universe", "world", and "all" in English works.'[26] In the Phalgun 1773 Saka (1851) issue of the *Tattwabodhini Patrika*, the first annual lecture of the Brahmo Samaj, delivered in the unmistakable diction of Akshay Dutta, was published.[27] The general subject matter of the talk was an apotheosis of Rammohun Roy as the founder of the Samaj. A close reading of the lecture may prove to be crucial in establishing certain pervasive commonalities between Rammohun's and Akshay's ideas of the 'global'. While deliberating on how the Brahmo Samaj, established by Rammohun, may be envisioned as the root cause of *aihik paratrik mangal*[28] (well-being in this world and the next), the lecture is peppered with the words *bhumandal*,[29] *viswa*,[30] *jagat*,[31] and *prithibi*,[32] all meaning the universe or the world. Undoubtedly, here, Akshay envisions the 'global' in terms of a universalist structure of moral practice qualified by the Brahmo Dharma and invested in an emancipatory rhetoric whose enunciative impulses reach out across spatial and temporal boundaries. He writes how Brahmo Dharma will reach 'every place of the earth' (*bhumandaler sarvasthane*)[33] and that the name of Rammohun will be celebrated 'from one corner of the earth to the other among every civilized human race.'[34] The pattern of unfolding of a rhetoric of universalism from Rammohun's *vishva*, *jagat*, and *sarva* to a similar, almost identical, vision of emancipation in Akshay's choice of words is conspicuous. Such a conception of the *jagat* or *bhumandal* is complemented by Akshay's engagement with and faith in the manifestation of the *parameshwar*'s handiwork in the phenomenal world around the human subject. For him, each of the infinite solar systems that constitutes the universe is a manifestation of a page from the one 'elementary book of the universe' (*viswa rup mul grantha*) that lies at the core of the entire system.[35]

Thus, the trajectory of the soteriological is embedded in the phenomenal world, and true knowledge (*prakrita jnan*)[36] is only achievable through an intense reading of this *mul grantha*. He also regards this intense close reading of nature and the phenomenal world as the only means of 'rightful moral education' (*jathartha dharmasiksha*).[37] Apart from the obvious reference to Rammohun's notion of the unitary or the Advaita, there are clear markers here of Akshay's familiarity with the works of George Combe. Incidentally, it was at the same time when this lecture was delivered that Akshay was also serially translating *The Constitution of Man*[38] by Combe in the pages of the *Tattwabodhini*. In fact, one instalment of the translation immediately followed this lecture in this particular *Tattwabodhini* issue. Akshay's notion of *parameshwar* or god as the determiner or governor (*sristi-sthiti-bhanga karta*)[39] of the universe and nature as the manifestation of the order ordained by god is reflected in almost similar terms in Combe's next book *On the Relation Between Science and Religion*[40] that Akshay must also have read. In a similar vein as Akshay imagines the world as a 'book', Combe imagines it as an 'institution' that unfolds itself subject to the authority of God. Combe writes:

> If this world is an *Institution*, and if God is its Author and Governor, it appears to be the duty and interest of man to regard it with reference, to study its arrangements ... to act in accordance with the rules which it indicates for the guidance of his conduct.... We must approach Nature in the spirit of little children, humble, eager for instruction, and willing to obey. To reach this state of mind, we must lay aside that practical atheism which blinds us to the laws of God's Providence, manifested in Nature, and devote our best energies to discover the Divine Will revealed in that record.[41]

From Rammohun to Combe to Akshay, it is not difficult to imagine a global intellectual connect in terms of the construction of a universal structure of morality mediated through god who is manifest as *brahman sarvavyapi*[42] (the pervasive brahman) for Rammohun, natural science and 'real order of the Divine government on earth'[43] for Combe, and *viswa rup mul grantha* as the site of faith for Akshay. This apparently universalist framework may, however, be further complicated by reading Ramohun's non-linear, un-Hegelian, assimilationist form of unitary divinity against the grain of Combe's phrenological analysis of 'Hindoo, Mahometan, or any other false religion',[44] or his insistence on Europe being 'the centre and focus of all the lights of the world'.[45] The confluence of both these disparate yet commensurate models of morality renders a complex contour to Akshay's conception of the universal, and this strand of the discussion will be taken up in due course. At the moment, while still closely reading this crucial and interesting lecture at the Brahmo Samaj, I intend to make two brief digressions.

In the first chapter I had briefly referred to the distinction that Brian Hatcher makes between eclecticism and syncretism. While syncretism was more of a synthesis of sorts keeping with the traditional, developmental narrative structure, eclecticism involved a hermeneutics of sorts that resisted symptoms of singularity while anticipating the universal. Hatcher sees in Rammohun one of the earliest practitioners of eclecticism in the debates concerning the comparative merits of the religious faiths of the colonizer and the colonized:

> One early and notable case occurred in Calcutta in 1820, when the polymath Bengali reformer Rammohun Roy locked horns with some of the first Protestant missionaries to preach the Gospel in Bengal. With his pride in Sanskrit and the Vedas, his training in Arabic and Persian, his fluency in English, and his knowledge of biblical Greek and Hebrew, Roy represented something of a living testament to eclecticism.[46]

Clearly, the comparative-historicist framework of universality is what Rammohun was taking recourse to. He was using a similar strategy in fending off his native interlocutors. To go back to Banerjee's important essay once again, he argues that it was the style and format of disputation 'which allowed an enunciation of the global and the historical in Rammohun'.[47] Banerjee claims that instead of resorting to dogma or mystical faith, Rammohun was using historically embedded argumentative frameworks where claims from the *shastras* were foregrounded with the help of *tarka* (debate) and *yukti* (reason). He believed that *dharma* (morality) could only be established by the *shastras* by using *tarka* and *vichara* (judgement). It is singularly interesting to notice how Akshay uses a similar rubric of analysis in his lecture while investing Rammohun with qualities that would later help him establish his own views on rationality and the practice of individual faith. In the lecture he focuses on two qualities in the human subject, those of *vichara* and *buddhi* (intelligence). He insists that the manifestation of the love for the grand design of the *parameshwar* was to follow the rules of nature and that this is immediately apparent to one who makes use of natural intelligence (*swakiya buddhibal*).[48] Likewise, he praises Rammohun's *sparshamani swarup ascharya buddhi* (touchstone-like wonderful intelligence)[49] and his sense of *vichara*, presumably more precious than *buddhi*, by which he combatted the *buddhi* of his adversaries.[50] Akshay makes another strikingly important point here by talking about another quality in Rammohun, radically distinct from either *buddhi* or *vichara*, and a quality that sets the tone for a kind of universalism that will be for Akshay one of the defining features of the *brahmanistha grihastha*, the quality of *karunya-swavab* (compassion).[51] It is by virtue of this quality of compassion that one makes *buddhi* or intelligence *dharma swarup* (akin to *dharma*).[52] This conception of *dharma* one needs to carefully distinguish from the sanctioned and institutionalized *dharma* of the *shastra*s. In this context, Brian Hatcher recalls the unresolved conflict in Vidyasagar's mind about these two sources of *dharma*: 'On the one hand, there are what he calls the holy sanctions of India's *sastras*; on the other there is the evidence of God's purpose revealed to us in creation – Aksay's modernist substitute for the *dharmashastras*'.[53] In fact, Hatcher argues that Vidyasagar prioritizes *sadharana dharma* (the religion of the common householder or *brahmanistha grihastha* based on rational principles and *karunya-swavab*) over and above the *varnashrama* structure foregrounded by the classical scheme of Hinduism and having shastric sanctions. It is interesting that Hatcher refers to this form of religious practice as 'Aksay's modernist substitute',[54] thereby claiming for Akshay a space of radical challenge to the established norms of discursive religious idiom, and also adding the spin of modernism which locates it within a larger global context. He makes Vidyasagar an accomplice of Akshay as well by claiming that 'for him the norms of the *dharmashastras* must conform to the universal norms that are expressed through the idioms of modernist rationalism and humanism'.[55] The discerning reader does not fail to notice the use of the word 'universal' in this context. It is quite possible, therefore, to argue that through his own pattern of disputation and rhetoric, Akshay was attempting to expand the boundaries of the debate concerning the constitution and practice of religion and morality. On the one hand, the strand of natural theology was introducing the notion of the rational and the empirical, thereby opening up the question of *dharma* towards global assumptions and interpretative possibilities; on the other, by investing the idea of practice with the notions of *buddhi*, *vichara*, and *karuna*, Akshay was both humanizing the religious and making it the householder's instrument, manifesting itself at a very local scale of his own milieu.

One crucial question needs to be addressed here and that is in the more immediate context of colonial rule and the reaction of Akshay's social milieu to this larger dynamic of administrative control related to global political dimensions. In the second chapter I have argued how as a 'science-worker' whose primary intention was to establish modes of rational thinking in the educated common person and writing textbooks on science and moral education, Akshay was largely at a cultivated and objective distance from the

more invested reformers such as a Vidyasagar or a Bankimchandra in later
years. Is it possible, therefore, to read Akshay as the kind of universalist who
assimilates, collates, and compares within a global network of knowledge
formation while categorically refusing the political intent of any such
network? It is here that I will place my second brief digression. However
imperceptibly, however incidentally, Akshay repeatedly raises the question of
the local, the immediate, and the space of the colonized in this same lecture
on Rammohun. It is crucial to notice how many times Akshay uses words
and phrases such as *pavitra bhumi* (the sacred land),[56] *janani janma-bhumi*
(motherland),[57] Bharatvarsha,[58] *swadesh*,[59] and Bharat *bhumi*[60] in the course
of the lecture. It is apparent that within the grand design of the *parameshwar*,
whereby the phenomenal world is manifested for comprehension as the *viswa
rup mul grantha* through the intelligence and compassion of the human subject,
the idea of Bharatvarsha as a singular space is also underlined repeatedly by
Akshay. The particularism implicit in this idea of the nation space as part of
the global is never overemphasized in Akshay's work. However, that it was
sometimes even an absent-presence, an implicit motif that would function
as a subtextual reminder of the political self, cannot be gainsaid in the entire
oeuvre of Akshay Dutta. The careful reader does not fail to notice the easy
movement between *jagat/bhumandal* and *swadesh*/Bharatvarsha in this talk,
the continuous movement from the universal to the particular and vice versa,
in the attempted realization of a moral order which is part of a larger, grander
design. Rammohun becomes the engineer, the maker's chosen one, who, with
the instruments of *buddhi*, *vichara*, and *karunya-swabhab*, designs the Brahmo
Dharma that is destined to eliminate all false religions (*samuday kalpanik
dharma*)[61] and usher in enlightenment (*jnan swarup suryodyay*).[62] The global
in the regional and the regional in the global are consistently implied in such
a way that the larger moral template or the category of the global is entangled
within a contingent local space, or emerging from it, where the priority of the
nation-space is often foregrounded as an almost political necessity. The local
needs to be accounted for in order that the global would make sense, and this
sense of the contingent has always been the argumentative crux in Akshay's
writings. Therefore, one would need to tread carefully at any attempt to
immediately map Akshay's ideological discourse within the larger framework
of global intellectual history, although undoubtedly it may turn out to be an
immensely enriching exercise opening up exciting possibilities of interpreting
the varied and multiple influences that ran through his mind.

How 'Global' Was Akshay Dutta?

Historians of modernity have written consistently about the reordering of discursive paradigms and transmission of ideological categories across geographical spaces that were opening up newer horizons of connection or exchange around the world for most of the eighteenth and the nineteenth centuries. Colonial modernity had its own equations of influence, control, assimilation, dispersal of systems of knowledge, and movement of capital that created its own peculiar network germane to the moment in history and the contingencies of geography. Within the same network, the colonial subject was curiously embroiled in devising an epistemology that spoke to and of multiple registers at the same complex moment. On the one hand, the native or colonized intellectual wanted to elicit from the system a form of emancipatory rhetoric that had all the symptoms of a Eurocentric version of enlightenment; on the other hand, there was a simultaneous dialogue with an indigenous premodern past that continuously qualified the implicit prescriptions of universalism that the former narrative entailed. In India, for example, and in the present context, Bengal, the native intellectual not only revived the immediate Perso-Islamic past, but also brought into the polemic a much older and traditional Hindu-Sanskritic context that lent depth and agency to the already fraught contours of the debate. However, it is necessarily noteworthy that such narratives of influence, each with its complex discursive apparatus, are not to be read as monoliths that were necessarily brought into the debate to oppose, reject, or counter the others. Given the tiered and embedded nature of these discourses with various internal contradictions, they would often either work in collusion or engage dialogically with each other in ways that created a large canvas which lent itself to multiple and nuanced interpretative mores. A moot point here would be to determine the method of reading or analysing this canvas of influences that formed both the imaginative geography and the ideological position of the subject located within such a space of colonial modernity, as well as determine if it is possible to derive categories of thought from such heterogeneous narratives. It is perhaps imperative that in trying to determine the position of the native intellectual in nineteenth-century Bengal, one must necessarily revisit this question of method, considering both the synchronic and diachronic nature of influences, and the narratives of global history that it encompassed. In due course, this analysis might help in situating Akshay Dutta within this framework and consider his agency as of an intellectual within such a purportedly global network.

Locating the 'Global'

In their now celebrated volume, Samuel Moyn and Andrew Sartori have attempted to define, underscore, or formulate a method of studying global intellectual history by problematizing the notion of the 'global'.[63] In their introduction to the volume, the editors try to deconstruct erstwhile notions of the global, closely read the possible correspondences between the global and the modern, and reconstruct them by attempting a redefinition of the boundaries of such global historical frameworks. They also raise and try to address such inclusive questions as 'Is a premodern global history possible?'[64] In attempting to conceptualize the global, Moyn and Sartori open up the debate to three possible narrative trajectories that would lend a perspective to the question of globality, or lend it more depth of analysis in terms of the question of representation. They write:

> We might begin by distinguishing among, first, the global as a meta-analytical category of the historian; second, the global as a substantive scale of historical process, and hence a property of the historian's subject matter; and third, the global as a subjective category used by historical agents who are themselves the objects of the historian's inquiry.[65]

The first principle, by a reduction of the global to a meta-analytical category (and not the analysis itself), divests the narrative of any claims to legitimize a universal paradigm of understanding the world, and denies discursive determinisms that reduce the subjects of history to easy self-other analytical tools. The second, by insisting on a 'process', resists the idea of closure and emphasizes the need to focus on particularisms rather than universalisms. The editors bring in the notions of 'intermediation', 'circulation', or 'transmission'[66] as implicit markers along which knowledge is transmitted in a holistic manner, implying that the politics of historical analysis will look for 'specific practices of mediation in particular times and places'.[67] The third offers a unique self-reflexivity to the discipline of historical practice by dismantling the object–agent binary and investing the object of historical inquiry with the agency of an active player within the system of knowledge dissemination. Incidentally, placed in the perspective of the third category, Akshay Dutta would simultaneously become an object and agent of history (read both as a reformist and a science worker), what Ranajit Guha would call the quintessential 'small voice of history'.[68]

The contention of Moyn and Sartori, especially in the second and third narratives of the global as process and as a subjective category, would help me in suggesting an ambiguous location for Akshay read in terms of Guha's argument. In the two previous chapters I have foregrounded the implicit suggestion that Akshay's location, due to the unfinished and staccato nature of his education, and his desire to befriend various categories of the underclass, was always on the fringes of the bourgeois, upper-class society of a Rammohun or a Debendranath. On the flip side, he became the editor of one of the most influential periodicals of his time, the *Tattwabodhini Patrika*. Therefore, on the one hand, he would be an unfinished subject of what Ranajit Guha notes as the 'statism of Indian historiography'[69] that was the result of western education within the colonized elite. While most of his upper-class, elite, bourgeois milieu would conform to the structure of the civil society as propagated by systems of state in modern Europe, and the consequent manufacture of 'consent' in terms of domination, particularly when speaking of reform, Akshay's location would unsettle this apparently obvious deterministic logic. Guha writes how 'it made no sense to equate the colonial state with India as constituted by its own civil society. The history of the latter would always exceed that of the Raj, and consequently an Indian historiography of India would have little use for statism'.[70] Akshay unerringly becomes this figure of ambiguity, occupying a liminal space, vacillating between these two kinds of historiographic formulations of the colonial state. Both as a quiet reformist and a science worker (who writes textbooks on science but is not an active participant in the process of an emergent science practice), the symptoms of his agency as an intermediary are not immediately apparent. It is perhaps this lack of closure in the way one might read the presence of this liminal but crucial figure that would make Akshay Dutta a critical subject and agent of global intellectual history. What Guha says about the small voices of history, the ones relegated to the background of a more visible, more articulate narrative, may also be said, in certain ways, of Akshay:

> These are small voices which are drowned in the noise of statist commands. That is why we don't hear them. That is also why it is up

to us to make that extra effort, develop the special skills, and above all cultivate the disposition to hear these voices and interact with them. For they have many stories to tell – stories which for their complexity are unequalled by statist discourse and indeed opposed to its abstract and oversimplifying modes.[71]

Is it possible that the principles of practising global intellectual history as suggested by Moyn and Sartori earlier would accommodate within them this small voice of history? This particular small voice, however, is more complex than the one Guha talks about. This is not the voice of the subaltern, the absent subject, but the one of the historical agent who is defined by his ambiguity, his liminality, his continuous resistance to closure. It is from such a complex location that Akshay Dutta registers his footprint within the sophisticated formulations of globality and the notion of intellectual history.

The 'Global' as a Subjective Category

We now need to understand how Akshay, as both a subject and an agent of history, anticipates what Moyn and Sartori call 'the global as a subjective category'. Further, what is the peculiar role of Akshay, as an intellectual in nineteenth-century Bengal, within the larger scope of what is being envisioned as the 'global' in this context? Clearly, we are looking at two different but related events here. In the first place, as a subject considerably invested in the mores of European modernity, with a reasonably wide exposure to social, political, and philosophical debates and discourses from the west, the editor of *Tattwabodhini Patrika*, one of the leading proponents of the contemporary Brahma Samaj, an ardent subscriber to scientific rationalism, Akshay was in some ways a typical product of colonial modernity and suitably exposed to a certain systematic enterprise of historiography that had its Hegelian and Eurocentric tilt. However, this discursive yet 'hyperreal'[72] imaginative geography was qualified by both a native understanding of a pastness and tradition, and an awareness of the ambiguous nature of the political space that he inhabited in a society fraught with differences of class, caste, religion, colour, and agency.

It may be interesting to read this difference in the context of the manner in which Sudipta Kaviraj understands the inflections of the word 'world' in the beginning of his book on Bankimchandra.[73] Kaviraj begins by saying that an artist creates a world, and then asks a leading question about how one may configure or conceive of the idea of such a 'world':

> First, what kind of a world is this – what is its structure, its limits of possibility, the inner logic of its working? Second, how did this world that the artist created relate to the world in which he lived?[74]

Kaviraj seems to be clearly sceptical of the extreme realist position that would deny agency to the world of the imagination unless it leads to historical material, and, instead of the overdeterministic ontological question, foregrounds the inherent paradox that lies at the heart of these questions, thereby anticipating the idea of 'play'. In a certain sense, this also anticipates Chakrabarty's contention of the 'hyperreal', while pithily noting that 'even if both are "worlds", even if they are both "real", they could neither be real nor worlds in quite the same sense'.[75] What Kaviraj says about the artist could easily be extended to the intellectual, or, for that matter, the historian as well. The many histories that came together through myriad pathways and timeframes inevitably created the world of play and inflicted meaning on the idea of the 'world'. It is difficult to deny that the colonial intellectual inhabited both these worlds and that it might be both futile and facile to try to solve the problem by creating separate compartments for each of these worlds. Although they could neither be real nor worlds in the same sense, they were both present, simultaneously, through various narratives – philosophical, social, or historical – and formed a network that was not opposed, but often contrapuntal. It is at this site of play that I would like to place the notion of the 'global' and read it symptomatically in terms of how Akshay reacted to this play. I have already pointed out how in the same lecture Akshay was positing the idea of the *jagat* or *bhumandal* with the contrapuntal notion of *swadesh* or Bharatvarsha. The difficult part is to determine how, or if at all, the conception of the 'global' could have emerged from such a contrapuntality, whether such a model of the world was at all conceptually tenable, and if it was possible to fit it within the framework of global intellectual history put forward by Moyn and Sartori.

Bharatvarsha, *bhumandal*, and premodernity

One of the important thrusts of writing the history of the modern world has been a focus on the movement of capital across the globe, and how the major narratives of change have had a direct and intrinsic relationship with the flow of capital and the narratives of production and circulation. A substantial part of the colonial and administrative tropes was predicated on the collusion between modernity, capital, and the modes of production, and how the colonized space, through an intervention of colonial modernity, was being witness to a global event that was instrumental in locating the colonized space on the geographical map of progress. However, as Sheldon Pollock has argued, modernity was a contrastive historical concept with an implicit yet inevitable link with what may be called 'premodern'. Therefore, in many instances it offered 'little in the way of a convincing account of the nature of the "premodern", at least in the case of South Asia'.[76] Thus, ideas of rationality, labour, economy, knowledge, or morality cannot be unequivocally assigned to modernity, or assumed to be 'entirely unknown to premodernity'.[77] Pollock asserts, 'European modernity and South Asian premodernity are obviously uneven and not absolute categories; the former displays premodern features, the latter modern ones, no matter what definitions we invoke'.[78]

Interestingly, Akshay Dutta writes a long essay in two parts in the pages of the *Tattwabodhini* on the global nature of premodern trade and commerce, and the epistemological exchanges that were part of this enterprise, much before modernity was imported through colonial praxis.[79] A close reading of the essay will reveal the strategy that Akshay employs in the essay. It is not a direct critique of the colonial enterprise in terms of trade, commerce, or the change in the nature of the movement of capital. Neither is it a call for opposing the trajectory of the colonial economy and its forms of economic and administrative reforms that had implicit support from the bourgeois elite.[80] Without getting into the immediate context of colonial economy and its many manifestations within the milieu in which Akshay incidentally belonged, he attempts, in the essay, a veiled critique of modernity through a comparative study of a Hindu past and present. He writes:

For the entrepreneurial Phoenicians it was quite possible to travel from Persia to India, and neither was it impossible for the Hindus to travel likewise. Although now they are pusillanimous and lacking in enterprise, and the imagination of various modernist mores has at some point of time led to stoppage of their voyages and foreign travel, they were not like this earlier. It is a duty, therefore, to elucidate on this while talking about the history of India's trade.[81]

In the paragraphs that precede or follow, Akshay meticulously maps the
footprints of the people of India across various nations, participating in trade,
commerce, culture, and information networks that bear the marks of a global
trajectory of transmission, circulation, and exchange. He culls references
from multiple texts and sources that bear testimony to his claim. He quotes
Theophrastus to provide evidence of the export of cinnamon, cardamom,
spikenard, and other spices and medicinal plants to the Arab world.[82] He
refers to the *Ramayana* to prove that in ancient India traders would travel
to China, Java, and Sumatra.[83] In this context, he refers to the works of
Ptolemy, Humboldt, Al Biruni, and the French archaeologist Reinaud and
concludes that their references clearly prove the journey of the Hindus to
China, Java, and Sumatra in ancient times.[84] He culls references from the
Mahabharata (the conquests of places outside India by Arjuna and Nakula),
the *Raghuvamsam* (references to Raghu's conquests in Persia), the *Varaha
Purana* (describing the trade ventures and travails of Gokarna, the trader),
and the *Yajnavalka Samhita* (reference to the custom of providing loans to
businessmen venturing into the sea); he also refers to the custom of marriages
to foreigners (the wedding of Ratnavaba the trader in *Dasakumaracharitam*);
and in Bengal itself, he recalls the journey of the traders Dhanapati and
Srimanta to Sri Lanka as described in the *Chandimangal*.[85] In due course he
reminds his readers that Indian rulers had sent diplomats to the courts of
the Roman emperors Antonius Pius, Theodosius, Heraclius, and Justinian
and refers to Juvenal's *Satires* to prove that in the first century, Indian experts
on astrology were employed in the city of Rome.[86] Akshay refers to the
annals of Cornelius Tacitus in his footnote, which says that around 60 BC
some Hindu traders travelled as far as Europe by sea, and claims how 'none
of the ancient races of the world (*bhumandal*) had undertaken such a long
voyage'.[87] In fact, he leaves it to his readers to decide whether these traders
and travellers could be compared to a Columbus or a Vasco da Gama.[88] He
also refers to Humboldt's *Cosmos* in the essay to point out how there is clear
historical evidence that Hindu pundits travelled to the Arab courts to teach
the *shastra*s.[89] He concludes the first part of the essay with the following
unambiguous declaration:

> Most of the examples provided here about the foreign travel of the
> Hindus are undoubtedly authentic; and, on comparison of the Hindu
> shastras with historical evidence it is unequivocally established that in
> earlier times Hindus would travel both within and outside Bharatvarsha

with great enthusiasm and an unflinching mind, and would often remain there for a period of time.[90]

He ends this part of the essay with the regret that it was a proof of the penuriousness of the Hindu mind that its *shastras* would now prohibit foreign travel. The only antidote, he declares, was education.

The second, shorter part of the essay, appearing in the Bhadra 1772 Saka issue, also delineates the extensive trade relations between the Indians and the Persians, Babylonians, and across the Mediterranean with the Europeans and Africans. Akshay quotes from various sources and cites extensive reference to establish how pearls, ivory, ebony, cinnamon, gold, dye, crops, perfumes, spices, liquor, and even animals such as dogs were exported from India. He draws comparisons between Ctesias's *On the Onyx Mountains of Ctesias in the Collection of the Treatises of the Count von Veitheim* and Valmiki's *Ramayana* to establish that products were sent from Kashmir and its adjoining areas to Africa and Europe by the Mediterranean route.[91] He is also particular in mentioning that in places such as Egypt the philosophy and religion of India were also especially celebrated.[92] In what may be called the companion piece, 'Prachin Hindudiger Samudrayatra', Akshay refers to the *Rigveda Samhita*, the *Manu Samhita*, and the *Ramayana* to establish that much before Europeans, Indians were adept at shipbuilding and trading across the seas.[93] To establish his argument, Akshay refers to several literary texts such as the *Avijnanasakuntalam* (the narrative of Dhana Vriddhi the trader), the story of Kandarpaketu in the *Hitopadesha*, the narratives of Chand Sadagar in *Manashamangal*, and Srimanta Sadagar in *Chandimangal*.[94] On a comparative note, he posits texts that have a non-Indian origin but also make similar claims, such as Arrian's *Periplus of the Erythrean Sea* or the opinions of Stamford Ruffles and John Crawfurd on Hindu influences in the islands of Java and Sumatra.[95] He concludes this essay by asserting that earlier, Hindus were used to being on the sea for several months, and there were no shastric sanctions that were imposed on them. It was only after the arrival of the Muslims and the spread of certain imaginary religions (*kalpanik dharma*)[96] that they have forgotten their glorious past.

This entire discourse, along with the extensive footnotes, bring several strands of the argument on modernity, India, and colonial rule together, and open up a curious and fraught set of narratives on the nature and impact of what one may call the 'global'. The epistemological thrust, very clearly, is the one adopted from the scientific model recently brought in by the colonial practitioner, with an emphasis on empirical evidence expressed through extensive cross-references in the footnotes. But the main text is also replete with references from earlier literary and cultural texts that emphasize the idea of the global in a premodern India. Clearly, there is an attempt to rediscover or revalidate a history of India's past in the manner of a contrastive recollection that places the idea of selfhood in the 'modern' context as the one that is restricted and bounded, as against a premodern self that was enterprising and adventurous. This revival is also meant to remind the present nineteenth-century readership of both an ontology and an epistemology of a global selfhood in premodern India that was as historically traceable and as real as the contemporary emancipatory and civilizational rhetoric assumed by the colonial ruler. On the question of space as a political construct, Akshay has carefully skirted the implications of nationalism for the time being. This would require a longer discussion, and I intend to address this in more detail when I read Akshay with Bhudeb Mukhopadhyay and Bankimchandra Chattopadhyay later on in the book. However, it may be topical to note here that Akshay's reference to Muslim rule or Islam as a religion is more complex than what is immediately apparent in the context of the present essays.[97] It is also interesting to see how Akshay uses the term 'Bharatvarsha' as a determinant of the geographical space instead of either Hindustan or India (both of which were current at the time Akshay lived and wrote). It is possible that for him the term 'Bharatvarsha' as a semantic label was more inclusive, wide, and neutral in terms of its political valency than either India or Hindustan. As Manan Ahmed Asif has contentiously, but astutely, noted:

> Much is made of the fact that both the words 'Hind' and 'India' are inventions of outsiders describing the subcontinent. In contrast are labels such as 'Jambudvipa' or 'Bharataavarsa', which represent emic or internal spatial labeling. The anxieties of insider/outsider, between languages that 'belong' to the subcontinent and those that do not, permeate much of such debates. The Sanskritic labels preserved in Vedic texts speak often of a cosmological conception of place – an all-world encompassing space. There is no delineation of insider/outsider in such a cosmology. There is also no sense of the political belonging and exclusion that modern invocations of these terms rely upon.[98]

In fact, while discussing the impact of colonial and nationalist cartography on the minds of such personalities as Rammohun Roy and Sahajanand Swami,

Brian Hatcher also points out how both of them found the classical idea of Bharatvarsha as a polity as a more inclusive and less contestatory category:

> Both Sahajanand and Rammohun drew on the idea of Bharatvarsha to think about their worlds (sometimes invoking cognate terms such as Bharata-khanda or Bharata-Bhumi).... But what did it connote for them? With roots in the Epics and the Puranas, the category speaks to an overarching, if nonempirical, cosmography, advanced in terms of a vast chronotope of worlds, continents, and eons (in Sanskrit, *lokas*, *dvipas*, and *yugas*, respectively).[99]

Evidently, as both Asif and Hatcher point out, the idea of Bharatvarsha opens up the polity of the geographical space to wider connotations of globality as an 'all-world encompassing space' or 'a vast chronotope of worlds, continents', thereby bringing to a crisis the notion of colonialist epistemologies and their claims of cosmopolitanism. The diachronic movement throughout the content and the footnotes of Akshay's essays refers to an already existing cosmopolitanism, one that emerges from the emic and encompasses the etic, and within an epistemological framework that belongs emphatically to the past. The idea of the global that it invokes is therefore one that has less of a derivative import, not being of European origin. However, there is clearly no intent of deliberate and symptomatic subversion of the colonial epistemology in Akshay's work. He uses their epistemological frameworks and cites sources that have a currency within colonialist pedagogy, but carefully through a consistent and almost deliberate overlapping of epistemic categories. In this particular set of essays, he even uses the strategy of the orientalist in speaking of a glorious past as opposed to a diminutive present in terms of the cultural and social exposure of his milieu. Also, the recently arrived 'new morning of knowledge' (*nutan jnan dibasher ushakal*) that should give hope to Bharatvarsha, the exhortation with which he ends the essay 'Prachin Hindudiger Samudrayatra', is undeniably predicated on the ideas of modernity brought in by the colonialist.[100]

The volumes of the *Tattwabodhini Patrika* under the editorship of Akshay Dutta bear testimony to a complex ideological map that had many inherent contradictions peculiar to the time and place in history. From the varied nature of the subject matter to the way it envisioned modernity, the *Tattwabodhini* was invested with a particularism that also, peculiarly, carried in its pages the indelible mark of its editor. The idea of India or Bharatvarsha, however one chooses to say it, was enunciated through multiple frameworks of the regional and the global, the premodern or the modern, and through a network of religion and science, rationality and belief systems, which had their impact on the lived experience of the educated middle class in nineteenth-century Bengal. This latter group of people, of the *bhadralok* category, was also not a homogeneous one and constituted of both the *kerani* and the deputy magistrate, the matriculate and the elite, Hindu College intellectual.[101] Evidently, the readership of the *Tattwabodhini* also constituted a motley group of people across sections of the *bhadralok* population, and also not restricted only to the members of the Brahmo Samaj. Therefore, whether it was religious or moral instruction, or dissemination of general knowledge or science education, the motley nature of the readership involuntarily created a network of influences and counter-influences that had both local and global connotations. Given the complex nature of the polity, and the range of influences that spanned centuries and continents, the editor and his milieu were wading through a series of rapid epistemic shifts and ideological manoeuvres that frequently ran into each other and yet were distinctly different. It was a time of considerable intellectual turmoil, and the global and the local were enmeshed in ways that could not be easily or immediately categorized. Thus, even though it is tempting to attempt to fit Akshay Dutta within a map of global intellectual history, the placement itself is a difficult task and needs careful meditation.

Towards the beginning of this chapter I was trying to figure out if it was possible to envision Akshay Dutta's intervention into the Bengali intelligentsia of the nineteenth century, primarily through his editorship of the *Tattwabodhini Patrika*, as a phenomenon that had certain global or universalist implications. Of the several models of global intellectual history that Moyn and Sartori foreground in their volume, the global as a native or actor's category would seem to be a framework within which it is possible to fit the role of Akshay Dutta in this context. Seemingly, it is a natural fit, considering how the object of history becomes the agent attempting to rewrite both the discourse and the contours of historical practice through a continuous reassessment of the location of the global within the local, and simultaneously engendering or provoking a refashioning of social and cultural praxis. The meta-analytical category of the historian or the investigator critically estimating the globality or reach of the passive subject is pushed back by these attempted epistemic shifts initiated by the agent or the actor, who has direct access to the narrative as a player. Also, these interventions by the agent or the actor have immediate contextual underpinnings both locally and globally, at the levels of both the real and the imaginary. This, in turn, also complicates the colonial polity with its almost simplistic insistence on the narratives of progress and modernity as linear mechanisms that constitute the notion of cosmopolitanism for the colonial subject. Interestingly and crucially, Akshay does not deny the rhetoric of the colonizer either. As a reformist and a science worker he both undercuts and underlines the notion of modernity and its associated claims to universalism, globality, and cosmopolitanism. In this context, I would once again like to emphasize the idea of 'play' that Sudipta Kaviraj has brought into his discussion of Bankimchandra. The real and the imaginary, or the historical and the literary, implode into each other in the cultural economy of the educated intelligentsia and are scattered unevenly across the various ranks of the *bhadralok*. The *brahmanistha grihastha bhadralok*, or the prospective member of the civil and political society, for Akshay, would be this individual with a number of innate or acquired qualities: a faith in the instrumentality of *parameshwar* in the well-being of the individual in this world and the next (*aihik paratrik mangal*); a rational view towards the connection between the existential and the phenomenal worlds through a universal system or design preordained by the inscrutable Brahma; a scientific and empirical approach towards the external world and natural phenomena; a general knowledge about the world through curiosity and exposure; an awareness of the idea of a contact between Bharatvarsha and its community with the world or the *bhumandal* through real and imaginary narratives of cultural encounters, historical evidence, and scientific and geographical inquiries.

The implicit particularism of such a model of the *grihastha*, or the educated common man in this case, qualified by a global awareness, would not necessarily conform to the immediate structures of modernity and cosmopolitanism brought in by the colonial ruler. However, there is no obvious subversive intent aimed at the modernist narrative either in such a nuanced model of colonial subjecthood. What it opens up are structures of play within which the notion of the global as a category is rendered unstable and contingent. A deliberate coalescing of categories – the religious and the scientific, the modern and the premodern, the past and the present, Bharatvarsha and *bhumandal* – unsettles (but does not upend) the stable narrative of progress, in global terms, that colonial modernity tried to bring in as a gambit of dominance and control. I also argue that it is in this singular manner in which Akshay Dutta, as the editor of the *Tattwabodhini*, wrote, chose, and published the articles in his periodical that the other relatively stable (albeit tiered and disjunctive) narrative of the *bhadralok* was also complicated. A significant section of the articles or printed lectures had elite, intellectual subject matter, those that would dally with the liberal fancies of the *bhadralok*: discourses on the Vedas and the Puranas; nuanced interpretations of the Brahma Dharma; condition of the peasants in rural Bengal; the educational principle of the Hindu College; the need for vernacular education; the ideological clash of religions; and female education, to name a few. However, a section of the periodical regularly printed articles on the minor religious sects such as the Nanakpanthis, the Kartavajas, the Shibnarayanis, the Babalalis, and their social and cultural practices; simple educative lessons on the volcano, the hot springs, practices of human sacrifice, or the walrus; moral dictums on drinking; or simple lessons on the right and virtuous way to lead one's life. In a way, this was also pushing the limits of the *jagat* of the *bhadralok*, of accommodating a world that was relegated to the fringes of elite aspirations of modernity or their definitions of enlightenment, an inclusive register that opened up the idea of globality to newer, contingent, and localized subcultural perspectives. It is in this context that I find useful the threefold problematic of global intellectual history that Moyn and Sartori speak of in their book:

> … a refusal to allow the global scope of particular colonial claims to obscure the local scope of their enunciation; a rigorous interrogation of the conception of the 'global' as a category of colonial exclusion; and the opening of historical investigation to forms of 'otherness' that exceed and disrupt the parameters of the uniformity, commensurability, and coherence of global space and time.[102]

I would like to read in Akshay's editorship of the *Tattwabodhini*, in his own writings, and the careful selection of articles (through the recommendations of a paper committee constituted by Debendranath and comprising elite, *bhadralok* intellectuals) an attempt at a rupture at the moment of enunciation. The category of the global is problematized in terms of not only iterating the presence of the local, but also fracturing the local at the moment of its articulation of the global. The global does not remain a mere inflow through colonial rhetoric, and its manifestation in tropes of modernity acquired by the colonized, but elite, subject. By a continuous reassessment of the fraught nature of the local, its many avenues of representation through othernesses that may barely be imagined, there is an outward, centrifugal movement towards the global that initiates a dialogue that unsettles the homogeneity of a centred causality. The hyperreal Europe is met by a hyperreal Bengal or a hyperreal Bharatvarsha on a level playing field of the global. The idea of the global is therefore brought out of the simple logic of hegemonic discourse, and an explicit Eurocentrism, to a more radical conception of space and its representability. The idea of unitarianism in religion, the contribution to global economy through travel, exchange, and business, the diffusion of ideas and epistemic practices across geographical spaces are all seen in a particularistic fashion, with a centrality accorded to the local or the regional. The possibility of Bharatvarsha as both a real and an imaginary space, of a native form of the hyperreal that needs to be assimilated within the dialogue of the global, is thus foregrounded by what Akshay was trying to achieve.

The transformative quality of a global history as against a universal history, if I understand correctly, is perhaps to be able to accommodate and articulate difference in ways that would create a space and a moment of enunciation that has possibilities of disruption or mismatch. It can therefore be imagined as a field of play, of possibilities, of randomness or diversions that could find comparable moments in other histories, other spaces, other temporal registers, and not be necessarily commensurate with any idea of totality or a narrative of progress. The question of culture, in the general sense, is indelibly grafted to such an idea of globality.[103] What I have tried to suggest in this chapter is how the *Tattwabodhini Patrika*, under the editorship of Akshay Dutta, was using the disjunctive agency of culture to unsettle a template of modernity that was firmly ensconced within the discursive apparatus that Akshay himself was a part of. What Akshay manages to achieve is to put his finger on a kind of elision of a cultural logic that accommodated both the colonizer and the colonized *bhadralok* within a narrative continuum of progress that pushes other narratives into disuse or as being less significant. By recovering these narratives, Akshay revitalizes the question of the hyperreal, but this time through a reversal of the focus from the colonizer to the colonized. The intensity of the act is multiplied by relegating the important native subject of colonial history of Bengal, namely the *bhadralok*, to a less active role and foregrounding the small voice of history. The idea of the hyperreal, or that which needs to be imagined, is now trained on the smaller voices of history, making the question of culture more eclectic and more fractured at the same time. An interesting example might elucidate this further. While discussing the minor religious sects of India, across various issues of the periodical, Akshay takes up the discussion on the Shibnarayani sect.[104] He begins with a mention of their faith in a unitary god, while clearly distinguishing them or setting them apart from the three major religious forms of Hinduism, Islam, and Christianity. He also mentions how the three main tenets of their religion are forgiveness, truth, and temperance. What truly sets them apart as a sect, however, is a liberal value system that opens itself up to forms of cosmopolitanism. Unlike their Hindu and Muslim brethren, they do not have any casteism, nor any prohibition on consumption of certain foods, or a structured set of rituals and forms of worship. However, in order that they are not judged harshly by members of other religious folds for their liberal values, they use an esoteric and symbolic language to signify certain common objects that have the potential of appearing contrary. Akshay gives us a somewhat lengthy list of these words, and some of them are as follows: *chandankhori* for pork; *duduyaram* for liquor; *anandaram* for hemp; *kabutari* for garlic; *akashkamini* for toddy, and so on, none of which are familiar words within the indigenous cultural milieu. The eclectic and the esoteric come together to dismantle the boundaries of expectation at multiple levels, thereby opening up the space for an otherness that demands comparison through global exposure, or, as Moyn and Sartori call it, 'subaltern internationalisms or globalisms'.[105]

Such examples of particularisms, unmediated by structured epistemic categories, constitute those moments of enunciation that render the articulation of essentialist universalisms contingent. The idea of nationhood implicit in Eurocentric formulations of modernity and progress is contextually intervened by the local claiming a global space, in what Homi Bhabha would call the nation as narration, of 'an expressive totality with its alliance between a plenitudinous present and the eternal visibility of a past'.[106] In fact, Moyn and Sartori would echo in their formulation of the actor's category what Bhabha refers to as the liminality of the colonized population as a double-inscription, 'as pedagogical objects and performative subjects',[107] a role that is disavowed within the discourse of a Eurocentric historicism. What Akshay manages to achieve in the pages of the *Tattwabodhini* is to provide narrative authority within a modern, secular space to the 'nonsequential energy of lived historical memory and subjectivity'.[108] The easy politics of a 'social and textual affiliation'[109] between the modernity that is imported by the imperial project and its local manifestation within the colony through tendencies of enlightenment in the cultural logic of the *bhadralok* has an epistemic validity that is naturally accepted within the domain of a Hegelian idea of universalism. The *Tattwabodhini*, through its ideological apparatus, mostly consolidates this affiliation, only to intervene at moments of enunciation of the universalistic with symptoms of contrariness that unsettle the narrative. The strategy that Akshay assumes, however, is not contestatory in nature, one that is predisposed to counter the colonial logic with a non-linear argument based on principles of indigeneity. In fact, such a confrontational strategy would only consolidate the narrative of progress and modernity by discovering for the latter an other of historicism that could be undermined. Rather, by carefully placing the non-conforming yet non-contestatory discourse within the axis of a pre-determined modernity, Akshay imperceptibly pushes it towards the more inclusive logic of globality where manifest difference only expands the horizon of understanding.

To conclude, I should say that the Tattwabodhini period, or the period of time when Akshay Dutta was the editor of the *Tattwabodhini Patrika*, was not only one of the most productive periods of his life, but also served to consolidate his ideological stand as an intellectual. This was also the period when he planned most of the rest of his oeuvre, and even published parts of them, either as separate volumes or in the pages of the periodical. *Tattwabodhini* therefore becomes an important site to explore the basis of the link that Akshay wanted to establish between his milieu, his *bhadralok* identity, the changing dynamic of the society around him, colonial modernity, and the larger context of the world or the globe that he imagined. In trying to locate the many particularisms in his writings, as I have done in this chapter, it will be unwise to neglect the inevitable generalisms that also formed part of his cultural and social discourse. The 'global' is a formula that may definitely help in setting Akshay Dutta apart from many of his contemporary intellectuals, and that is the point of my argument in this chapter. However, a conception or possibility of the global will not be laid out in a vacuum. The very fact of the birth of a periodical such as the *Tattwabodhini Patrika* is predicated on a positive consensus within a certain cultural milieu about certain forms of knowledge and epistemic practices that had colonial and Eurocentric roots. The trope of particularisms that opens out towards possibilities of the global emerged from a need for a different kind of articulation that both assimilated and critiqued assumptions of colonial modernity as a lived reality. Akshay's attempts may not have been born out of the notion of universal history, but carried its symptoms as a trace. It may have been about forging an identity that could be placed within the larger and more egalitarian rubric of the global instead of the universal, but one must remember Frederick Cooper's conception of 'flexible networks' that 'do not argue for a more refined or precise word to replace *identity*, but rather for the use of a range of conceptual tools adequate to understand a range of practices and processes'.[110] In the 'Concluding Reflections' section of Moyn and Sartori's volume, Cooper once again warns us against 'a too hasty leap to the "global"'[111] and incisively points towards the right question to ask:

> ... we need to ask whether we are still writing about a few thousand people, linked with one another across great distances but perhaps poorly connected to millions who live a few miles from each of those centers and who do not speak the language of 'global' intellectual communication.[112]

I would argue that in the pages of the *Tattwabodhini*, Akshay was attempting to forge this connection between the well-connected few and the poorly connected millions through a process of iteration and familiarization. To call it 'global', therefore, is to think about it from the perspective of a new paradigm, to understand the process as a form of disclosure that wades through practised amnesia or deliberate forgetting, and foregrounding a connectivity that is both wider and older. It cannot be denied that such an understanding of connectivity also presupposes, in complex ways, the idea of the nation and its people in terms of colonialism and its epistemic discourses that include but are not restricted only to the movement of capital.[113] The references to Bharatvarsha, *swades*, or *matribhumi* read against the grain of references to *bhumandal* or *jagat* or *viswa* throughout various articles and debates published in the pages of the *Tattwabodhini* remain as a continuous reminder of an implicit but not imperceptible thrust that may not be denied. I shall take this up for detailed discussion in the next chapter, where I will take up the question of culture in more detail. While I will remember Sanjay Subramanyam's important caveat in his review of the volume of *Global Intellectual History* that '[not] all intellectual history ... has to be "global" for it to be persuasive and intelligent',[114] I would still consider the framework to be a powerful tool to read Akshay's intervention as a historical agent who uses the global as a subjective category to unpack or represent difficult knots of the 'cultural' within the conventional modes of understanding the history of Bengal in the nineteenth century.

Notes

1. It is interesting to note, however, that some commentators on this debate between Debendranath Tagore and Akshay Dutta have tried to absolve the former entirely of the responsibility of the claim of the infallibility of the Vedanta. Benoy Ghosh, for example, in his introduction to selected issues of the *Tattwabodhini Patrika*, transfers the entire responsibility of this opinion to Ramchandra Vidyabagish. He even goes on to suggest that Debendranath did not find such an argument rational or acceptable. See Benoy Ghosh, *Samayikpatre Banglar Samajchitra*, vol. 4 (Kolkata: Prakash Bhavan, 2016), pp. 27–28.

2. Prasad Sengupta, 'Akshay-Manas', in *Anustup* 54, no. 1 (2019): 176–177.

3. See Nakurchandra Biswas, *Akshay-Charit* (Calcutta: Adi Brahmosamaj Press, 1891), pp. 25–26.

4. As quoted in *Akshay-Charit*, p. 28.

5. Amiya Kumar Sen, *Tattwabodhini Sabha and the Bengal Renaissance* (Calcutta: Sadharan Brahmo Samaj, 1979), pp. 194–195.

6. See especially chapters 6 and 7 in Brian Hatcher, *Bourgeois Hinduism, or the Faith of the Modern Vedantists* (New York: Oxford University Press, 2008).

7. Hatcher, *Bourgeois Hinduism*, p. 114.

8. Ibid., p. 122.

9. Ibid., p. 123.

10. For example, Hatcher talks about a characteristic theme of *paropakar* (service to others) in Akshay's writings (ibid., p. 123) or Vidyasagar's typical use of words such as *lopapatti* (meaning destruction or disappearance) or *jathestachari* (instead of *jathecchachari*, meaning one who does as he pleases) in his writings (ibid., p. 128) or Ramchandra Vidyabagish's frequent use of citations from the Upanishads or other Sanskrit texts (ibid., p. 129).

11. Akshay Dutta, *Bhyavastur Sahit Manab Prakritir Sammandha Vichar*, vols. 1–2, in *Akshaykumar Dutta Rachana Sangraha*, vol. 1., ed. Swapan Basu (Kolkata: Paschimbanga Bangla Academy, 1852/2008), pp. 113–316.

12. Akshay Dutta, 'Dharmaniti', in *Akshaykumar Dutta Rachana Sangraha*, vol. 1., ed. Swapan Basu (Kolkata: Paschimbanga Bangla Academy, 1852/2008), pp. 431–528.

13. Akshay Dutta, *Bharatvarshiya Upashak Sampraday*, vols. 1 & 2 (Kolkata: Karuna Prakashani, 1870/2015–1883/2013).

14. Akshay Dutta, 'Palligramastha Prajader Durabastha Barnan', in *Akshaykumar Dutta Rachana Sangraha*, vol. 1, ed. Swapan Basu (Kolkata: Paschimbanga Bangla Academy, 1852/2008), pp. 586–606.

15. See Swapan Basu (ed.), *Akshaykumar Dutta Rachana Sangraha* (Kolkata: Paschimbanga Bangla Academy, 1852/2008), pp. 529 – 653.

16. See Sengupta, 'Akshay-Manas', pp. 174ff.

17. *Tattwabodhini Patrika* 2, no. 17, 1 Paush 1766 Saka, pp. 135–137, 138–139.

18. *Tattwabodhini Patrika* 1, no. 103, Phalgun 1773 Saka, pp. 146–150.

19. Later, *Atmatattwavidya* was published as a separate volume. See Debendranath Tagore, *Atmatattwavidya* (Calcutta: Tattabodhini Sabha Press, 1852).

20. The paper committee of the *Tattwabodhini Patrika*, the committee that was responsible for determining the content to be published in its pages, consisted of the following individuals, along with the editor himself: Anandakrishna Basu, Rajnarayan Basu, Rajendralal Mitra, Iswarchandra Vidyasagar, Radhaprasad Ray, and Syamacharan Mukhopadhyay. It is rather debatable whether Prasannakumar Sarbadhikari and Anandachandra Vedantabagish were also members of the committee. It is well known that at some point in time Debendranath had regretted that the paper committee was constituted of a team of atheists. See Asitkumar Bhattacharya, *Akshaykumar Dutta Ebong Unish Sataker Banglay Dharma o Samajchinta* (Kolkata: K. P. Bagchi and Co., 2007), pp. 128–129.

21. See David Kopf, *The Brahmo Samaj and the Shaping of the Modern Indian Mind* (New Jersey: Princeton University Press, 1979), p. 3.

22. Ibid.

23. Milinda Banerjee, '"All This Is Indeed Brahman": Rammohun Roy and a "Global" History of the Rights-Bearing Self', *Asian Review of World Histories* 3, no. 1 (January 2015): 83.

24. See Samuel Moyn and Andrew Sartori, 'Approaches to Global Intellectual History', in *Global Intellectual History*, ed. Samuel Moyn and Andrew Sartori (New York: Columbia University Press, 2013), pp. 3–32.

25. Banerjee, 'All This Is Indeed Brahman', p. 83.

26. Ibid., p. 89.

27. *Tattwabodhini Patrika* 1, no. 103, Phalgun 1773 Saka, pp. 146–150.

28. Ibid., p. 146.

29. Ibid., pp. 146, 147, 149.

30. Ibid., p. 148.

31. Ibid., p. 148.

32. Ibid., p. 150.
33. Ibid., p. 146.
34. Ibid., p. 147.
35. Ibid., p. 148.
36. Ibid., p. 148.
37. Ibid., p. 148.
38. George Combe, *The Constitution of Man* (Cambridge: Cambridge University Press, 1828/2009).
39. *Tattwabodhini Patrika* 1, no. 103, Phalgun 1773 Saka, p. 148.
40. George Combe, *On the Relation Between Science and Religion* (Cambridge: Cambridge University Press, 1847/2009).
41. Ibid., p. 191.
42. Banerjee, 'All This Is Indeed Brahman', p. 92.
43. Combe, *On the Relation Between Science and Religion*, p. 71.
44. Ibid., p. 72.
45. Ibid., p. 87.
46. Brian Hatcher, *Eclecticism and Modern Hindu Discourse* (New York and Oxford: Oxford University Press, 1999), pp. 31–32.
47. Banerjee, 'All This is Indeed Brahman', pp. 91ff.
48. *Tattwabodhini Patrika* 1, no. 103, Phalgun 1773 Saka, p. 148.
49. Ibid.
50. Ibid., p. 149.
51. Ibid.
52. Ibid.
53. Brian Hatcher, *Idioms of Improvement* (New Delhi: Oxford University Press, 1996/2001), p. 259.
54. Ibid.
55. Ibid.
56. *Tattwabodhini Patrika* 1, no. 103, Phalgun 1773 Saka, p. 146.
57. Ibid., p. 147.
58. Ibid.
59. Ibid., pp. 147, 148.
60. Ibid., p. 149.
61. Ibid., p. 150.
62. Ibid.
63. Samuel Moyn and Andrew Sartori (eds.), *Global Intellectual History* (New York: Columbia University Press, 2013).
64. Ibid., p. 5.

65. Ibid.

66. Ibid., pp. 9–16

67. Ibid., p. 10.

68. See Ranajit Guha, 'The Small Voice of History', in *The Small Voice of History: Collected Essays* (New Delhi: Permanent Black, 2002), pp. 304–317.

69. Ibid., p. 306.

70. Ibid.

71. Ibid., 307.

72. I borrow this word from Dipesh Chakrabarty. For an informed discussion on the nature of the 'hyperreal', see his essay 'Postcoloniality and the Artifice of History', in *Provincializing Europe* (New Jersey: Princeton University Press, 2000), pp. 27–46.

73. Sudipta Kaviraj, *The Unhappy Consciousness* (Delhi: Oxford University Press, 1995), p. 1.

74. Ibid.

75. Ibid.

76. See Sheldon Pollock, 'Cosmopolitanism, Vernacularism, and Premodernity', in *Global Intellectual History*, ed. Samuel Moyn and Andrew Sartori (New York: Columbia University Press, 2013), p. 70.

77. Ibid., p. 71.

78. Ibid.

79. Akshay Dutta, 'Bharatvarsher Sahit Anyanya Desher Purbakalin Banijya Bibaran' (parts 1 and 2), *Tattwabodhini Patrika* 3, no. 78, Magh, 1771 Saka, pp. 153–166, and part 4, issue 85, Bhadra, 1772 Saka, pp. 68–76. Although both these essays are unsigned, they bear the indelible marks of Akshay's language, style, and ideological opinion. Swapan Basu has included both these essays as uncollected works of Dutta in *Akshaykumar Dutta Rachana Sangraha*. Much after Akshay's death, these were edited, interpolated, and reprinted as an independent volume by Akshay's son Rajaninath Dutta as *Prachin Hindudiger Samudrayatra o Banijyavistar* (Calcutta: Sanskrit Press Depository, 1901). Parts of another essay, 'Prachin Hindudiger Samudrayatra', published in *Tattwabodhini Patrika* 3, no. 71, Asad, 1771 Saka, pp. 44–48, were also included in this volume. Although Akshay Dutta's name appears as the author, Rajaninath declares that Akshay's original essay only constituted the backbone of the present volume.

80. In an interesting essay on the 'elective affinity' between the form of the Vedanta practised and promoted within the Tattwabodhini Sabha and the socioeconomic activities of its bourgeois promoters, Brian Hatcher

writes about how the discourses of the Sabha were 'a redefined theology of the Vedanta set to the task of naturalizing the economic privileges of the Sabha's bourgeois members'. See Brian Hatcher, 'Bourgeois Vedanta: The Colonial Roots of Middle-Class Hinduism', *Journal of the American Academy of Religion* 75, no. 2 (2007): 298–323, 308.

81. *Tattwabodhini Patrika* 3, no. 78, Magh, 1771 Saka, p. 163.

82. Ibid., pp. 156. See reference to Theophrastus in a footnote.

83. Ibid., pp. 157–158.

84. See ibid., footnote on p. 158.

85. Ibid., pp. 158–159.

86. Ibid., p. 161.

87. Ibid., p. 162.

88. Ibid.

89. Ibid., p. 163.

90. Ibid., pp. 164–165.

91. *Tattwabodhini Patrika* 4, no. 85, Bhadra, 1772 Saka, p. 70. See also A. H. L. Heeren, *Historical Researches*, vol. 1 (Delhi: Daya Publishing House, 1985), p. 421, n. 24.

92. *Tattwabodhini Patrika* 4, no. 85, Bhadra, 1772 Saka, p. 73.

93. *Tattwabodhini Patrika* 3, no. 71, Asad, 1771 Saka, pp. 44–45.

94. Ibid.

95. Ibid., p. 45. In the context of the ideas and opinions of Ruffles and Crawfurd, see also John Bastin, 'Sir Stamford Ruffles and John Crawfurd's Idea of Colonizing the Malay Archipelago', *Journal of the Malayan Branch of the Royal Asiatic Society* 26, no. 1 (July 1953): 81–85. In the context of Akshay Dutta's claim, see also Benoy Kumar Sarkar, *The Positive Background of Hindu Sociology* (Delhi: Motilal Banarasidass, 1985), pp. 381–393.

96. *Tattwabodhini Patrika* 3, no. 71, Asad, 1771 Saka, p. 48.

97. The complexity of the religious views and positions adopted by Akshay Dutta and his contemporaries such as Tarachand Chuckerbutty, Ramtanu Lahiri or Rajnarayan Basu is discussed by Brian Hatcher in his essay 'Varieties of Eclectic Experience: The Case of Colonial Bengal', in *Eclecticism and Modern Hindu Discourse* (New York and Oxford: Oxford University Press, 1999), pp. 95–128.

98. See Manan Ahmed Asif, *The Loss of Hindustan* (Cambridge, MA: Harvard University Press, 2020), p. 32.

99. Brian Hatcher, *Hinduism Before Reform* (Cambridge, MA: Harvard University Press, 2020), p. 43.

100. *Tattwabodhini Patrika* 3, no. 71, Asad, 1771 Saka, p. 48.

101. There have been many informed discussions on the category of the *bhadralok* in nineteenth-century Bengal. For a contemporary discussion on the various tiers of the *bhadralok* category, see Bhabanicharan Bandopadhyay, *Kalikata Kamalalaya* (Calcutta: Ranjan Publishing House, 1936). See also Tithi Bhattacharya, *The Sentinels of Culture* (New Delhi: Oxford University Press, 2005), pp. 35–67; Sumit Chakrabarti, *The Calcutta Kerani and the London Clerk in the Nineteenth Century* (London and New York: Routledge, 2021), pp. 19–62.

102. Moyn and Sartori, *Global Intellectual History*, p. 18.

103. I say 'in a general sense' to indicate a broad meaning of the word 'culture'. Andrew Sartori uses this word in a more limited and interesting sense in his book *Bengal in Global Concept History* (Chicago: The University of Chicago Press, 2008). I shall take up this narrower sense of 'culture' in the next chapter.

104. *Tattwabodhini Patrika* 2, no. 112, Agrahayan, 1774 Saka, pp. 89–93.

105. Moyn and Sartori, *Global Intellectual History*, p. 19.

106. Homi Bhabha, 'Dissemination: Time, Narrative and the Margins of the Modern Nation', in *The Location of Culture* (London and New York: Routledge, 1994), p. 151.

107. Ibid.

108. Ibid., p. 141.

109. Ibid., p. 140.

110. Frederick Cooper, *Colonialism in Question* (Berkeley: University of California Press, 2005), p. 9.

111. Frederick Cooper, 'How Global Do We Want Our Intellectual History to Be', in *Global Intellectual History*, ed. Samuel Moyn and Andrew Sartori (New York: Columbia University Press, 2013), p. 290.

112. Ibid., p. 291.

113. See, for example, Sanjay Subrahmanyam's review of Moyn and Sartori's volume, 'Global Intellectual History Beyond Hegel and Marx', *History and Theory* 54 (February 2015): 126–137.

114. Ibid., p. 136.

4

Reconstructing Bengali Selfhood

The Conception of *Dharma*[1] in Akshay and Bankim

History and Bengali Selfhood

The writing of history will always seek out narratives. If one were to look around the cultural, social, religious, or economic tropes scattered across the nineteenth-century Bengali society, it would not be difficult to discover the many reconstructivist narratives that define what may be described as 'threshold moments'[2] in the history of the Bengali people. So many of these narratives employ, implicitly or explicitly, tropes of representation that may be read through lenses of globality, global intellectual history, the world historical, or the universalist, and put into critical categories that bring out differential moments of enunciation which may be interpreted variously. Similarly, while some historians and commentators will tend to read nineteenth-century Bengal as one whole block divided into separate but connected narratives, others would discover a more well-defined disjunction between the first and second parts of the century. Likewise, both the principles of reconstruction and the way the ethos of the Bengali people were interpreted may be seen as different ways of reading history. Or, in other words, different ways of framing a narrative. As I have tried to understand in the last chapter, Akshay Dutta's intervention as both an object and an agent of history involved a rather complicated cultural politics due to his interstitial location within *bhadralok* Calcutta society, the contingent and unfinished nature of his academic training, and what one might call a certain ideological evasiveness that refused nomenclatures, boundaries, or categories. With time, the debates on representation became more fraught and by the middle of the century, the principles of reconstruction or avenues of representation were complicated by too many interconnections, cross-currents, and hermeneutic challenges that were not easy to grapple with: the modern and non-modern debate; the good and evil of imperialism; the principles of education; nationalism and its manifestations, and the corresponding idea of *swadesh*; religion, religious practice, and debates on conversion – to name a few. Out of these debates and discussions emerged the question of selfhood, of fashioning the self as a representative body of Bengali (or sometimes national) identity and defined within a moral or cultural register that had a commensurate relationship with modernity. A substantial part of intellectual life in the city of Calcutta throughout the nineteenth century was qualified by its sustained attempts at defining an acceptable selfhood within an imperial apparatus that was simultaneously determined by colonial oppression, European education and the ethic of enlightenment, revivalist modes of indigenous epistemic systems, and, most of all, a historical consciousness.

Within the scope of such a complex web, the articulation of a historical consciousness that would suitably represent a 'civilized' Bengali selfhood (and, in turn, the wider formulations of indigenous *bhadralok* identity) had its own problems. The constitution of an authentic self had manifest contradictory or intertwined impulses within the religious, cultural, and social reformisms that underlined the epistemic categories prevalent throughout the nineteenth century. The discipline of history as a tool for validation of a possible and traceable past was also new and brought in by the imperial master as a mode of dominance and a mark of superiority.[3] The educated Bengali *bhadralok* was almost unwittingly both a symptom and a victim of an essentialist elision of the past. On the one hand, he could not trace an authentic narrative and lay claim to a documented past that could be placed within the sophisticated evidential and empirical epistemic system brought in by the master class. On the other hand, the manifestations of disciplinary rigour within colonial modernity and its systems of knowledge formation had their own charm for the recent entrant into such a space of liberal education and rationalist discourses. Therefore, the question of culture for the native intellectual, retrospectively understood, was entrenched within a lack that needed to be addressed urgently. I shall address the specific problem of the question of culture presently.

Sudipta Kaviraj makes an interesting intervention within this idea of history as a narrative and reads an alterity in the way the colonial intellectual would grapple with this particular disciplinary formation. While principles of rationalism and order drew him naturally towards a historical consciousness of the self, the nineteenth-century Bengali intellectual was also becoming aware of the constructed nature of the historical narrative. As history was majorly 'the myth of a people, its construction of its self',[4] the performative role of the ideological was also a continuous and commensurate presence. Kaviraj argues how the 'Europeans were constructing an essentialist image of a subject people',[5] and therefore it was imperative that such a construction of history needed to be countered by an indigenous narrative with revivalist intentions. As one would understand, such a construction of a counter-narrative would be a project fraught with many contradictions. In the first place, is it at all possible to determine the exact historical moment when such a counter-narrative of representation or construction of the self as a non-essentialized subject might have begun? Why I raise this question will be apparent soon, when I bring up the notion of a well-defined ideological division between the two parts of the century that some historians have argued in favour of. Second, in terms of the notion of culture, the ideological apparatus of such a construction within the *bhadralok* milieu was largely borrowed from colonial registers of enlightenment education. In order that the intellectual would need to represent the self and the society (or the nation) through those very epistemic constructions that it needed to either critique or dismantle needed a complex self-reflexive manoeuvre. Third, a revival of the past as the precursor of the present cultural self within a set and traceable historical narrative was also not ideologically tenable. The nineteenth century may be seen as the most prominent timeframe of what Brian Hatcher has described as 'the empire of reform'[6] when traditional forms of belief and practice, both social and religious, directly encountered colonial modernity as a contrastive form of episteme. While the trajectory of colonial modernity was trained as a narrative of forward movement and progress, the amorphous or ill-defined past of the native subject was constructed, in the terms of such progress, as essentially regressive. While contrasting the two religious polities of the Swaminarayan Sampraday and the Brahmo Samaj, both born around the same time, Hatcher writes: '... these two early colonial religious polities were to become exemplars of two contrasting historical trajectories – one that spoke to the tenacious grip of tradition and the other to the promise of reason, progress, and freedom.'[7] Therefore, for the native intellectual, western educated and by default 'enlightened', a simple backward movement laced with revivalist intentions would entail the risk of an evident slippage into such a narrative of regression.

A good question to ask at this moment, therefore, would be whether the notion of selfhood is to be articulated solely as a question of culture that is epistemically entrenched within the practice of imperialism. To address this, one has to go back once again to the question of narrative and the need for a structural framework of articulation. Kaviraj insists that the cultural structure of the imagination and the articulation of selfhood were 'created by colonialism'[8] and writes:

> … Bengalis initially, but later Indians, must win the right to their own history. They must assert the right to narratives of the self.... To tell a series of infinite incidents is impossible. The conversion of an infinite material into a finite form, which alone could be *told*, is to turn it into a narrative. It appears to the intelligentsia in the late nineteenth century that they must exercise this pre-political right to the narrative of their own people.[9]

Thus, as a condition of epistemic necessity, the question of culture becomes enmeshed in the need for a narrative, and thereby in the larger disciplinary rubric of history. Kaviraj goes on to talk about the proliferation of writing historical narratives, both real and fictional, among the Bengali intelligentsia from the later years of the nineteenth century.[10] While one cannot deny such a contention, it is perhaps imperative to point out a couple of things in this context. In the first place, is it necessarily true that historical consciousness and, by extension, the practice of writing real and fictional historical narratives towards an articulation of selfhood were a peculiar phenomenon that began only in the later years of the nineteenth century? In his book Kaviraj was talking specifically about Bankimchandra, but would it perhaps be a narrow view of history if one were to collate the notions of selfhood, nationalism, and history into a singular (and the only possible) narrative of anti-imperial or post-colonial representation? Is it possible that the manifest and various churning of identities that was evident throughout the nineteenth century due to a continuous and multi-layered cultural encounter with the imperial presence and beyond was unable to produce any worthwhile narrative of selfhood? Does one therefore read the narrative of the birth of the historical narrative in Bengal, and by extension, India, as a manifestation of either militant or cultural nationalism of the late nineteenth century? These are the questions I will try to address in this chapter through a close reading of some of Akshay Dutta's works.

On another but related note, the relationship between culture and history is one of complex collaboration, as perhaps this sentence from Kaviraj may well express: 'Novels are a continuation of history, uttering what history could not.'[11] Thus, history, or the writing of history, may not be understood as a singular register of empirical data, merely a revival or analyses of past events for the purpose of a counter-narrative or the articulation of nationhood vis-à-vis a framework of colonialism. The introduction of the 'cultural' within the rubric of the 'historical' entails certain abstract or implicit articulations of selfhood that have a life of their own within such a narrative.

As I will read closely some of the works of Akshay Dutta along with continuous cross-references to the writings of Bankimchandra Chattopadhyay, my contention here will be to answer or address some of the questions I have raised above. In the first place, if historical representation of the Bengali self is read in terms of a lack due to the absence of a disciplinary or epistemological narrative, I would argue that from the middle of the nineteenth century some of the works of Akshay Dutta and Bhudeb Mukhopadhyay, to take two significant examples, measured up to a kind of attempted narrativization of a historically located selfhood through an exploration of traditional cultural registers. Such cultural registers might not have spoken to a structured and epistemically closed historical narrative. But they would open up an indigenous past towards a dialogue with history through the articulation of a social and moral thematic that borrowed from traditionalist models of understanding lived experience. Such attempts, consistent as they were, would also address the question of the clear rift between a tentatively 'loyalist' first half of the nineteenth century and the more nationalist and militant second half. While the peculiar thrust of the cultural politics of the later years of the nineteenth century would clearly push towards forms of militant nationalism, the seeds of a counter-narrative were already in place much earlier. That this counter-narrative did not have a militant or nationalist form does not necessarily take away the implicit insurgent motive of these attempts. Considerably influenced by western forms of knowledge and scientific progress, the likes of Akshay Dutta, Bhudeb Mukhopadhyay, or Iswarchandra Vidyasagar were nevertheless aware of the importance or necessity of *remembering* the past through ideas that had percolated across time but lacked a systematic rhetoric within the discourse of colonial modernity. Many of these ideas constituted an ethic that had informed lived experience and cultural patterns through centuries of practice, and thus it was possible to elicit the semblance of a narrative out of them. Systems of nomenclature would not categorize them as 'history', but attempts at remembering and validation would render them open to epistemic systematization by western forms of knowledge and 'curiosity'.[12] Therefore, on the one hand, such attempts would have a revivalist intention in mind, a move that would elicit the response of the native reading public towards indigenous cultural mores that could be traced back to the past and validated; on the other hand, such narratives were often put into frameworks that suited the Victorian inclination for moral reform and creating a morally sound middle-class citizenry,[13] and thus a natural curiosity in exploring the indigenous morality of the colonized subject, which in its turn could lead to an epistemological validation of such narratives by the master class.

The Liberal–Cultural Divide

Here I would like to foreground and briefly discuss an interesting distinction between the liberal and the cultural forms of the native intellectual reaction to the various mores of colonialism that Andrew Sartori reads as a crucial trope by which to analyse the imperialism and modernity debate in nineteenth-century Bengal vis-à-vis the global unfolding of such ideas.[14] While locating Bengali culturalism within a global framework, Sartori refuses to see the idea of the culture concept in Bengal as a derivative form (either as 'local deviation' or as 'late reiteration'),[15] and therefore a subordinate of the western idea of culture, but as 'a spatially and temporally specific moment in the global history of the culture concept'.[16] He also categorically rescues Bengali culturalism from the abstract notion of timelessness or the more specific one of regionalism and locates it instead within structures of 'social practice' that render 'the culturalist imagination meaningful as a lens for thinking about self and society'.[17] It is at this confluence of the notions of social practice and selfhood that Sartori locates his distinction of the liberal and the cultural:

> … I argue that Bengali culturalism emerged in the 1880s as a reaction against a liberal ideological paradigm that had emerged to dominance in the early nineteenth century. I thus elaborate culturalism and liberalism as distinct ideological paradigms.[18]

Sartori does, however, add as a disclaimer that both these paradigms may exist side by side as a synthesis or a jumble, but that his contention is to read the trajectory of the historical development of Bengal in the nineteenth century as a discontinuity rather than as a continuity. In fact, he discovers a 'sharp interruption' of liberalism by culturalism in the later years of the nineteenth century.[19] Reduced to simplest terms, Sartori's distinction may perhaps be read in the following manner: the 'liberal' Bengali intellectuals of the nineteenth century (till before the 1880s) were a category of the *bhadralok* who were western-educated, good subjects of colonial modernity, who would critique the imperial government through petitions, appeals, and pamphlets, engage in debates and discussions through articles in newspapers and periodicals, would be either staunch or moderate reformists (or prone to such impulses), upholding the ideals of universal progress and emancipation, and inclined towards a capitalist mode of production narrative; the 'culturalist' Bengali intellectual, on the other hand, belonged to the later years of the nineteenth century (1880s onward), of a similar *bhadralok* disposition, with most of the qualities of the former in terms of education and class identity, but more invested in the revivalist model of a more relatable indigenous past, the unearthing of a historical identity of the native subject, and promoting forms of nationalism (militant or otherwise) that would celebrate or uphold indigeneity as opposed to structures of cultural discourse borrowed from the colonial master class. Of course, this is a rather bare and reductionist reading of Sartori's argument, but if we set aside his focus on political economy and the various machinations of abstract capitalist social relations for the time being, this would be the core of his argument. As Sartori underscores in his reading of the nature of this return to the past or remembering, in his revival of the technical word *anushilan* (the rough English equivalents being 'cultivation' or 'culture') as used by Bankimchandra, this 'return' that the culturalists of the later years of the nineteenth century envisioned was 'not to return the fractured present to the past, but rather to use the forms of the past as the vehicles that would carry it to a new future'.[20] What Sartori also contends is that it was Bankimchandra who 'was to raise *culture* to the status of an explicitly formulated concept for the first time in Bengali'.[21]

It is imperative at this moment, once again, to return to the question of narrative that Sudipta Kaviraj mentions. Earlier in the chapter I had raised the question whether it was possible to determine the moment in time of the articulation of a counter-narrative to the epistemic paradigms of culture that colonial modernity had set in motion within the native intelligentsia. Interestingly, here is Sartori providing us with a framework, an almost exact historical moment, for the rise of Bengali culturalism in both the causal and the teleological sense. There is a certain pattern in this argument that consolidates the rationale of narrativization, and therefore the coming of age of Indian historiography. It is not by accident that both Sartori and Kaviraj discover in the figure of Bankimchandra the prime mover of such a newly narrativized culturalist ethic. A few years earlier, Partha Chatterjee had also discovered in Bankim a similar historical consciousness that led him to establish in *Krishnacharitra* 'the historicity of the character'.[22] In almost the same vein as Kaviraj later on, Chatterjee asserts that Bankim would use Sanskrit literary texts as his historical archive in the same manner as the Greeks and Romans would use Herodotus or Livy.[23] This was, therefore, Bankim's method of establishing a narrative of native or indigenous historiography. Chatterjee writes:

> Bankim's method, concepts and modes of reasoning are completely contained within the forms of post-Enlightenment scientific thought. One major characteristic of this thought is its celebration of the principle of historicity as the essential procedure for acquiring 'objective' knowledge. History, indeed, was seen as reflecting on its surface the scientific representation of the objective and changing world of being.[24]

Somewhat contrary to this claim by Chatterjee, in the chapter 'Hinduism as Culture' in his book, while discussing the differences that Bankim had with Akshay Dutta in terms of their understanding of the duties or responsibilities of the human subject (particularly in terms of the distinctions between spirituality and worldliness) within the specific historical context, Sartori asserts how '... Bankim was clearly hesitant to accept Dutt's dissolution of human subjectivity into the lawlike regularities of the object world'.[25] Although not necessarily opposing views, the way Chatterjee and Sartori read Bankim's historical consciousness leaves scope for a more detailed engagement. I shall take up this strand of the discussion later in the chapter.

For the moment, I intend to closely analyse some of the theoretical strands that Chatterjee, Kaviraj, and Sartori use to locate Bankim within the domain of Bengali cultural history. It would be interesting to examine whether such theoretical markers were unique to Bankim and the way he and his allies were envisioning Bengali culture, or if a historical trajectory of similar ideas could be traced back to someone like Akshay Dutta. The tracing of such a genealogy is necessary for a couple of reasons. In the first place, one would need to understand if the 1880s indeed marked a clean break of sorts from earlier forms of Bengali selfhood and their representation; second, what was the nature, if at all, of historical consciousness within the Bengali fashioning of the self in the face of a largely hegemonic imperial polemic of cultural superiority. A related question, peculiar to my concern here, would be if a figure such as Akshay Dutta was merely an incidental liberal presence in the early part of the nineteenth century, or could we locate traces and determine the nature of indigenous selfhood in his writings?

The Conceptions of *Dharma, Anushilan,* and *Parishram*: Bankim and Akshay

Kaviraj writes about the necessity of a narrative to foreground or establish the foundational structure of an indigenous historiography. This is sometimes achieved, as he argues, through the 'conceptual indeterminacy' of imaginary histories. In Bankim he discovers such an attempt unfold through two strategies – the ambiguous use of the word *jati* and 'gradually conceiving a community called the nation'.[26] Likewise, Sartori discovers in Bankim 'a doctrine of agential subjectivity grounded in the concept of culture'.[27] He reads this culturalism in the light of history understood as 'social practice' and through this a discovery of Bengali 'selfhood'. Partha Chatterjee in his discussion on Bankim finds in the latter the conviction that 'the validation of truth had to lie in a rational demonstration of its historicity'.[28] In thinking about Bankim all these three historians of nineteenth-century Bengal focus on Bankim's idea of *anushilan* as elaborated in his long essay *Dharmatattwa,*[29] published in the form of a catechism between a guru and his disciple on the principles of what constitutes *dharma*. However, before engaging with the text of *Dharmatattwa*, it is perhaps necessary to ask how these three commentators on Bankim have grappled with the important question of indigenous historiography. Kaviraj focuses on the notion of conceptual indeterminacy as a ploy to include the literary, the imagined histories, and other kinds of writing as part of the historiographical construction of Bengali selfhood. On a more curious note, Sartori brings in the idea of 'social practice' within the historiographical and therefore considerably widening the scope of the historical beyond the epistemological domain laid down by the tropes of colonial modernity. Such a notion opens up the scope of a dialogue between the disciplinary and the representational that both accepts the need for and in the same breath dismantles the disciplinary framework of the epistemology. Social practice as a narrative would not only address the gap due to the supposed absence of historicity that western epistemology of the colonial master class has used as a symptom of 'lack', but would at the same time import 'culture' as a raw material for history. The everyday, which has an easily traceable past and a narrative of tradition to fall back on, would thus become the source of history, and help in determining notions of Bengali selfhood. Partha Chatterjee, much earlier, had already brought in the question of rationality, which adds a rather intricate charge within the domain of history. The rationalism that was an essential condition of modernity, to be traced back to European enlightenment, needed to be discovered within the traditional and cultural praxes of Bengali life. Thus, questions of religious practice, moral principles, and the larger spheres of social and cultural life of Bengal in particular, and Bharatvarsha in general, had to be revisited, and, if necessary, the rhetoric had to be refashioned to fit in the principles of rationality.

What is crucial to understand from the ongoing discussion is that most historians and social scientists deliberating on the construction of Bengali selfhood within the domain of an imperial cultural politics see Bankim's writings as a kind of starting point or a watershed moment for the germination of an indigenous historical consciousness predicated on all of the above factors. Whereas, undoubtedly, Bankim was a formative figure shaping the discourse of nationalist historiography, he was perhaps not as foundational as he is possibly made out to be. I would want to argue that in an inconspicuous and less deliberate manner Akshay Dutta was already, a few years before Bankim, tracing a trajectory of Bengali selfhood through his writings. If one were to consider the development of a historiography as a fluid and contingent process, culling its material more from cultural practice and social norms (both of which had easily traceable pasts), rather than from a disciplinary framework of historical development, then Akshay Dutta may very well be considered as a precursor of Bankim in the attempt to construct a selfhood for the Bengali people. After all, Bankim was primarily a fiction writer rather than an essayist, for whom history as epistemology would generally be of lesser interest than history as a cultural construct. The primary material for his construction of Bengali selfhood was cultural in nature. In a certain sense, therefore, his claim to historical truth or authenticity could only be comparable or equal to that of Akshay's and not greater in any manner. One also needs to consider that Akshay Dutta rarely ever wrote any fiction. Also, in terms of Bankim's idea of *anushilan*, which most historians consider to be his crucial contribution to the development of Bengali selfhood, I would suggest a close reading of some of Akshay's works along with Bankim's to discover startling commonalities in terms of both theory and practice.

The idea of *anushilan* is scattered across Bankim's rather long deliberation, of twenty-eight chapters and four appendices, published in 1888, called *Dharmatattwa* which is a catechism between a guru and his disciple on the nature of *dharma*. Towards the beginning of the dialogue, in chapter 3, titled 'What Is *Dharma*?', the guru tries to define the idea of *dharma* as distinct from the idea of religion. He asserts how 'religion' is a western word, and western pundits have many and different definitions of the word, and that there is a general disagreement between them.[30] However, it is the *nitya padartha* or the constant substance in all of these that will be called *dharma*. Soon Bankim asserts, through the words of the guru, 'The Substance of Religion is Culture'.[31] In a letter to Benoykrishna Deb dated 27 July 1892, Bankim writes: 'Whatever is beneficial to people (*lokahitakar*) is *dharma*'.[32] In the first place, therefore, Bankim tries here to set his idea of *dharma* aside from a supposedly narrow or limited western construct of religion. Second, by reaching out to the idea of culture through *lokahita*, Bankim attempts a wider and more inclusive definition of *dharma*. Through an exploration of the various human faculties (*vritti*), Bankim ventures to define the essence of his notion of *dharma*. The essence of man, for Bankim, is the congruence (*samanjasya*) between the physical (*shaririki*), the intellectual (*jnanarjani*), the causal (*karyakarani*), and the aesthetic (*chittaranjani*). Among these *vritti*s, however, there are some, Bankim says, that have an ability to accommodate or expand more than the others. One such is the *karyakarani vritti* whose chief qualities are those of *bhakti* (devotion), *priti* (love), and *daya* (compassion).[33] These qualities, Bankim believes, should be foregrounded by the true practitioner of *dharma*, and should be the major focus of *anushilan*. Bankim also speaks about other *vritti*s such as the physical that are capable of similar expansion, but it was *akartavya* (or contrary to one's duty) to allow such lower *vritti*s to expand.[34] *Dharma* is constituted of the right balance or congruence (*samanjasya*) between these various *vritti*s. What then would be the relationship between the human subject who practices these *vritti*s and the external world? Bankim contends that the relationship between the external world and the human being is predicated on the idea of *mangal* or well-being:

More one would discuss the theory of the world, it will be more apparent that the relation between the world and us is through *mangal*. The universe in its entirety is conducive to all of man's *vritti*s. Nature helps our *vritti*s. Therefore, down the ages, mankind has generally progressed, and not the contrary. *Dharma* is the cause of such progress.[35]

Bankim also insists that the non-believer or the *nastik* who argues that science is the cause of progress does not realize that science is also a part of this *dharma*.[36] He also ascertains that this entire discourse of *anushilan* is meant for the householder and not the *sanyasi*, that it belongs to the *pravrittimarga* (or the path of engagement) and not *nivrittimarga* (or the path of abstention).[37] The nature of *anushilan* is related to *karma* or work and not abstinence.

I shall come back again to the close reading of Bankim's *Dharmatattwa*. In the meanwhile it may be interesting to compare this basic argument in Bankim's text to some of Akshay Dutta's writings and see if there are commonalities that may lead us to rethink the way historians have distinguished between the early and later parts of the nineteenth century in terms of the fashioning of Bengali selfhood, and the way most of them envision Bankim's intervention into the cultural history of the Bengali self as a watershed moment. In 1856, Akshay Dutta published a tract comparable to Bankim's *Dharmatattwa*, calling it *Dharmaniti*.[38] Earlier, around 1853–1854 he published the second part of *Charupath* in which, I would suggest, the seeds of *Dharmaniti* were already present.[39] In this second volume of *Charupath*, Akshay writes an essay titled 'Parishram'[40] (literally meaning labour or toil), which fits into a schematic framework on the subject of *dharma* to be taken up later by him in *Dharmaniti* and by Bankim in *Dharmatattwa*. In this essay he talks of the two *vrittis* – *buddhivritti* and *dharmapravritti* – as the touchstones of human excellence. Akshay insists that the development of these two faculties would lead to safeguarding the sovereignty of the self (*swia swatantrata raksha*).[41] Through the practice of one's *buddhi* (read either or both as intelligence and rationality) and *dharma*, one would be able to ascertain one's individuality. Is it possible to read this prescription as an early articulation of the idea of selfhood for the Bengali subject?

In the same manner as Bankim speaks of a balance between the various faculties of the human subject, those of the physical, the intellectual, the causal, and the aesthetic, Akshay Dutta also gives us a four-tier model in this short essay. For him, the four necessary aspects of a balanced existence are: the physical (*jibika nirbaha* as in performing the daily chores), intellectual (*jnananushilan* or the practice of acquiring knowledge), spiritual (*dharmanusthan* or religious rituals), and aesthetic (*pavitra pramod* or pure forms of entertainment).[42] It seems that Akshay's term *parishram* is closely proximate to the way Bankim uses the word *anushilan*, of course notwithstanding the fact that the two words have a somewhat commensurate connotation in the Bengali language. *Parishram*, for Akshay, involves a proportionate balance of both physical and intellectual labour. In a similar vein as Bankim he insists on the importance of physical labour, particularly its manifestation in the forms of labour required for agriculture and industry. The discerning reader would not miss the point that Akshay foregrounds through his insistence on the need for the development of these two particular aspects within the Bengali cultural milieu. I have mentioned earlier in this book how Akshay, in spite of his metropolitan location through most of his working life, had a peculiar distance from the *bhadralok* population of Calcutta and its suburbs. He was defined by a liminality that resisted a fixed location and set him apart from most of his colleagues and fellow intellectuals. In this essay Akshay chides the *bhadralok*. He writes how the *bhadralok* would take great physical pain to go hunting or gaming in high summer heat but consider it shameful to lend their labour to agriculture and industry.[43] It is at this point that Akshay goes back to the question of society (or *janasamaj*), and to what Bankim would later call *lokahita*. *Parishram*, for Akshay, is a natural culmination of the faculties of *buddhivritti* and *dharmapravritti*. It is for the sake of one's selfhood and sovereignty that a person should realize that it is not shameful to use the plough or use one's own hands for the purpose of labour. And it is through a balanced combination of *buddhi* and *dharma* leading to *parishram* that one contributes to the larger scheme of social life around the self:

> To lead life all must work according to ability, and those that live in a society must engage as a rule in some form of welfare (*hitakari karma*) for their own society, and such a dictum for well-being is prevalent everywhere.[44]

Evidently, it is through such a mechanism of participation that the individual and the society come together as a cultural unit, and a part of Akshay's idea of *parishram* resonates organically with Bankim's notion of *anushilan*. It is this that Sartori possibly understands as 'social practice', and the idea of an indigenous community evolves, as Partha Chatterjee indicates, towards the conception of a nation. Likewise, the emergence of a narrative that traces the historicality of social practice helps to disengage lived experience from traditional epistemology and the limitations of discipline, while claiming for itself the validity of 'prevalent everywhere' (*sarvatra prachalita*) and therefore giving it a global spin. Towards the end of this short essay Akshay talks about the importance and necessity of both forms of labour – of the body and the mind – and of a necessary combination of labour and capital for the improvement of the society.[45] Akshay praises all those who create or manufacture machines or formulate theories for the advancement of technology, those that write moral tracts, or those who elaborate on discourses of wisdom or knowledge through their writings. He ascertains that in the same way as the morning sun rises in the eastern part of the world and gradually enlightens the west, so would the *jnan* and *dharma* of these men gradually travel across the globe.[46] While he ends the essay with a note of disdain for his *swadesh* and *swajati* (both of these ideas will be familiar to readers of Bankim) where the rich indulge in the lowly faculties and neglect improvement of the indigenous society (*janasamajer srivriddhi*), the careful reader will not fail to notice three separate and connected tropes that emerge from his argument. In the first place there is a hint at the reversal of the narrative of enlightenment (from the east to the west and not the other way round), thereby confronting the existing and hegemonic narrative of imperial historiography, and suggesting the possibility of a historical counter-narrative through the notion of the cultural. Also, by dovetailing this entire narrative of prosperous social living with the idea of prosperity as conceived around the world (*sarvatra prachalita*), Akshay is opening the debate towards global history rather than the narrower and more immediate domain of colonial history. Second, the reference to *swadesh* and *swajati* clearly suggests a framework of nationhood that would emerge from the idea of a society and its welfare, and one that could be read as the simultaneous possibility of the emergence of a historical narrative based on the contingent model of an indigenous society and its practices.[47] Third, by emphasizing the notion of prosperity (or *srivriddhi*) instead of progress (or *pragati*) Akshay places the argument within the domain of what Kaviraj has called conceptual indeterminacy, thereby skirting the discipline-centric arguments of historical authenticity foregrounded by colonial modernity. In fact, like Bankim, Akshay also uses the idea of *jati* (he uses the word *swajatiya* in the last sentence of his essay) and the tries to conceive of the possibility of a nation within the community.

Dharma as a Cultural Question: Consolidating Global Narratives

I will return here, once again, to the conception and framing of *dharma* as a major concern in both Akshay Dutta and Bankim in *Dharmaniti* and *Dharmatattwa* respectively. I would try to understand if Bankim's *Dharmatattwa* was an evolved and more sophisticated rendition of some of the main arguments that Akshay puts forward in *Dharmaniti*. In the course of this argument, I would intend to examine if it is possible to push back Sartori's idea of culturalism as an ideological paradigm into the domain of what he understands as liberalism, thereby problematizing the pre- and post-1880s division that he suggests. That is to say, is it possible to push back the 'threshold moment' of the conceptualization of identity and Bengali selfhood into the domain of the 'liberal' period? This would then open up the debate about identity and selfhood towards various and complicated manifestations of indigeneity and globality beyond the immediate categories of the modern and the non-modern (or premodern) that were identified by imperial epistemologies. The manifestation of selfhood within the domain of the cultural as a narrative would disrupt the easy essentialisms of colonial modernity not only by complicating the notion of the historical as epistemology, but also by eliciting paradigmatic structures of morality, ethic, and community that would act as pre-existent narrative frameworks that would defy the monochromatic representation of the enlightened and colonized *bhadralok*. Akshay Dutta, incidentally, would be the perfect candidate for such a disruptive presence, inhabiting the interstitial space, as he did, between the *bhadralok* elite and the common colonized subject.

Akshay begins his argument in *Dharmaniti* with the assertion that *dharma*, imagined as a gem, is the most precious material in the universe (*dharmarup maharatna sarbotkrishta padartha*).[48] He also asserts that one of the ways to be initiated into the path of *dharma* was to learn about those that have embraced immense pain and torture to uphold *dharma*, and those that were ready to sacrifice their lives for the independence of their nation (*swadesher swadhinattwa*).[49] Thus, to begin with, it is imperative to point out that the idea of the independence of the nation, and the sacrifice of one's life for the sake of such an idea, was not alien to the intellectuals belonging to the 'liberal' half of the nineteenth century, and, in fact, knowing about their lives, Akshay insists, constituted one of the primary parameters for beginning to understand the nature of *dharma*. As in his essay 'Parishram', Akshay reiterates that the faculties of *buddhivritti* and *dharmapravritti* are key to the constitution of selfhood. *Buddhivritti*, read as both intelligence and rationality, would lead the self towards acquiring knowledge of the material world and develop the power of judgement (*vichar*). And *dharma* is manifested in the self through a concerted practice of the qualities of benevolence (*upachikirsha*), devotion (*bhakti*), and justice (*nyayparata*). It is important to keep in mind that Akshay here uses the term *nyayparata* to literally mean justice, but extends the meaning and relates it closely to the notion of duty or *kartavya*. The idea of *kartavya* needs an informed discussion, and I shall come back to it later in the chapter. It is not difficult to immediately relate Akshay's idea of *dharma* with that of Bankim's. The major focus of Bankim's idea of *dharma* manifested as *anushilan* is the practice of the causal faculties that constitute the qualities of *bhakti*, *priti*, and *daya*. The commonalities are obvious in the emphasis on the qualities of devotion (*bhakti*) and benevolence (both *daya* and *upachikirsha* are acceptable translations of the word). There is clearly a similar kind of instrumentalism in the way in which both Akshay and Bankim conceive of the idea of *dharma* outside the domain of the religious and within the domain of the social and cultural.

However, two crucial pointers need to be emphasized in this context. In the first place, rescuing the notion of *dharma* as lived experience from the constricted framework of organized religion was not new, and had a tradition within Bengali conceptions of social practice. Much has been written about how the likes of Rammohun Roy or Iswarchandra Vidyasagar had tried to read *dharma* as moral practice outside the onerous rubric of shastric Hinduism and emphasized the need for compassion as central to the idea of *dharma*.[50] Within folk culture, the figures of Fakir Lalon Shah and Sri Ramakrishna Paramahansa tried to unravel narratives of social practice divested of immediate religious practice through their songs and teachings respectively.[51] But it was probably in the writings of Akshay Dutta, and later on in Bankim, that an instrumentalist and rationalist framework emerged for the first time providing a model for the possibility of the practice of *dharma* as social behaviour.[52] Both Akshay's *Dharmaniti* and Bankim's *Dharmatattwa* were thus treatises that were tentatively modelled on epistemological foundations borrowed from the west, but deeply entrenched in indigenous social and cultural practices that had both an immediate relevance and a tradition, in the form of a narrative, to fall back upon. The moral framework promoted or prescribed by both the texts were specific to emic cultural practice lifted directly out of lived experience, yet continuously in a dialogue with texts, philosophers, or ideas from across the eastern and the European worlds. It would perhaps not be off the mark, therefore, to claim that these texts were not only opening up a global dimension for locating indigenous cultural practices, but also simultaneously establishing a narrative of comparative cultural history vis-à-vis the global that was crucial for reclaiming selfhood for the Bengali subject. The idea of *dharma*, for both Akshay and Bankim, was a means to establish or examine a set of social and cultural practices for the householder based on parameters set by both indigenous and foreign traditions that could be diachronically connected to the present in either the form of a critique or as an existent narrative that needed to be rescued. Akshay's *Dharmaniti*, for example, is peppered with references to a past, globally imagined, based on the idea of *dharma* as social responsibility. Writing on the evils of child marriage, for example, Akshay points out how such heinous practice did not exist in a Bharatvarsha of the past where women could choose their partners and widows could remarry: 'The Hindus of that period were no doubt more honest and virtuous than the superstitious, corrupt Hindus of today.'[53] Immediately after, he holds up Germany as an example from the present time where men and women are not allowed to marry unless they are twenty-five and eighteen respectively, and how in ancient Greece, Lycurgus ruled that men and women could not marry unless they were thirty-seven and seventeen respectively.[54] While speaking of the evils of consanguinity he culls his examples from indigenous past as well as traditions prevalent in Rome or Athens.[55] In the matter of female education Akshay clearly states that they should be educated in the same subjects and with the same rigour as their male counterparts as they are capable of training themselves in 'various immensely difficult fields of knowledge, and like the male learners acquire pleasure out of intellectual labour'.[56] He points out how in ancient India such education of women was common, and mentions several contemporary European women as examples. He particularly mentions the Scottish scientist Mary Somerville whose knowledge of astronomy was well known and whose treatise on the physical sciences was, according to Akshay, regarded as one of the finest books in contemporary times.[57] In the matter of the education of children Akshay points out how their teachers should acquaint them with the works of those who from an early age were known for their intellectual and moral mettle such as Socrates, Bacon, Newton, Franklin, Pascal, Washington, Aryabhatta, Bhaskaracharya, Rammohun Roy, and others.[58] He also mentions how Germany and America have turned out to be pioneers in education.[59] The reader will not fail to notice the almost deliberate empiricist rigour in Akshay's examples.

If one were to turn to Bankim it would not be difficult to notice a similar kind of instrumentalism in his conception of *dharma*. At the same time, it also had a similar global outlook and cosmopolitan range in the way Bankim enumerates his concept of *anushilan*. Towards the beginning of *Dharmatattwa* Bankim makes an important observation regarding the scope of *dharma*. While praising Krishna as the embodiment of perfection, Bankim writes: '*Dharma* is not in the Vedas, *dharma* is in *lokahita*.'[60] This is of course an almost exact echo of Akshay's opinion on the matter of *lokahita* as expressed in *Bahyavastur Sahit Manabprakritir Sammandha Vichar*: 'The need of all our *dharmapravritti* is to strive for the benefit of the commoner (*sadharaner hita*) with due reverence towards *Parameshwar*.'[61] Thereafter, while delineating the nature of *dharma* Bankim argues how there is a similarity between the philosophy taught by such nineteenth-century philosophers as Herbert Spencer and Auguste Comte and those of the Vedantic insights on *advaitavada* and *mayavada*. Likewise, parallels may be drawn between Spinoza's thoughts and those of the Vedanta.[62] Interestingly, Bankim insists on referring to Spinoza or Spencer as 'European Hindus' who have been able to comprehend only the basic tenets of Hinduism. For the Hindu, on the other hand, 'the present, God, human beings, all beings, the entire universe – all taken together is *dharma*.'[63] A crucial contrary logic to the almost concerted emphasis on Bankim's militant nationalist self is, however, rather evident in *Dharmatattwa*, and that is in his deep faith in monarchism and the need for faith in the king (*rajbhakti*) for social good. Bankim insists that in the same way as the child should have *bhakti* for the father, so should the subject have *bhakti* for the king:

> Even if not in the English religion, in English social practice devotion towards the king had its pride of place. Nowadays such devotion for the king is no longer evident. But those regions where this is still prevalent, such as Germany and Italy, the state is progressing.[64]

It is through this trope of *bhakti* among the common people that Bankim broaches the idea of a global notion of *bhakti* that has an inherent and inclusivist social principle. He says that more than the king, the teachers of social ethics and principles are the subjects of *bhakti*. Their role as arbiters of principles extends from the household towards the society at large. Interestingly, Bankim uses the word *parishram* here to denote how these gurus shape the foundation of a society.[65] They are gurus of the kings as well, across continents. Thus, as in Bharatvarsha there are figures such as Vyasa, Valmiki, Vasistha, Vishwamitra, Manu, Yajnabalka, Kapila, and Gautama, in Europe there are Galileo, Newton, Kant, Comte, Dante, and Shakespeare.[66] Quite obviously, one does not fail to notice the striking parallels between the ways in which both Akshay and Bankim imagine the shaping of an emergent social space with an evident narrative that is both synchronic and diachronic, indigenous and global at the same time. There is evidently a narrative intent in the way both of them imagine the past of Bharatvarsha as a social space both through real and imagined narratives of the consolidation of community. Bankim even uses the compound word *puranetiha*s (a mix of the Puranas and history) to validate diverse ways of constructing a narrative outside the epistemological foundations of colonial historiography.[67] One daresay, in terms of the instrumentalist vision of *dharma* as a narrative of lived social experience, and in terms of the cosmopolitanism of the approaches, there is an immediate comparability between the 'liberal' and the 'cultural' ways of social thinking.

The second pointer relates to another noticeable comparability between Akshay and Bankim (that is the 'liberal' and the 'cultural') in the way both of them choose to talk about god as generally separated from religion in the scriptural, and hence a narrow, sense. God as the maker or the arbiter of the universe was an idea that both of them largely subscribed to in a purely instrumental way, in a way that was directly commensurate with *parishram* or *anushilan* and hence, in the larger sense, their conceptions of *dharma*. Akshay clearly suggests that god is the primary destination of *bhakti*.[68] The entire body of *Dharmaniti* (and for that matter almost his entire oeuvre) is peppered with references to god, but rarely does Akshay ever mention organized religion as part of such a practice of *dharma*. Rather, the central focus of Akshay's conception of *dharma* is how the individual 'in a pure and sinless manner abides by all the rules laid down by *Parameshwar*'.[69] The idea of retributive justice divined by *parameshwar* is also predicated not on the institutional practice of religion, but on the social and individual behaviour (*sadasad–byabahar*) of the human subject, and this, Akshay insists, is accepted by pundits across the world.[70] Thus, in spite of the fact that Akshay was one of the founder members of a particular religious fold, his use of the word *dharma* and its conception were peculiarly instrumentalist in nature, predicated more on the social function of the subject rather than any pronounced spiritual manifestation. For Bankim as well, the relationship between god and religion, although more complex than Akshay's, was typically invested with an instrumentalism that went beyond the spiritual. In the first chapter of *Dharmatattwa*, Bankim describes the structure of *dharma* as a 'system of culture', a system beyond the conception of such British practitioners of *anushilan* as Matthew Arnold.[71] Culture lies at the core of *dharma*, Bankim argues, and the kind of *dharma* (*param pavitra amritamay dharma*) that lies at the core of the *Gita* is based on this idea of *anushilan*.[72] The reason the western version of *anushilan* is incomplete and undeveloped, according to Bankim, is its atheism, or vice versa. For the Hindus, on the other hand, their *bhakti* leads their *anushilan* towards the *jagadishwar*, and is therefore the desirable version.[73] For Bankim, god is immanent, the manifestation of all virtue (*guna*) and the only example of ripeness (*parinati*).[74] It is the intention of *anushilan* to guide all the *vritti*s towards this god.[75] There is a continuous reference in Bankim's idea of *dharma* of the need to engage with the world through *anushilan*, and the possibility of the dissolution of the man–god divide through a global engagement of ideas: 'The day European science and industry, and the *niskama dharma* of Bharatvarsha will come together, man will become God.'[76] This is not a trivialization of the god-figure, but a symptom of Bankim's faith in worldly and communitarian engagement, a conflation of global practices, which is not to be confused in any way with the discourse of militant nationalism. Rather, this idea is closer to Akshay's idea of the *brahmanistha grihastha* – the image of the householder who goes about his personal and social duties in the name of god. It was important for both Akshay and Bankim to reiterate in their works the crucial role of the householder in terms of the building of a *samaj* or society, of the communitarian responsibility of the man who followed a life of *dharma*. That is to say, it was clear in both of their works that they did not endorse the renunciation of the world, or the life of a *sanyasi* devoid of all responsibility for the society. Akshay asserts in *Bahyavastu*:

> Those that relinquish worldly labour in the cause of whiling away their time in hearing, thinking, contemplating, or ideating about *Parameshwar*, must admit their grievous mistake. The one and only *Parameshwar* is the guardian of this world, and He has established all the benevolent rules required to sustain it. His desire is the gradual progress (*unnati*) of the world; the abiding responsibility of man is to work towards this prosperity as intended by Him.[77]

Earlier in the same book he clearly asserts that there are some people who, in the hope of some special favour of the *parameshwar*, relinquish the labours of family life (*sangsarshram*) and become *sanyasi*s. But, Akshay asserts, 'that is to transgress the orders of the *Parameshwar*, and become in his judgement, an offender'.[78] We see Bankim speak in a similar vein in *Dharmatattwa*. According to him, *jagadishwar* has designed the world according to certain utilitarian principles. It is due to such a design that the world has generally moved towards progress (Bankim uses the same word *unnati* as Akshay did). *Dharma* is the cause of such *unnati*.[79] *Dharma*, once again, is a combination and balance or congruence (*samanjasya*) of various *vrittis*. The *yogis* or ascetics, on the other hand, teach how 'some vrittis need to be completely eradicated, some neglected, and only some others to be practiced and expanded – this is the goal of yoga'.[80] Bankim is of the opinion that their *dharma* is *adharma* and that they are as *adharmik* as the glutton or the lustful, who similarly neglect certain *vrittis* in preference for certain others.[81] It is noticeable how both Akshay and Bankim, separated by decades, are prescribing a similar kind of social engagement that would go on to consolidate an idea of a *samaj* – a crucial marker of identity and selfhood. Their continuous need to connect this entire project not only to the design of an all-encompassing god figure, but to an indigenous past as well as a global endorsement of such a set of practices across time is perhaps a deliberate encroachment into the fold of the historical, the attempt at discovering a narrative for locating this project of selfhood. Interestingly, though, neither Akshay in *Dharmaniti* nor Bankim in *Dharmatattwa* engages at any length in discussing the relationship between *dharma* and organized religion. For both of them *dharma* remains a primarily empirical and largely secularized model of social practice, a narrative of engagement with the everyday world through such simple household qualities as *upachikirsha*, *bhakti*, and *nyayaparata* (for Akshay) or *bhakti*, *priti*, and *daya* (for Bankim).

Bahyavastu as the Master Text: Seeds of the Conception of *Dharma*

It will be topical in this context to briefly talk about a longer text by Akshay Dutta *Bahyavastur Sahit Manabprakritir Sammandha Vichar*.[82] Parts of this text were published serially in the *Tattwabodhini Patrika* before it was published as a separate volume in two parts (the first part was published in 1851 and the second in 1853). By Akshay's own admission, this volume is a rough summary of George Combe's 1828 book *The Constitution of Man*,[83] but not an exact translation: 'Those examples that are relevant and beneficial for the Europeans, but not suitable for Indians, have been replaced by those examples that are relevant and beneficial for the latter.'[84] Written before *Dharmaniti*, and much before Bankim's *Dharmatattwa*, *Bahyavastu* is a rigorous and detailed prescription for indigenous ways of life, a primer of sorts that provides a structure of conduct for personal, family, and social life lived according to a combination of the rules of the universe laid down by the *parameshwar* and shastric doctrines of the Hindus (*Hindushastra-sammata*).[85] To put it simply, there is an easy cohabitation of the 'liberal' and the 'cultural' dynamics in the text: on the one hand, a consolidation of Akshay's faith in a colonial system of knowledge, and the fact that Combe's dependence on phrenology in *The Constitution of Man* was not unknown to Akshay, and his endorsement of it; on the other hand, a structured attempt to indigenize the principles of social practice in ways that would consolidate the notion of community living through the path of *dharma* and according to scientific principles of rationalism. He asserts that through the investment of the various faculties (*vrittis*), it is undoubtedly the utmost intention of the maker to discover in us the qualities of being *grihastha* (householder) and *jana-samajastha* (part of the society).[86] The quality of being a householder (one immediately remembers the phrase *brahmanistha grihastha*) and part of the larger social fabric (*jana-samaj*) was of crucial importance to the notion of a narrative in Akshay. What I would contend here is that as early as the *Tattwabodhini* days, when parts of *Bahyavastu* began to appear in a serial form, Akshay was already trying to establish a framework of social living that constituted a holistic narrative that could be traced back to an indigenous past and yet be located within a global perspective of progress and modernity. The ideological framework of *dharma* that he later publishes as *Dharmaniti*, or what is prescribed by Bankim in *Dharmatattwa*, were expressed more elaborately earlier, in the pages of *Bahyavastu*. What is also noticeable is that there is already, in *Bahyavastu*, a clear and harsh critique of imperialism that runs parallel to a narrative of admiration for European sciences. He writes in almost unadulterated praise of the European sciences in the introduction to the book: 'The way in which contemporary European pundits by virtue of their extraordinary intelligence have made progress in such subjects (as astronomy), Sanskrit astronomy would appear miniscule in comparison.'[87] However, there is no doubt in Akshay about the way in which imperial rule was contrary to *dharma* and violated the rules laid down for the world by *parameshwar*:

> The English have captured Bharatvarsha by virtue of *adharma*, and rule by the principles of *adharma*. But there are repercussions if the rules laid down by the *Parameshwar* are not obeyed. Thus, the intensity of all

those lowly instincts that have led them to capture Bharatvarsha and be unjust to their subjects has led to much harm of the state (*swadesh*). The *adharma* inherent in both the ruler and their rules have led to much suffering of the people. However, it is to be noted that one's independence (*swadhinattwa*) is not compromised if the conquered are themselves not afflicted by *adharma*. It is their physical weakness, and the lack of *buddhivritti* and *dharmapravritti* that is the root cause of such an event.[88]

A little earlier in this chapter, Akshay had already delineated the general character of the English. Akshay writes: 'For a very long while the English have worked under the influence of their lowly faculties (*nikrishta pravritti*). Imperturbable greed, very intense self-love and tremendous malice have been instrumental in all their work.'[89] The reader will not fail to notice the parallels between these contentions and the ones made either in *Dharmaniti* or Bankim's *Dharmatattwa*. The idea of *anushilan* that was so central to Bankim's argument, and the impetus of a nationalist ideological shift that was so crucial to the debates about forms of resistance to empire, had their seeds already in *Bahyavastu* as early as the middle years of the nineteenth century. Although Akshay calls George Combe a 'mahatma',[90] there is a clear repudiation of imperial governance and a call for physical and intellectual prowess in the native subject for the implicit purpose of resistance, at the core of *Bahyavastu*.

I have said in an earlier chapter that unlike a Rammohun or a Vidyasagar, Akshay was rarely involved as a direct agent of social reform who would participate in social movements or reformist programmes that would require dialogue or confrontation with the imperial system. He was less of a leader in this sense, and more of a quiet reformer who would want to elicit a response from his milieu in the form of a measured afterthought. While Bankim is generally conceived of as the one to have given a clarion call for resistance in the name of the nation (or *swadesh*), one would frequently discover in Akshay a quieter, but equally firm, reiteration of the idea of *swadesh*. In *Bahyavastu*, for example, a treatise clearly modelled on a western text, Akshay would emphatically foreground his notion of the *swadesh* and try to inspire in his readers an identical concern. Towards the end of the fourth chapter he writes: 'It is our foremost duty to purify the minds of the people by preaching the enlightened knowledge of those that are inclined towards benefitting the nation (*swadesher subha sadhan*).'[91] He would take up social evils of the contemporary period and trace a trajectory of reform that would go back to a genealogy of social practices from the past, and come back to the idea of emancipation of the *swadesh*. In the matter of marriages, for example, Akshay would critique current practices in terms of those that were practised in the times of the *Ramayana*, the *Mahabharata*, or the Puranas.[92] In the same vein, he would insist that those laws that were once relevant in the indigenous society needed to be reformed or revisited in terms of the present social needs. He argues that if one were to go back to the pundits of the past, they would agree that although such extant laws were not against the *shastras* (*shastra-biruddha*), they were nevertheless against contemporary practice (*byabahar-biruddha*).[93] Through all of these, Akshay was trying to imagine a model or a form of indigenous social living that had both a traceable history and contemporary relevance. He talks about the *swadesh-hitaishi* or the *swadesher suvanuragee* (the well-meaning native) invested with the emotions of *karunya* and *daya-dharma* (both forms of compassion) who works tirelessly for the alleviation of poverty and uplift of the 'family-like people of the country' (*swaparibar swarup deshastha lok*).[94] This imagining of the nation as one's own family (*swadesh* as *swaparibar*) while tracing the forms of social living to an indigenous past and yet investing it with a rationalist contemporaneity was Akshay's very own conception that clearly predated Bankim's ideas of *swadesh* and *swajati*.

To briefly return again to the trope of *samanjasya* or congruence between the various human faculties that Bankim uses categorically as a pivotal logic in his *Dharmatattwa*, one would discover a similar emphasis on the idea of *samanjasya* in Akshay's *Bahyavastu*. Akshay begins by emphasizing the need for *samanjasya* between the various physical and mental faculties, manifested through the workings of *buddhivritti* and *dharmapravritti* in the form of good work (*satkarya*).[95] Soon, he unambiguously asserts how 'it is the corresponding congruence (*samanjasya*) of all our faculties that is the cause of happiness (*sukha*)'.[96] Soon after Akshay suggests that it is only possible to perform one's *kartavya* or duty if there is a complete congruence of all the faculties of the human being (*sampurnarup samanjasyibhuto*).[97] As for this sense of *kartavya*, one needs to direct it towards the self, towards one's relatives, towards *swadesh*, towards all mankind, and towards the *parameshwar*.[98] It is interesting to notice the structural pattern of this map of *kartavya* that extends from the self towards *swadesh*, the world, and finally towards the *parameshwar*. It is not difficult to derive from this the worldview that Akshay subscribed to – to reach out towards the global through *swadesh*, and an ultimate and abiding faith in the *parameshwar*. There is a curious link between Akshay's and Bankim's conceptions of the notion of *samanjasya* as well. For Akshay, *buddhivritti* and *dharmapravritti* are the two larger rubrics within which the various manifestations of *dharma* may be placed. If there is a supposed conflict between the various *vrittis*, it is through the mediation of these two that the conflict needs to be resolved, and *samanjasya* established.[99] Now, the major focus in Akshay's idea of *dharma* has been on the manifestation of such qualities as *upachikirsha*, *bhakti*, and *nyayaparata* – and these qualities are to be foregrounded as the principle elements for establishing *samanjasya*. Likewise, Bankim argues in *Dharmatattwa*: 'Some faculties – such as *bhakti*, *priti*, *daya* – have a greater capacity for expansion; and in the greater expansion of these is the root of the rightful fruition and *samanjasya* of all faculties.'[100] It is indeed quite possible, therefore, that Bankim was considerably influenced by Akshay in placing *samanjasya* as a crucial pivot within his conception of *dharma*, especially as it is probable that Bankim had read *Bahyavastu* as a prescribed text while in college.[101]

Conclusion

It has been my intention in this chapter to use a contrastive argument that uses the trope of comparatism not only to read native forms of narrativizing lived life against the grain of western epistemic historiography, but also to understand an implicit and perhaps inadvertent myopia while studying the ideological dimensions of nineteenth-century Bengal. In most of the important historical works, written either in the North or the South, there is a grand ideological sweep where significant yet relatively smaller voices are lost. Either there have been histories of class or caste, religion or culture, and social movements, or there are histories of individuals whose voices could not be heard. Implicitly, there is a grand design within the writing of intellectual histories, where the historical players have always been in the middle of things as icons of ideological confrontation, either in the form of a Rammohun or a Vidyasagar in the early part of the century, or in the form of a Bankimchandra or a Rabindranath in the later part. Akshay Dutta has rarely, or cursorily, featured in major historical narratives on nineteenth-century Bengal, unless one was discussing Brahmoism, and the Akshay–Debendranath debate.

Through my discussion of the principles of *dharma* in this chapter, I have tried to understand if the foundational role assigned to Bankim by historians has, more often than not, eclipsed an almost identical cultural politics foregrounded decades earlier by Akshay. Whereas, in his discussion of Bankim's *anushilantattwa*, Sudipta Kaviraj does not mention Akshay Dutta at all, the two cursory references to him in Andrew Sartori's *Bengal in Global Concept History* are interesting. In the first instance, Sartori sets Bankim apart from Akshay by asserting that the former 'wanted a theory that overcame the dichotomy between spirituality and worldliness' and therefore introduced the idea of *anushilan* as a concept of culture.[102] In the second instance, while still on the subject of *anushilan* and the idea of culture Sartori writes:

> One was no longer stuck in the dilemma of the mid-nineteenth century between objective necessity and subjective freedom, between Akshay Dutt's dissolution of subjectivity into the natural order and Debendranath Tagore's assertion of a spiritual subjectivity outside the material world.[103]

In this chapter I have tried to argue that in his works, Akshay Dutta was already, through his discourses in *Dharmaniti* or his essay 'Parishram', dissolving the gap between spirituality and worldliness, much before Bankim. In fact, one could find in Bankim's works an immediate affinity with Akshay in terms of the rationalist model that the latter foregrounded in *Dharmaniti* and before that in *Bahyavastu*. The divide between Akshay and Debendranath that Sartori refers to, and which I have discussed in detail in the first chapter, had already been resolved during Akshay's *Tattwabodhini* days. Debendranath had conceded the fallibility of the *apaurusheya* model of the Vedanta, and accepted (or given way to) Akshay's more rational model for the conception of *brahma* as manifest in the phenomenal universe. By the time Akshay was writing *Dharmaniti* in 1856, he had already moved on to more intricate questions about his immediate society or the *janansamaj*, and ways of its emancipation, rather than debating on the nature of *brahma* and its relationship with the individual subject. Likewise, the Comtean model of the philosophical contemplation of labour that Sartori discovers in Bankim was an almost exact replica of Akshay's model in both *Bahyavastu* and *Dharmaniti*.[104] In fact, the question of narrative within the social and cultural space, and the place of the *swadesh* within the larger historical scheme of labour and capital were already being explored by Akshay, as early as 1849, in such tracts as 'Prachin Hindudiger Samudrayatra'.[105]

The cultural polemic on Bengali selfhood – its search for a historicity within the social and cultural space of lived experience – was a complex process that had its own gradualist narrative with multiple trajectories that were spread across the globe. The performativity implicit in the very act of foregrounding a notion of *dharma* as social practice based on certain empirical principles rather than on religious discourse had its own contingencies. The manifestations of Akshay's *upachikirsha*, *bhakti*, and *nyayaparata* or Bankim's *bhakti*, *priti*, and *daya* as cultural models of *dharma* would create performative ambiguities that would continuously redefine the space of culture and widen the scope of the possibility of a narrative. I would therefore contend that it is difficult to sustain the liberal contra cultural model, albeit tentatively, as such a model has the possibility of compromising the performative fluidity of representations of Bengali selfhood. In the act of setting up Bankim as a role model of change, or a new beginning, the origin of the culturalist narrative of Bengali selfhood is established in such a way that the ambiguous moment of performative possibilities that would help in imagining a historical narrative (always/already present) is being compromised, along with the crucial role played by such apparent liberalists as Akshay Dutta. In the next chapter I will read Akshay along with Bhudeb Mukhopadhyay to see if their different notions of imaginary histories had created other possibilities of narrative performativities that subverted western epistemological expectations.

Notes

1. For a detailed discussion on the implications and the idea of dharma in nineteenth-century Bengal, see Amiya P. Sen, 'Hermeneutics and Ethical Theory: Re-visioning Dharma in Nineteenth-Century Bengal', in *Explorations in Modern Bengal c. 1800–1900: Essays on Religion, History and Culture* (Delhi: Primus Books, 2010), pp. 121–164.
2. See Samuel Moyn and Andrew Sartori (eds.), *Global Intellectual History* (New York: Columbia University Press, 2013), p. 4.
3. See the discussion on the lack of a conception of history within traditional thought before western education in Sudipta Kaviraj, *The Unhappy Consciousness: Bankimchandra Chattopadhyay and the Formation of Nationalist Discourse in India* (Delhi: Oxford University Press, 1995), pp. 107ff.
4. Ibid., p. 108.
5. Kaviraj, *The Unhappy Consciousness*, p. 108.
6. Hatcher, *Hinduism Before Reform* (Cambridge, MA: Harvard University Press, 2020), p. 4.

7. Ibid.

8. Kaviraj, *The Unhappy Consciousness*, p. 110.

9. Ibid., p. 109.

10. Ibid., p. 111.

11. Ibid., p. 111.

12. I use the word 'curiosity' here in the Arnoldian sense. Matthew Arnold writes in *Culture and Anarchy* (published as a single volume in 1869):

> Montesquieu says:-'The first motive which ought to impel us to study is the desire to augment the excellence of our nature, and to render an intelligent being yet more intelligent'. This is the true ground to assign for the genuine scientific passion, however manifested, and for culture, viewed simply as a fruit of this passion; and it is a worthy ground, even though we let the term curiosity stand to describe it.

Matthew Arnold, *Culture and Anarchy* (London: Smith, Elder & Co., 1869, Reprinted with an introduction and notes by Jane Garnett [New York: Oxford University Press, 2006]), p. 33.

13. For a discussion on this, see M. J. D. Roberts, *Making English Morals: Voluntary Association and Moral Reform in England, 1787–1886* (Cambridge: Cambridge University Press, 2004).

14. See Andrew Sartori, *Bengal in Global Concept History* (Chicago: University of Chicago Press, 2008).

15. Ibid., p. 5.

16. Ibid.

17. Ibid.

18. Ibid., p. 6.

19. Ibid., p. 7.

20. Ibid., p. 110.

21. Ibid., p. 111.

22. Partha Chatterjee, *Nationalist Thought and the Colonial World* (London: Zed Books, 1986), p. 59.

23. Ibid.

24. Ibid., p. 58.

25. Sartori, *Bengal in Global Concept History*, p. 117.

26. Kaviraj, *The Unhappy Consciousness*, p. 113.

27. Sartori, *Bengal in Global Concept History*, p. 117.

28. Chatterjee, *Nationalist Thought and the Colonial World*, p. 59.

29. Bankimchandra Chattopadhyay, *Dharmatattwa*, in *Bankim Rachanabali*, vol. 2, ed. Jogeshchandra Bagal (Calcutta: Sahitya Samsad, 1954), pp. 584–679.

30. Ibid., p. 589.

31. Ibid., p. 591.

32. See Alok Ray, *Bankim-Manisha* (Kolkata: Ebong Mushayera, 2014), p. 87.

33. Chattopadhyay, *Dharmatattwa* , p. 596.

34. Ibid., p. 597.

35. Ibid., p. 598.

36. Ibid.

37. Ibid., p. 600.

38. See Akshay Kumar Dutta, *Dharmaniti*, in *Akshaykumar Dutta Rachana Sangraha*, ed. Swapan Basu, vol. 1 (Kolkata: Paschimbanga Bangla Academy, 2008), pp. 431–528.

39. For all the parts of *Charupath*, see Swapan Basu (ed.), *Akshaykumar Dutta Rachana Sangraha* (Kolkata: Paschimbanga Bangla Academy, 2008), vol. 1, pp. 317–384. Also, many of the short tracts on general knowledge or moral improvement were published earlier in the pages of the *Tattwabodhini Patrika*.

40. See 'Parishram', in *Charupath*, vol. 2, in *Akshaykumar Dutta Rachana Sangraha*, ed. Swapan Basu, vol. 1 (Kolkata: Paschimbanga Bangla Academy, 2008), pp. 345–348.

41. Ibid., p. 346.

42. Ibid., p. 347.

43. Ibid., p. 346.

44. Ibid., p. 348.

45. Ibid. Akshay Dutta uses the phrase *janasamajer sribriddhisadhan*, once again reiterating the idea of a society (*janasamaj*) and the narrative of improvement or prosperity (*srivriddhi*).

46. Ibid., p. 348.

47. It is important here to make note of the fact that the ideas of *swadesh* or *swajati* were borrowed from the ideas of nation or nationhood in western epistemology. The liberal versus cultural divide that historians such as Sartori suggest implicitly create a demarcation between the supposed sympathy for the colonial master in the liberal versus a form of militant nationalism in the cultural that stands in complete opposition to colonial rule. A close reading of Bankim's *Dharmatattwa* would bring out a slightly contrarian note. In chapter 8 of *Dharmatattwa* the guru talks about how the

word *swadhinata* is a direct translation of the word 'liberty'. The significance of the word 'liberty', Bankim says, lies in the fact that the king may not necessarily be a native. In fact, the indigenous ruler might sometimes be an enemy of liberty, while a foreign ruler might be sympathetic to the idea of liberty or *swadhinata*. This is an interesting argument that needs to be taken into account while discussing Bankim's notion of nationalism and liberty. See Chattopadhyay, *Dharmatattwa*, p. 609.

48. Akshay Kumar Dutta, *Dharmaniti*, in *Akshaykumar Dutta Rachana Sangraha*, ed. Swapan Basu, vol. 1 (Kolkata: Paschimbanga Bangla Academy, 2008), p. 440.

49. Ibid.

50. Rammohun's emphasis on *daya* and Vidyasagar's insistence on *karuna* (both translated as compassion) are well-known examples of this. For more information on the subject, see Ranajit Guha, *Daya: Rammohon Ray o Amader Adhunikata* (Kolkata: Talpata, 2012), and Brian Hatcher, 'The Stuff of Legends', in *Vidyasagar: The Life and After-life of an Eminent Indian* (New Delhi: Routledge, 2014), pp. 78–106.

51. See, for example, Shaktinath Jha, *Fakir Lalon Sai: Desh Kal Ebang Shilpa* (Kolkata: Sambad, 1995), and Ayon Maharaj, *Infinite Paths to Infinite Reality: Sri Ramakrishna and Cross-Cultural Philosophy of Religion* (New York: Oxford University Press, 2018).

52. One cannot discount the importance of Bhudeb Mukhopadhyay in this context, particularly his lengthy treatises on model practices of social and family living in 'Paribarik Prabandha', 'Samajik Prabandha', or 'Achar Prabandha'. See Bhudeb Mukhopadhyay, *Prabandha Samagra*, ed. Manaswita Sanyal and Ranjan Bandopadhyay (Kolkata: Charchapad, 2010). However, there was no sustained emphasis on the idea or question of *dharma* in Bhudeb, although he was indeed writing on similar lines.

53. Dutta, *Dharmaniti*, p. 469.

54. Ibid., pp. 469–470.

55. Ibid., pp. 471–472.

56. Ibid., p. 495.

57. Ibid., p. 495. Also see T. M. Bruck, 'Mary Somerville, Mathematician and Astronomer of Underused Talents', *Journal of the British Astronomical Association* 106, no. 4 (1996): 201–206.

58. Dutta, *Dharmaniti*, p. 505.

59. Ibid., p. 506.

60. Chattopadhyay, *Dharmatattwa*, p. 594.

61. See Akshay Dutta, *Bahyavastur Sahit Manabprakritir Sammandha Vichar*, in *Akshaykumar Dutta Rachana Sangraha*, ed. Swapan Basu, vol. 1 (Kolkata: Paschimbanga Bangla Academy, 2008), p. 142.

62. Chattopadhyay, *Dharmatattwa*, p. 596.

63. Ibid., p. 596.

64. Ibid., p. 616.

65. Ibid., p. 617.

66. Ibid.

67. Ibid., p. 612. Bankim points out the existence of, and validates, oral narrative as history and considers such *puranetihas* as the source of knowledge that would feed the *jnanarjani vritti* across generations. It is also interesting how he finds such a tradition easily and suitably comparable with the European pedagogical traditions.

68. Akshay Kumar Dutta, *Dharmaniti*, p. 441.

69. Ibid., 445.

70. Ibid., p. 450. In this particular context Akshay also mentions the need for the readers of *Dharmaniti* to refer to his earlier book *Bahyavastur Sahit Manab Prakritir Sammandha Vichar*.

71. Bankimchandra Chattopadhyay, *Dharmatattwa* in *Bankim Rachanabali*, vol. 2, p. 585.

72. Ibid.

73. Ibid.

74. Ibid., p. 593.

75. This god that Bankim refers to, however, is not an impersonal god of the Vedanta or the Advaitavadis, but a personal god (*saguna*) of the Puranas (or as Bankim says, *puranetihas*), a god closer to being human, a god found in communitarian narratives, for example. Bankim's god is a god of the householder and not the ascetic, one who drives the *vrittis* towards fruition through *anushilan*. Many of Bankim's novels are expressions of such worldly *anushilan* rather than ascetic renunciation, where to turn towards the human is to turn towards god. There is a fine analysis of this (and the way many critics misread Bankim's intention in his *anushilantattwa*) in Tapobrata Ghosh's *Je Bhabe Bankim Pari* (Kolkata: Tobu, 2012).

76. Chattopadhyay, *Dharmatattwa*, p. 633.

77. Dutta, *Bahyavastur Sahit Manabprakritir Sammandha Vichar*, p. 290.

78. Ibid., p. 226.

79. Chattopadhyay, *Dharmatattwa*, p. 598.

80. Ibid.

81. Ibid.

82. Dutta, *Bahyavastur Sahit Manabprakritir Sammandha Vichar*, pp. 113–316.

83. George Combe, *The Constitution of Man: Considered in Relation to External Objects* (Cambridge: Cambridge University Press, 2009).

84. Dutta, *Bahyavastur Sahit Manabprakritir Sammandha Vichar*, p. 116.

85. Ibid., p.117.

86. Ibid., p. 231.

87. Ibid., p. 118.

88. Ibid., p. 250.

89. Ibid., p. 248.

90. Ibid., p. 251.

91. Ibid., p. 164.

92. Ibid., p. 187.

93. Ibid., p. 187.

94. Ibid.

95. Ibid., p. 142.

96. Ibid., p. 154.

97. Ibid., p. 158.

98. Ibid.

99. Ibid., p. 154.

100. Chattopadhyay, *Dharmatattwa*, p. 596.

101. See, for example, Alok Ray, 'Bankim-Manisha', in *Unish Satake Nabajagaran: Swarup Sandhan* (Kolkata: Akshar Prakashani, 2019), p. 303.

102. Sartori, *Bengal in Global Concept History*, p. 117. In fact, Amiya P. Sen, while discussing Bankim's *anushilantattwa* (he calls it *anushilan dharma*) would go so far as to say that it was an idea borrowed from the west, but would not even mention Akshay Dutta in this context. See Amiya P. Sen, *Hindu Revivalism in Bengal, 1872–1905* (New Delhi: Oxford University Press, 1993), p. 112.

103. Sartori, *Bengal in Global Concept History*, p. 134.

104. Ibid., p. 135.

105. See *Tattwabodhini Patrika* 3, no. 71, Asad, 1771 Saka, pp. 44–48.

5

On the Question of the Public Sphere

Civic Life, Polity, Dissent, and an Affective Engagement with the *Janasamaj*

In the previous chapter I have argued how the major templates of post-colonial historiography have largely engaged with figures who could be drawn larger than life with broad brushstrokes, and how the categorical divisions within historiographic practice have led historians to formulate ideological divisions (such as 'liberal' and 'cultural') to make sense of the complex reactions to imperial governance in nineteenth-century India and Bengal. Both these tactics – of nominating and focusing on important ideologues on the one hand and designing binary or incommensurate ideological templates on the other – were perhaps necessary to comprehend, in a generalized sense, the structure of post-colonial historical practice. Such broad templates would also consolidate a framework that would typically register and establish the reactions or responses to the colonial project of transposing its narrative of modernity and progress, and set off a critique that could also be understood as a narrative within the disciplinary formations of historiography. If one were to follow the development of post-colonial Indian historiography, it would not be difficult to discern such a claim towards a narrative, either as a derivative discourse or a global engagement or as a result of inevitable or incidental entanglements, to name a few.[1] I have expressed a measured scepticism about the tentatively closed templates that would discount the contingent nature of ideology critique and the fluidity of cultural resistance through praxis that is possible within a colonized space that has deep traditional roots and those that try to re-articulate the notion of the historical narrative through a lens of lived experience within the *samaj* or indigenous society. More often than not, there is a certain performative spin to the articulation or representation of identity even

within closed and well-defined contexts that engenders the notion of a
slippage or a spillage. Such slippage or spillage may not always be due to
excess, but due to a leakage or a gap within the set discursive rhetoric of
a narrative. The performative moment within indigenous polity is capable
of such complexities, whereby an act of continuous mimesis or mimicry of
the master-narrative might surreptitiously provoke that contingent moment
of alterity by which to identify or posit the question of selfhood. While
such moments may not be the defining moments of the larger narrative of
epistemic historiography, of the foundational tack towards post-colonial
history writing, they nevertheless remain as continuous reminders of the
various and fraught nature of the representation of the colonized space as
one that grapples with too many alternative narratives of representation
or resistance. In what I have discussed in the previous chapters, I hope I
have been able to put my finger on why a figure such as Akshay Dutta was
crucial to the project of narrativizing the historical identity of a colonized
race, and how it was possible to claim for Akshay a formative role in the
way rationalism, science education, or a technical training in the vernacular
were popularized in nineteenth-century Bengal. It is also important to note,
however, that Akshay Dutta either does not feature or only cursorily features
in most discussions on the way representative politics, the writing of history,
or the articulation of the post-colonial self has been narrativized or spoken
about within the various academic disciplines that talk about colonial Bengal.
No doubt the diminutive and perpetually sick figure of Akshay Dutta, a
recluse of sorts for the larger part of his adult life, without formal degrees
or professional training in the strictest senses of the terms, could not have
been in the centre or at the forefront of the project of informed resistance
that would produce disciplinary narratives of resistance. Undoubtedly, the
production of post-colonial historiography for the colonized state needed
heroes with myth-generating potential, and Akshay was not one of them.
A Rammohun Roy or an Iswarchandra Vidyasagar in the first half of the
nineteenth century or a Bankimchandra Chattopadhyay or Keshub Chunder
Sen in the latter half were larger-than-life figures who could comfortably fit
the cultural template of representative politics that could bring in epistemic
change. Akshay Dutta, on the other hand, would remain as an aporia,
sometimes for either side of the bargain, one who would inconspicuously
unhinge the carefully determined gates of epistemic certainty, but always
like the careful practitioner of a method, and never like a rebel.

Dissent within Method: A Sly Civilian?

If one were to carefully read the entire oeuvre of Akshay Dutta, one would discover symptoms of direct dissent only on rare occasions. Other than the long and protracted debate with Debendranath Tagore about the origin and authorship of the Vedas, Akshay would rarely be discovered at the forefront of an ideological debate with far-reaching political implications. However, Akshay would produce pieces of writing at regular and consistent intervals. Much of what he produced, primarily in the vernacular, were school textbooks or moral tracts for the householder, articles on popular science or the natural world. There was no myth generating potential in Akshay. It was as if the entire discourse of colonial governance and its social, cultural, or political implications were unfolding in a world that had no immediate relevance for the hermit practitioner of knowledge whose location was far removed from the larger, important, and foundational events of history. By all means, Akshay would come across as a dispensable figure in history. Yet one cannot fail to notice how Akshay was selected by Debendranath to be the editor of what was going to be (under Akshay's leadership) one of the most influential periodicals of the time (the *Tattwabodhini Patrika*). Likewise, on his resignation from the editorship of the *Tattwabodhini Patrika*, he was invited by Vidyasagar in 1855 to become the principal of the first government-run teachers' training school in Kolkata. Akshay assumed several roles that had significant intellectual impact on his milieu at a crucial moment in history when the Bengali subject of the empire was beginning to articulate a sense of selfhood in a way that would have a far-reaching impact on the larger scheme of the history of imperialism in Bengal. He was an editor, a patron of vernacular education, an administrator, an advocate of religious reform, and a science worker. What was imperative in all of these roles was that Akshay was writing, expressing himself, giving an opinion – and doing it from such a professional capacity that it reached the reading public of the time. In a certain sense, therefore, Akshay was playing the role of a public intellectual within a milieu that was developing a sense of native autonomy and a consequent articulation of selfhood within a cultural space where the imperialist had already and convincingly claimed an epistemic superiority.

My intention here is to argue that Akshay had never or rarely ever played the role of the dissenting intellectual who would challenge the foundational claims of colonial modernity towards a superior racial identity, and try to establish an oppositional framework that would have a directly confrontational agency. I would rather argue that like the typical deconstructionist, Akshay would unsettle the claims of superiority of the imperial narrative by reading a cultural text against its grain, by rendering an absolutist tract open to native interpretation through the act of translation. Akshay had translated many English tracts into Bengali, but most of them were invested with a peculiar native spin that would not confront the claims of the tract directly, but carefully unsettle the foundation of its thesis. A good example of this could be found in Akshay's translation of Combe's *The Constitution of Man*.[2]

In his introduction to *Bahyavastur Sahit Manab Prakritir Sammandha Vichar*, Akshay praises Combe's analysis of the relationship between *parameshwar* and the natural laws by which He governs the universe.[3] In fact, for most of the tract Akshay seems to be following the design set down by Combe in his book:

> If, then, the reader keep in view that GOD is the creator; that Nature, in the general sense, means the world which He has made; and, in a more limited sense, the particular constitution which he has bestowed on any special object, of which he may be treating, and that a Law of Nature means the established mode in which that constitution acts, and the obligation thereby imposed on intelligent beings to attend to it, he will be in no danger of misunderstanding my meaning.[4]

Although this is more or less the template that Akshay has followed in *Bahyavastu*, he insists in the introduction that his tract is not an exact translation of Combe's work. In fact, he admits to have suitably indigenized the text to suit the purposes of his countrymen by interpolating relevant examples that would be 'proper and directed towards their well-being' (*sangata o hitajanak*) and by omitting those examples that would be peculiarly relevant to Europeans.[5] There are a few crucial things that need to be noted here. First, Combe's *The Constitution of Man* was published in 1828, and Akshay's *Bahyavastu* appeared in print as a volume in 1851. A substantial part of the text was serialized in the pages of the *Tattwabodhini Patrika* from 1849, and with the necessary emendations that Akshay thought were relevant to his reading public. Therefore, in spite of his great admiration for the works of Combe, a cultural shift was being foregrounded to set the needs of the native subject apart from those of the colonial master class. Second, in the couple of decades between the publication of the original text and its native rendition, the symptoms of readjustment, or the need for a revision, point towards an active intellectual agency that was both informed about global advancements and invested in the peculiar need of the native subject. Third, a careful analysis of both the omissions and the interpolations might be crucial in unfolding the ideological departures that could help in determining Akshay's role within the larger scheme of the participation of the liberal intellectual in the colonial logic of modernity and progress.

It will be topical to note here that phrenology, along with the writings of George Combe, had made considerable inroads into the native Calcutta society during this period, and his works were being read and circulated among a section of the English-educated Calcutta intelligentsia. Cally Coomar Das, for example, a student of the Calcutta Medical College, was an ardent follower of Combe's works and had established the Calcutta Phrenological Society in 1845. The society had its own library, which had books and journals sent by Combe himself. James Poskett writes:

> The books and journals sent by Combe sat alongside copies of Spurzheim's *Outlines of Phrenology* and Mackenzie's *Illustrations of Phrenology*. Like many colonial libraries, the collection represented the different ways in which India was connected to the wider world.[6]

Soon after, in February 1850 the society started its own periodical, *Pamphleteer*, a monthly number, steeply priced at a rupee per copy and clearly meant for the English-educated upper echelons of the native Calcutta society. Poskett writes how the members of the society met frequently at Das' house for traditional *adda* sessions and discussed books from Europe and the Americas, or blending together national and world politics, thereby imagining 'reform within India as part of a global history of human improvement'.[7] Interestingly, in spite of Akshay's keen interest in phrenology, the medical sciences, and particularly the works of George Combe, he never became a member of the Calcutta Phrenological Society. Neither is there any reference to the *Pamphleteer* in his works or any proof of correspondence between him and Cally Coomar Das.[8] Intriguing as this may be, the possible reason for such a sense of alienation could be the fact that the 'prestige and respectability associated with English were much more important for the Calcutta Phrenological Society than the prospect of addressing a broader audience'.[9] As the editor of the *Tattwabodhini Patrika*, Akshay was not only keen to disseminate knowledge in the vernacular but also moulding such knowledge to fit a wider native audience and bring the latter within the fold of global advancement as it were.

It is not difficult to see how Akshay would occasionally deviate from Combe's contentions in order to address his own audience. One of the foundational claims in Combe's book, for example, is one of racial superiority of the European vis-à-vis the other races of the world. He bases his analysis on the science of phrenology: 'Mental talents and dispositions are determined by the size and constitution of the brain.'[10] In this context, he refers to India. Combe writes:

> It is well known that the caste of the Brahmins is the highest in point of intelligence as well as rank of all the castes in Hindostan; and it is mentioned by the missionaries as an ascertained fact, that their children are naturally more acute, intelligent, and docile, than the children of the inferior castes, age and other circumstances being equal.[11]

It is interesting to discover that although Akshay does depend on Combe's phrenological analysis in terms of how the behavioural and intellectual pattern in children are often determined by their parents and genealogy,[12] his translation of Combe's text completely misses out on this remark by Combe that is specifically relevant to the Indian context. While it is possible to read this omission as contrary to Akshay's claims of indigenizing the text, and that this particular example would be exactly relevant to the reading public that he was addressing, the intervention of Akshay as a reformist is immediately relevant in this case. Not only does he ignore this part of Combe's analysis, but Akshay's interpretation (and, by extension, translation) of Combe's text also gives it a contrary spin. Largely, throughout the text of *Bahyavastu*, Akshay maintains the logic of the master-text that claims the superiority of European culture following the trajectory of progress and modernity through scientific advancement. He also insists how most of the 'English-speaking natives' are exactly aware of the various traditional practices and superstitions that are part of daily existence. Among these he lists kulinism (*kaulinya maryada*), child marriage, and the resistance to the remarriage of widows.[13] Clearly, this is a direct attack on the existing Brahminical (and upper caste) practices of the time. This implicit subversion of the intention of Combe's text translated in the way Akshay does is a telling example of reading against the grain and, therefore, of deconstructive practice. Whereas Combe upholds racial superiority as a primary strand in his text, Akshay consistently but implicitly undercuts such a claim in his translation while keeping with the spirit of order, rule, and progress.

Likewise, it is only in the larger framework of the argument that Akshay follows Combe in *Bahyavastu*: that all external objects have a natural constitution, are governed by a natural law, and there is a divine presence that has created the universe as it is; and that it is through the practice of moral sentiments and following the laws that govern the natural world that universal happiness may be achieved. Other than this and the upholding of the general spirit of scientism, Akshay carefully avoids many of Combe's peculiar racial observations on the one hand and interpolates many of his own on the other. As I have already pointed out, even Combe's particular observations about India are often summarily ignored by Akshay. For example, while talking about mixed race marriages and the corresponding impact of such union on cranial capacities of the offspring, Combe makes an interesting observation about the future of the Anglo-Indian race in India:

> So much is this the case in Hindostan, that several writers have already pointed to the mixed race there, as obviously destined to become the future sovereigns of India. These individuals inherit from the native parent a certain adaptation to the climate, and from the European parent a higher development of brain, the two combined constituting their superiority.[14]

Evidently, there is no mention of this in Akshay's text. On the other hand, unlike Combe, Akshay makes some astute and politically topical observations in his translation. Combe's text, if one were to consider phrenology as a scientific field of study, is purely a textbook of scientific observations framed by a belief in god as the maker. While Akshay follows this general structure, he interpolates observations that are directly relevant to imperial governance. For Akshay, *buddhivritti* and *dharmapravritti* are two abiding virtues that should guide the human subject. Those that do not possess these are guided by their lowly instincts or *nikkrista pravritti*.[15] He discovers in the English merchants doing business in Calcutta a strong affinity towards *nikkrista pravritti*. Akshay writes how they are dishonest as businessmen, have a dubious reputation about repaying loans, prone to sins of the flesh, lead lavish lives beyond their income, have no propensity towards religion, and are completely unashamed of their deeds. In fact, it was due to the excessive greed of some of these dishonest merchants that indigo cultivation became so exploitative. They would acquire huge loans from banks and would be unable to pay back, leading in the end to the dissolution of the Union Bank.[16] This is evidently a political comment, a direct critique aimed at the economic imprudence of Company rule or the economic decline of Bengal at the behest of imperial governance.

In a similar vein, Akshay talks about the miserable condition of civic life in the native part of the city of Calcutta, which, according to him, was the reason for the ill-health and weak constitution of the inhabitants of the city compared to the residents of the village. He makes a list of the civic deficiencies of the city such as stinking waterworks, lack of garbage disposal, inadequate living quarters, and air pollution. Clearly, he views such sordid living conditions to be a violation of the principles laid down by god (*aiswarik niyam langhan*).[17] He compares Calcutta to a prison and directly blames the imperial government for such neglect of its citizenry:

> It is regrettable that the administrators turn a blind eye to such misery and death of the people on a daily basis. Can the merciless king who in spite of his power does not protect his subjects from the clutches of death, be called a decent king (*bhadra raja*)? To not save the miserable, and to behead one's subjects with one's own hands are but similar acts. The rulers have theoretically employed some commissioners, but in vain. The commissioners are a laughing stock. It is the duty (*kartavya*) of the rulers to be mindful of this and protect hundreds from dying and millions from their misery.[18]

Once again, in both the above instances, Akshay is using a deliberate strategy of quiet disruption backed by the logic that he borrows directly from Combe's text. In the section titled 'Calamities Arising from Infringement of the Moral Laws', Combe critiques the tendency of 'unbridled Acquisitiveness'[19] of the master classes or the manufacturing classes. As a critique of the effects of the Industrial Revolution in England, Combe writes how the 'extraordinary demand for labourers in 1825 was entirely factitious, fostered by an overwhelming issue of bank paper, much of which ultimately turned out to be worthless'.[20] In a comparable section, Akshay thus brings in the reference to the excessive greed of the indigo cultivators and traders that subsequently led to the dissolution of the Union Bank.[21] Likewise, in the latter instance of the rulers and the commissioners turning a blind eye to the fate of the citizenry of Calcutta, Akshay turns to the basic template of morality that lies at the heart of Combe's treatise:

> A practical faith in the doctrine that the world is arranged by the Creator, in harmony with the moral sentiments and intellect, would be of unspeakable advantage both to rulers and subjects; for they would then be able to pursue with greater confidence the course dictated by moral rectitude, convinced that the result would prove beneficial....[22]

It is through a close reading and translation of Combe's *The Constitution of Man* that Akshay places his critique of colonial rule – one that is not guided by moral sentiments or intellect (the two touchstones that should, according to Combe, guide both the rulers and the subjects), but by greed and neglect.

Likewise, it is crucial to notice how Akshay is using the translation of Combe's text as a ploy to consistently read it against the grain of colonial governance. The apparent respect for George Combe and his treatise is quite evident in the introduction to the first volume of the translation. In his introduction to the second volume, Akshay emphasizes the importance of *Bahyavastu* within the fold of school education, particularly for the principals of these schools who would plan ways to inculcate these natural laws in their students.[23] A considerable part of this introduction is spent on the relationship between education and the corresponding duties of the ruling class, their ways of facilitating modes, means, and strategies for formulating a good education for their subjects. Akshay emphasizes the 'rule of law' or *rajniyam* and the *kartavya* or the duty of the ruler to reflect his benevolent intention (*mangaldayak abhipray*) through the appropriate policy of school education.[24] Interestingly, in this context, he once again refers to the importance of civic amenities, which should be provided by the rulers according to *rajniyam*, for the smooth running of the project of education: a clean city, potable water, a waste disposal system – clear markers of the project of modernity upheld by the colonial master.[25] Towards the end of this introduction, Akshay perceptively but almost incidentally deviates towards his political intention. He suggests that it is the duty of those who have embraced Brahmoism to read and continuously discuss the contents of the volumes of *Bahyavastu*.[26] Throughout both volumes of the text, otherwise, he has rarely and only incidentally referred to Brahmoism or its practices. However, in the first volume of *Bahyavastu* he has expressed his discontent at the way the English schools of the country have consistently failed to educate their pupils about the necessary balance between physical and mental labour:

> It is a cause of grave regret that most students of the English schools of our country, by neglecting physical labour and through excessive mental labour have transformed their bodies into useless temples of disease. The principals of these schools do not consider that this needs to be urgently addressed.[27]

The careful observer will not fail to notice the performative intent of this political moment. First, there is a deliberate but not forceful foregrounding of indigenous methods of schooling as a substitute for western methods; second, the original theoretical framework is still borrowed from the narrative of the colonial master, which proclaims the superiority of the European, intellectual and otherwise, only given a subtle spin that serves as a critique of contemporary governance and its failures; third, Akshay is not upholding the traditional education of the *tol*s and the *madrasah*s, but veering towards a newly established system of education and religious formation (Brahmoism) that is laced with symptoms of modernity in terms of cultural practice, and yet whose roots could be dragged back to a foundational past. One could therefore say that Akshay's narrative, in its performative principle, was already proposing a reform without revolution, subtle shifts of focus while apparently pandering to an epistemic system that carried a European template. The deconstructive intent is implicit in Akshay's claim of translation, where he both translates and deviates, a continuous process of re-formation that pushes his work towards what Emily Apter calls the 'zone', where she imagines 'a broad intellectual topography that is neither the property of a single nation, nor an amorphous condition associated with postnationalism, but rather a zone of critical engagement that connects the "1" and the "n" of ranslation and transNation'.[28] The political intent of such a 'zone' that Akshay creates through his lengthy translation of Combe's work may not be easily discounted. It is through both an acceptance and a critique that Akshay formulates a necessary intervention into the almost opaque epistemic superiority of the colonizer. Yet he does this with the least disruption, almost a surreptitious act of destabilizing without motives of subversion.

Affect, Governance, Disaffection, and the Question of Legitimacy

If one were to closely read Akshay's works – either the primers written by him, or textbooks for schools, or the moral and ethical tracts, or the short caveats on the ill-effects of drinking, or the long essays on trade relations of ancient Hindus in the pages of the *Tattwabodhini Patrika* – it is possible for the reader to conclude that Akshay's intention was to intervene into the affective materiality of his cultural milieu. At the core of Akshay's work was a realignment of certain indigenous cultural mores, based on principles of rationalism and aspects of modernity, while retaining the affective values that connected them immediately to a past and therefore established a continuity in terms of community and history. Apparently, such a generalized assessment of Akshay's work may appear to be essentialist in intention, but let us break it down. More or less throughout his oeuvre Akshay has highlighted the importance of the two qualities of *buddhivritti* and *dharmapravritti* as the touchstones of ethical existence. He has broken the concepts down, piecemeal, analysed various tributaries and distributaries of each, and subsequently placed them at the centre of his ethical compass. Akshay has defined both these ideas for his readers in multiple tracts, and always on the basis of their affective and communal function, and in terms of what the practice of these qualities bring back to the *janasamaj* or community.[29] His insistence on rationalism and empirical evidence were not merely part of his training in the western texts and other influences brought in by colonial modernity. It is topical to remember that Akshay's protracted debate with Debendranath Tagore on the nature of the Vedas had its rational foundation within the shastric doctrines. Likewise, to take the immediate example of his translation of Combe's *The Constitution of Man*, one does not fail to notice the invested communitarian thrust in continuously trying to indigenize the text and connect it affectively to a past and the immediate concerns of the society and cultural practices around him. However, as I have already pointed out, Akshay's writings would generally avoid the confrontational rhetoric, any clear intent of subversion, and depend more on the incidental, the performative, and the contingent to establish his point. The affective principle that Akshay generally used was based on tracing a narrative back to an indigenous past, but rarely to place it alongside the present in a confrontational manner in order to establish any equation of superiority over the colonizer's narrative. One would wonder why Akshay was so careful with his rhetoric. Was it deliberate or incidental? Is it possible to explain this as Sartori does with the simple binary between the liberal and the cultural?

I would suggest that it is possible to read deeper into this. I have argued earlier that it would perhaps be unwise to draw a line between the liberal (till the mid-seventies) and the cultural (eighties and after) tendencies in nineteenth-century Bengal. Dissent, dissatisfaction, unrest were all part of the affective reality of the milieu of the colonized subject, and expressions of such unrest assumed myriad forms of expression through both the written and spoken words. That resentment against the ruling class and volatile expressions of such a sentiment were not unknown before the eighties of the nineteenth century may be symptomatically understood. With various forms of resentment brewing immediately after the 1857 unrest, the colonial government found it imperative to add Section 124a to the Indian Penal Code in 1870. The section reads:

> Whoever by words, either spoken or intended to be read, or by signs, or by visible representation or otherwise, excites or attempts to excite feelings of disaffection to the Government established by law in British India, shall be punished with transportation for life or for any term, to which fine may be added, or with imprisonment for a term which may extend to three years, to which fine may be added, or with fine.[30]

The notion of 'disaffection' therefore becomes an important juridico-legal framework that would help us read the reaction of the native commentator and the nature of affect that he would try to elicit from his constituency in terms of a reaction to colonial governance. But, more importantly, the government also felt it imperative to understand, interpret, and censure a notion as contingent and arbitrary as affect within the public sphere. In a fascinating analysis on the questions of affect and disaffection Tanya Agathocleous, in her book *Disaffected*, analyses the centrality of affect to governance in the colonial period and argues how 'the law against disaffection created a bifurcated public sphere in which British speech was associated with reason and detachment, and Indian speech with affect and atavism. The colonial public sphere … was defined by the state and racialized.'[31] While Agathocleous focuses chiefly on the Indian Anglosphere, and trains her critique on the analysis of the native Anglophone press from the late nineteenth century into the early decades of the twentieth, it might be valuable to read her analysis of disaffection closely with what someone like Akshay Dutta was already doing with his work around the middle of the nineteenth century.

As is evident from the disaffection clause (Section 124a of the Indian Penal Code), the phrase 'feelings of disaffection' has an arbitrary juridical bearing and may be interpreted freely and contingently. Agathocleous lists a series of emotions that could be held potentially seditious according to this clause, among them hatred, enmity, dislike, hostility, contempt, aversion, disloyalty, and so on.[32] She therefore suggests, and quite correctly, that disaffection was 'a state of mind, a feeling, and a political stance'.[33] What I am trying to argue here is that in terms of a narrative, such a state of mind, or 'feeling', was already present within the native public sphere, much before a legal code had to ratify or accept it as real. The section was added to the penal code in 1870; the rebellion that nurtured the direct possibility of such disaffection happened in 1857. It is not difficult to imagine that the rebellion also had a past, a narrative of dissent, dissatisfaction, or hostility, or however one chooses to name it as a state of disaffection, that was brewing in the native society before the rebellion actually happened. The affective community in nineteenth-century Bengal, for example, particularly with the proliferation of print culture, was reacting to the questions of governance in a way that involved the political with the literary, the historical with the cultural, the real with the fictional. The lived experience of metropolitan life in the city of Calcutta, for example, could be transformed in the public imagination to a fictional narrative whose central focus would be the affective, and yet a narrative that would engender a critique of contemporary colonial governance and the various associated dissatisfactions. I am particularly thinking here of the *naksha* narratives that had begun to infiltrate the native public sphere from the early years of the nineteenth century, such as *Kalikata Kamalalaya* (1823), *Nababubu Bilas* (1825), *Aalaler Ghorer Dulal* (1858), or *Hutom Pynachar Naksha* (1861).[34] Whereas none of them could be read as direct critiques of colonial governance, such farcical narratives were masters of dissembling, with myriad modes of self-reflexivity embedded within native cultural practice. Most of them, through their affective consolidation of a heterogeneous public sphere, would carry on a veiled critique of the empire and its modes of functioning.

In my opinion, the role of figures such as Akshay Dutta was crucial within the affective reality of the complex social space that he was addressing through his writings and editorial work. There was a confluence in his work of many strands of public culture manifested in a way that was far more complex than something like a disaffection clause could address. In the first place,

Akshay was addressing both the English-speaking and the non-English-speaking public. The *Tattwabodhini Patrika* had a curious sophistication in both its subject matter and the general use of rhetoric which invested in its readership a sense of subscribing to something that was both intellectually and culturally important. The debates or topics addressed in the pages of the periodical had an eclectic range that constituted relevant and contemporary debates on religion on the one hand[35] and discourses on the method and practice of education[36] or the ill-effects of consuming alcohol[37] on the other. The immense popularity of the periodical during Akshay's editorship goes on to suggest that there was both an immediate relevance and interest in the periodical and that there was a certain kind of social mobility associated with subscribing to it. This is where the role of the *Tattwabodhini Patrika* became crucial in involving what Agathocleous calls the counterpublic.[38] Whereas the public is the imagined audience or participant addressed in texts and circulated discourses, the counterpublic is the more contingent and arbitrary presence that resists the idea of a closed space of circulation and points 'to fissures in the idea of the public'.[39] Agathocleous raises an important question here: '… what happens when the audience interpellated by a particular form of print culture was both bourgeois and oppositional, both public and counterpublic at once?'[40] It is interesting that Agathocleous is speaking here of the Indian Anglosphere only, the English speaking native subject of the empire. The constitution of the vernacular counterpublics was evidently far more complex, arbitrary, and heterogeneous in nature.[41] Evidently, Akshay's readers constituted both the public and the counterpublic. The eclectic subject matters of his periodical, including, for example, a serialized and lengthy study of fringe religious and spiritual sects spread across both the urban and rural parts of Bengal (an empirical study that later developed into the *Bharatvarshiya Upasak Sampraday*[42]), would attract the curiosity of a range of consumers, across caste, class, and gender, who could not generally be included within the rubric of the reading public of the time. For most of the counterpublics, therefore, uninitiated to the rigours of formal education, the affective would play a major role in the way their opinion would be shaped. Along with this, the evident *bhadraloki* (the symptoms of being a *bhadralok*) associated with being a subscriber of the *Tattwabodhini Patrika* led to the immense popularity of the periodical. I have argued in an earlier chapter how through the pages of the *Tattwabodhini* Akshay was attempting a gradual epistemic shift in terms of the way the vernacular reading public would be acquainted with patterns of modernity and scientism. While it is evident that such a principle was foregrounded by the general choice of subject matter and through the debates and discussions published in its pages, it is not difficult to pick out consistent strands of the affective that found their place. Also, it is not difficult to presume that without an affective thrust, the periodical would not be as popular with the reading public of the time.[43]

Akshay's Affective Turn: A Carefully Crafted Strategy

A few examples from the pages of the *Tattwabodhini Patrika* and other writings might help to illustrate the kind of affective polity that Akshay intended to be a part of his constituency. Of course, imagining such a polity, or a readership, was possible because of the vernacular mode of communication that was able to reach out to the various reading public and counterpublics who would create continuous fissures and contingent moments of articulation. An implicit emphasis on the affective would lead to opening up the polity towards an articulation of selfhood or identity that was both performative and political. In such a case, the notion of disaffection would be both intricately heterogeneous and implicit, and veiled within multiple cultural and social discourses not immediately apparent to the ruling class. I would argue that as an author and editor, Akshay was intensely aware of his constituency, and went on to carefully influence his readership through affective dislocations of the ideological, positioning his voice at the liminal space between the public and the counterpublic, as well as the ruler and the ruled.

The opening piece of the Agrahayan 1765 Saka issue of the *Tattwabodhini Patrika* carries one of the rare signed pieces by Akshay. The piece is a lengthy apotheosis of god, the creator of the universe. In an earlier chapter I have mentioned the popular apocryphal story about Akshay dismissing the role of prayer as a means for growing crops.[44] The simple, empirical equation reveals a scientific and rational mind with little or no space for the affective. In this particular piece, however, it is interesting to note how Akshay emphasizes the need for feeling or *anuvaba* as a means for realizing the love of god: 'So he feels a love for God in his heart, and there is born a strange mixed feeling of pure bliss (*bimal ananda*), which is superior to all the feelings of this world, and which may only be felt by the worshippers of the Brahma.'[45] The emphasis on the affective need not be overemphasized. It is such a strategy of affect that Akshay carries across the various issues of the journal. However, the individual call for a worship of the Brahma is frequently transformed into a communitarian affectivity with a covert political and cultural intent. In the piece titled 'Bartaman Byabahar' (Current Behaviour) for example, published in the Bhadra 1771 Saka issue of the *Tattwabodhini*, there is a comparative analysis between the English-educated youth of contemporary times and the older generation of the society trained in the vernacular tradition. It begins with the regret that it was an ominous sign (*amangal*) that there was a clear rift between the educated youth of the community and the general public, and that this was a constraint to the happiness of the nation.[46] Akshay initiates the affective turn by asserting soon that the heart is at the root of all action (Akshay uses the Bengali word *mon* which may both be translated as the 'heart' or the 'mind'; in the context of the piece it seems that the former is more appropriate). In the following paragraphs he narrates how the contemporary English-educated youth indulge in various acts of imprudence including those of drinking and carousal. The older generation believes such violent and subversive acts to be the direct consequence of English education: 'At a time when English education has become imperative, they feel that too much education would lead their sons to forget tradition and become addicted to alcohol. So much so that they send their sons to common institutions instead of the Hindu College....'[47] Likewise, the behaviour of these educated youth will lead to parents from the older generation refraining from sending their daughters to school. And this, the tract continues, will be one of the reasons for the failure of the benevolent and noble mission of John Bethune for the spread of female education. At the end of the piece Akshay appeals directly to the affective instincts of the English-educated youth in order that the true ideal of education is achieved: 'You be staid and humble, show respect to *Parameshwar* and love to human kind, charm the hearts of the people by good behaviour, only then will you be invested with the power to do something for your country, you'll be celebrated by the society (*lok-samaj*), and achieve satisfaction.[48] The reader will notice the implicit strategy that Akshay has used in this piece. In the first place, this is a critique of the indigenous society – the privileged section that has access to elite institutions and an English education. It is, according to Akshay, a failure of their affective principles that has led to an alienation of this group of people from an earlier generation and their vernacular ethics. The *lok-samaj* has to be won over by love and understanding and humility. At the same time, there is a deliberate and strategic upholding of the intention of the sahib – the benevolence of his educational project that extends beyond the male population to the women of the colony. It is as if that the affective failure of the educated interlocutor is responsible for the larger population of the natives to be deprived of a glimpse of modernity, and a chance to be educated through the enlightenment that has been brought in by the master class.

Akshay's admiration and praise for John Bethune was expressed in an earlier piece in the *Tattwabodhini* as well. The piece titled 'Swadeshiya Bhashay Vidyabhyash' (Education in the Native Language), published in the Baisakh 1771 Saka issue of the *Tattwabodhini Patrika*, begins with profuse praise for the educational project that Bethune had undertaken, and his consistent emphasis on the need for proficiency in and the use of the vernacular by the native population.[49] Akshay elaborates on the three-fold principle that Bethune prescribed for the spread and prosperity of the vernacular: first, those that were educated in English should try to translate their acquired knowledge into their native tongue so that it was accessible to the masses; second, those that came to Bethune with their English works were encouraged by him to write rather in their vernacular, as that was the path to fame and glory; third, all native authors should try to produce books in the vernacular, or translate English books into Bengali if they desired to have a permanent place in the intellectual history of Bengal.[50] In this context, Akshay also praises the role played by the Deputy Governor of Bengal, Thomas Herbert Maddock, for being instrumental in emphasizing the importance of Bengali in his lecture to the students of the Hindu College. To this praise, crucially, Akshay adds: 'It is of great regret that after having spent thirty-five years as an administrator in India, it is only when he is about to leave that he expresses such enthusiasm.'[51] The perceptive reader will not miss Akshay's strategy of critiquing by comparison that he uses here. How is the reader supposed to deconstruct this strategy? Is it possible to read this merely as a comparative analysis between two representatives of the colonizing class, or is it a more nuanced critique of the sustained neglect of vernacular education by a class of administrators? I would contend that here is Akshay's deliberate ploy to work around the possibility of disaffection. The clause was still a few years ahead, but the symptoms and the consequent anxiety that led to it were already suitably ensconced within the narrative of the imperial discourse. Also, a critique based on discrimination or judgement in terms of culture and tradition had a more affective quality than one based on logic and empiricism. Akshay, the empiricist that he was, was also using the affective charge of culture and language to elicit a reaction from his heterogeneous readership. On the other hand, by getting Bethune on his side, he was also being complicit in the larger project of modernity, playing suitably into the trope of the civilizing mission. This is what Agathocleous calls print mimicry in her book:

> Disaffection was thus at once a political, criminal, and peculiarly Indian emotion hidden in words whose galvanizing power would be unleashed once it reached its target audience – unless it was intercepted along the way. In order to perform this interception, judge, jury and public had to become literary critics – analyzing tone, searching texts for hidden meanings, and producing plausible interpretations. This rigid governmental oversight inevitably produced the practice of print mimicry, a phrase that I use to evoke Homi Bhabha's 'colonial mimicry' while drawing attention to the crucial role of print culture, periodical form, and censorship in the production of mimic effects.[52]

I contend that through the various tracts that Akshay wrote, or edited, in the pages of the *Tattwabodhini* or elsewhere, he was quite deliberately foregrounding this strategy of print mimicry years before the government felt the need to censure any attempt at surreptitious and strategic subversion.

There is another more insidious strategy involved here. If one were to closely read the tracts of Akshay, it will be curiously apparent that Akshay would rarely or never train his invective on a particular person in the colonial administration or the civil society. Rammohun Roy and Iswarchandra Vidyasagar were known for their epistolary exchanges or lengthy public debates with important officials in the church or the educational administration demanding various reforms or emendations in the existing state of things.[53] For Akshay, on the other hand, there is no evidence of a direct personal confrontation, or even a letter or tract addressed as a critique to a particular person. He would confront a collective that could not be given a face, and hence was more difficult to censure or reprimand. Later on, in the same tract, 'Swadeshiya Bhashay Vidyabhyash', for example, he comes down heavily on the 'government'. He writes that in spite of the good intentions of the likes of Bethune or Maddock, it was the apathy of the government that was directly responsible for the lack of training in the vernacular:

> Till date there has been no facility provided by the government for the teaching of the Bengali language. No matter how much the newspaper editors will cry hoarse, and others would reason about its necessity, they

will not be moved. They remain deaf. At the moment the Hindu College does teach Bengali, but it is a mere formality. There is no pedagogic discipline, there are no teachers, no books, and no one to supervise. The process of learning depends on the whim of the student.[54]

It is not difficult to see how Akshay is strategically placing the figure of the benevolent and reformist individual member of the colonialist class contrapuntally against the inconsiderate and almost indifferent albeit impersonal form of the colonial government. His critique continues in the same vein for the rest of the piece, elaborating on the state of neglect of Bengali education across Bengal, from the cities to the district towns. He does not forget to mention the prosperity of the English schools, flush with funds and instructors, and how, in these English schools, special care is taken to ridicule vernacular education.[55] It will not elude the reader how the piece progressively unfolds the affective as a strategy. That the vernacular is being neglected deliberately by the government at the expense of the colonizer's language, and that it is being exposed to ridicule in the English schools, will immediately involve the emotion of his readership – both the public and the counterpublic – and will engender a series of implicit and sustained reaction. It is as if to stoke such a reaction that Akshay ends the essay with another statement that has a considerable affective charge: 'This kind of disinterest and neglect of the rulers about the education of their subjects arouses a feeling of deep unrest in the heart!'[56] One need not emphasize the presence of the overtly affective in this statement.

The Bengali Press and Disaffection: A Brief Digression

The eclectic nature of subjects and themes discussed in the pages of the *Tattwabodhini Patrika* had its own way of balancing pieces with a direct affective and incendiary intent with those that had absolutely no political charge. For example, a piece such as 'Swadeshiya Bhashay Vidyabhyash' in the Baisakh 1771 Saka issue would immediately be followed by a textual analysis of a section of the *Rigveda Samhita*, or an informative and apparently neutral piece on the 'Vaishnava Sampraday';[57] likewise, another piece titled 'Avichar' (Injustice) criticizing the practice of coercive Christian conversions that appeared in the Bhadra 1773 Saka issue of the periodical is enveloped by a piece on the natural laws of punishment (within *Bahyavastu*) and another on the physical sciences (the qualities of inert matter).[58] It is quite possible that such a balancing act, of placing a piece with subversive or critical intent carefully between other pieces of pure intellectual curiosity, was a deliberate ploy that Akshay was using as a subterfuge to ward off unnecessary political attention. As Agathocleous asserts, the public sphere within which the various trajectories of print mimicry played themselves out was a space rife with 'hybridity, ambiguity, excess, splitting, and subversion'.[59] I would argue that for most of his intellectual life as a writer and an editor, Akshay was keenly aware of his instrumentalist function, as a facilitator of both a dialogue between the colonizer and the elite, upper class section of his milieu through the pages of the *Tattwabodhini* on the one hand, and an affective churning of the public and the counterpublic through his interpretation of colonial governance in the vernacular on the other. Whereas in the former role he always chose his place in the background of the larger political and social debates that involved pamphleteering, petitioning, court proceedings, or a direct debate or confrontation with the colonizer class, in his latter role he was quietly subversive and often oppositional in a way that stoked the affective instincts of his native readership. It needs to be emphasized that although Akshay's intellectual milieu was composed of some of the most important reformists of nineteenth-century Bengal, who were writing and arguing in both English and Bengali, Akshay would rarely write in English. Although quite conversant with the nuances of the language, and engaging with many important philosophical, social, and scientific texts written in the language, it was undoubtedly a conscious decision on his part to choose Bengali over English as his medium of intellectual practice. The political intent for such a decision was not misplaced. In the first place, the erudition that Akshay brought into the vernacular press through the *Tattwabodhini*, and earlier through his *Bidyadarshan*, called for a sustained and serious engagement of his readers with pedagogy and knowledge formation in the vernacular. Also, he was mixing simple scientific or general knowledge with articles on social reform, thereby continuously expanding the range of his readership within the vernacular reading public. While the scientific articles might have had a niche readership, articles on society and culture would be able to penetrate a larger section of his audience. Most issues of the *Tattwabodhini*, for example, would bear testimony to the eclecticism and varied curiosity of its editors, writers, and readers. In a way, through such a strategy Akshay was also acting as a conduit between the elite and the commoner. The commoner had the feeling that he was subscribing to the same periodical as the elite and was a vicarious participant in the same debates and discussions, while the latter, already invested with reformist tendencies, had the feeling of a direct engagement with the common public through either contribution (as an author) or subscription to the periodical. I believe that one of the reasons for the popularity of the *Tattwabodhini* was the feeling of a connect that was established across sections of the native population. Second, at the time of Akshay's editorship of the *Tattwabodhini*, the vernacular press had not yet developed into a cause for concern for the colonizer. It was going through its own phase of experimentation, both in terms of writing in the vernacular, and methods and strategies of circulation.[60]

While still on the subject of disaffection it is crucial to understand that between the time of the passing of the Press Act under the aegis of Lord Metcalfe in 1835 that assigned freedom to the vernacular press and the disaffection clause of Section 124a added to the Indian Penal Code in 1870, the dynamics of imperial governance, and the native reaction to it, had gone through several phases of revision and assessment. In 1835, while repealing the Licensing Regulations of 1823 that had considerably censured the vernacular press, Metcalfe had declared: 'Freedom of public discussion, which is nothing more than the freedom of speaking aloud, is a right belonging to the people which no government has a right to withhold.'[61] The reaction through the years to the vernacular press had been one of mixed indulgence and light censure from the imperial government, till perhaps the disaffection clause tried to comprehend the hybrid or ambiguous or contingent nature of subversion that was intrinsic to the native writing in his own language. Print mimicry, therefore, was a late realization on the part of the colonial government. In fact, as Bose and Moreno assert in their book, even during the mutiny of 1857, the possibility of any subversion was a minor distraction set against the generally loyal and subservient vernacular press:

> There has been an attempt in some direction to denounce the Vernacular Press as disloyal and revolutionary, but here is a testimony, which proves that even the early Bengali Press helped the Government in 'strengthening the principal of loyalty'. Even the Report of Administration by the Bengal Government for 1917, frankly states that 'the tone of the Bengali Press is loyal.' It must not be lost sight of that even in the troublesome days of the Sepoy Mutiny, when the whole country was up against British authority, the Bengali Press continued to be loyal, without lending any help to the revolutionary party, supporting

firmly the British Government, and many a journal, like the *Subodhini*, sang songs of victory for the British, *Jay Britisher Jay*.[62]

Bose and Moreno also narrate another interesting incident that happened in the wake of the foundation of *The Bengal Spectator* in 1842, a few years before the *Tattwabodhini Patrika* was started. As part of a meeting of the Society for the Acquisition of General Knowledge (famously founded by the students of Derozio, such as Ramgopal Ghosh, Ramtanu Lahiri, Peary Chand Mitra, and others), Raja Dakshinaranjan Mukherjee delivered a talk, at the premises of the Hindu College, titled 'The Present Condition of the East India Company's Courts of Judicature and Police under the Bengal Presidency'. On this lecture being termed treasonous by the principal D. L. Richardson,[63] the committee walked out, soon founded the British Indian Society, and Ramgopal Ghosh along with his friends began to publish *The Bengal Spectator*. What is singularly interesting is how the *Bengal Hurkaru* reported this incident and Dakshinaranjan Mukherjee's talk in its pages: 'We have in vain sought for any proof of the charges of disloyalty, ignorance and *disaffection*, which have been so profusely heaped upon the Baboo'[64] (italics mine). Evidently, therefore, it was from as early as roughly the middle of the nineteenth century that 'disaffection' as a symptom of disloyalty to the empire was being spoken of.

However, if one were to study the many vernacular periodicals that proliferated between the forties to the sixties of the nineteenth century in Bengal, it would be evident that such instances of disaffection were indeed rare. Most of the periodicals that made their mark on the native intelligentsia were progressivist in content, speaking of reform of existing social and cultural mores, and celebrating forms of colonial modernity in their pages. While use of the affective as a strategy of critiquing native customs and superstitions was quite common, a corresponding critique of imperial governance was rare. The tone acquired by most of these progressive or 'modern' periodicals as they spoke to the imperial master class was mostly one of respectful request or pleading for justice or a plea to intervene in the customs and practices of the natives that were considered regressive or non-modern. A longer discussion on the content of these periodicals will be a lengthy digression in the present context, and may be taken up elsewhere. However, most of the well-known newspapers and periodicals that were published from the vernacular press, such as the *Sambad Prabhakar*, the *Jnananwesan*, the *Sambad Purna Chandradaya*, the *Sambad Bhaskar* or the *Sarba Subhakari*, did not pose a problem for governance for the empire. Rajat Ray also mentions how, even though there was a perceptive dissatisfaction that was being articulated in the Bengali press around the sixties, the imperial government was not too worried about it:

> The emergence of the educated public as a growing force outside the restricted participatory system of municipal government was reflected in a new tone in the vernacular press of Calcutta in the 1870s. Among ICS officers Richard Temple, now Lieutenant-Governor of Bengal, had seen the signs as far back as 1860, when a quasi-disloyal dissatisfaction in the columns of the Bengali newspapers first came to his notice.... Temple was not unduly disturbed by these symptoms of discontent and concluded that there was a natural desire on the part of qualified, professional Bengalis to get a larger share in 'the loaves and fishes of their Native country'.[65]

Although I do not claim any such a subversive intent for the *Tattwabodhini* under the editorship of Akshay Dutta, it cannot be denied that there was a sustained focus on disaffection aimed at the imperial administration in many of the articles that were consistently published in its pages. I shall end this chapter with a close reading of a series of three articles that Akshay published in the pages of the *Tattwabodhini* in 1850, titled 'Palligramastha Prajader Durabastha' (The Misery of the Subjects from the Villages) that might help us understand better his politics of affect.

Strategizing Disaffection in 'Palligramastha Prajader Durabastha'

The essay titled 'Palligramastha Prajader Durabastha' was published in three parts in the pages of the *Tattwabodhini Patrika*. They appeared in the Baisakh, Sraban, and Agrahayan issues in 1772 Saka.[66] If one were to read the three parts closely it would not be difficult to notice the emergence of a pattern that deftly albeit carefully unpacks the trajectories of misrule that were at the heart of imperial governance, and prodded the affective propensities of the native reader, and a consequent feeling of disaffection, by consistently highlighting the agential despondency of the agricultural class of rural Bengal. Akshay was employing a number of narrative strategies in this long essay. In the first place, he was addressing the affective guilt of the largely urban readership of the periodical. With the emergence of Calcutta as the most important urban centre for the empire, it had inevitably also become the nerve centre of much intellectual churning. Most debates around modernity, colonialism, education, rights and privileges, and civic or religious reforms would have their focus inevitably in and around this urban space. Only sometimes, if at all, would the locus shift to district towns and suburbs. The milieu that Akshay uneasily represented largely constituted of a category of the urban, middle-class *bhadralok* whose intellectual, cultural, and social concerns were wired around urban existence. I would say that Akshay slowly pushed the limits of the periodical beyond the immediate concerns of his urban milieu towards the rural, the subaltern, and the precarious as he gained substantial control of the workings of the *Tattwabodhini*. From his serial publication about the minor religious sects, most of whom would be discovered outside the urban orbit, to his engagement with the lived experience of the villages of Bengal was perhaps a deliberate attempt at an affective engagement with a premodern commonality and communalism that would revive for his readers a substantial cultural narrative they could use as a counter-argument against tropes of colonial modernity. This long essay involving the *palligram* was, therefore, playing the dual role of reviving a less remembered narrative on the one hand, and, on the other, investing in the urban reader an engagement with concerns that did not affect them immediately. The latter provided, for the urban readership, a sense of intellectual engagement with the problems of the less privileged, subaltern members of their own community. Second, by stretching the essay across three issues that were not even consecutive, he was in a way forcing his readers to remember, across a span of several months, the issues that he was trying to highlight. I would contend that it was a deliberate journalistic ploy to keep an issue alive across a space of time. Third, Akshay uses a clever and well-structured narrative strategy in the way he develops the essay. The first part, for example, is a protracted critique of the landowning class or the *zamindar* class of the villages, and their deeply exploitative behaviour towards the class of peasants and labourers. The second is a continuation of the critique, with occasional reference to the original master class or the imperial administration (*rajpurush*) that was squarely responsible for the exploitative relationship between the landowner class and the subaltern peasants, and how the imperial administration was equally collusive in the scheme of exploitation. The third part is a direct attack on the indigo traders belonging to the imperial master class, carefully separating them from the individual, benevolent *sahib* figure, along with a critique of the *bhadralok* category. If one were to assess the entire oeuvre of Akshay, the sentiment of disaffection is perhaps most pronounced in this essay, and it deserves a closer and more detailed reading.

The first part of the essay begins with the simple affective turn asserting the place of the peasant or the farmer as the one whose role is to sustain us by tilling the land and growing crops, and how it is the sustainer who has been rendered vulnerable by the system: 'What a pity! The heart despairs witnessing the utter misery of those that are our well-wishers, the cause of such happiness for the world!'[67] The reason for such misery, of course, is the presence of exploitative landowners (*bhuswami*) whose unbridled greed lies at the root of such evil. Akshay laments how the landowners remain completely unmoved by the miserable condition of the peasant: 'Their poverty, frail frame, pale features, tattered garments, nothing would sway the stony heart of the landowner – nothing is able to bring tears to their stern eyes.'[68] It is not difficult to notice the almost exaggerated tone in Akshay's diction, meant to elicit an affective response from his readers. Soon, however, the rhetoric switches to a more empiricist and nuanced critique of polity and the illegitimate means by which the landowners impose road taxes and customs duty, or establish a forced monopoly within their areas of rule or jurisdiction. Akshay goes so far as to say that the peasants are deprived of the sovereignty over their own bodies.[69] It is here that he carefully, for the first time in the essay, broaches the topic of the imperial government. He says how the strategies of exploitation employed by the landowners is an imitation of the ruling class: 'Those who have, by means of their native intelligence, been able to manufacture the various means of exploitation, will definitely imitate the strategies manufactured by the workings of multiple intelligent minds of the rulers of the nation.'[70] Akshay asserts that in spite of such virulent exploitation, in spite of having lost the right to their own labour and their own bodies, the peasants and workers have not deserted their motherland. Whereas this latter argument could have been easily put differently – as the complete loss of agency and therefore even the will or means to leave their homes – Akshay chooses to use the affective rhetoric of their attachment to their land:

Praise these subjects! One must salute their endurance. They are scorched by the heat of such suffering throughout their lives, and yet don't leave their country. If they were bereft of tenderness and as loveless as their landowners, and had deserted their mother-like place of birth, by now Bangabhumi would have been rendered as barren as a crematorium.[71]

Clearly, therefore, the author attempts to establish a binary here – between the faithful sons of the soil, the peasants, and the exploitative imitators of the colonial master class, the landowners. Whereas, the feeling of disaffection is trained on the landowning, or *zamindari*, class in this first part of the essay, it will gradually diffuse through an expansion of the orbit of exploitation towards the imperial rulers. Interestingly, in speaking of the misery of these marginalized peasants in the villages of rural Bengal, Akshay gives it a global spin by mentioning that they remain unfed and unclothed, while the fruits of their labour (the food crops and cotton they cultivate) reach far-off foreign lands.[72]

Akshay begins the second part of the essay directly with the question of polity and the larger structure of imperial misrule within which he places the problem of the rural subjects:

> If the land where there is a sovereign and a rule of law, and where the subjects pay necessary taxes for the employment of bureaucrats, remains thus ungoverned where the subjects with their property, respect, and lives do not feel sovereign themselves, it is the fault of governance.[73]

Although this part is once again dedicated largely to an analysis of the condition of the peasant at the hands of the landowners and the various middlemen, their fates sealed by moneylenders, their inability to fight for their cause in the courts of law – the onus of such a condition of the peasantry is squarely laid by the author on bad governance and a corrupt and self-serving bureaucracy. He writes how the bureaucracy is not incompetent, but active and efficient, and ready to use their effort, skill, and labour if there is some personal gain involved in any enterprise: 'They can gamble their lives and fulfill the most difficult of tasks if there is a cause for personal profit. Selfish gain incites their intellectual faculties, and they acquire double the physical strength.'[74] There is also the crucial discussion in this part about the dynamics of bureaucratic governance and its implicit relationship with the native sources of power. For example, sometimes the landowners acquire so much wealth and power that they can afford to ignore the lower level (albeit white) bureaucrats and are directly in collusion with the immensely more powerful bureaucrats from the upper echelons of the colonial administration.[75] In this part, Akshay traces a web of power and corruption that involves both the native landowner and the representative of the colonial government in the bureaucracy – a vicious partnership that he believes has undermined the entire framework of production and distribution, and therefore the healthy correspondence between labour and capital. This is the underlying cause, he concludes in this part, for 'the decline of wealthy native entrepreneurs in Bengal, and the cause of annihilation of the laboring class that has remained forever afraid, restless and impoverished'.[76]

The notion of sovereignty as a corporeal rather than a political question is a trope that repeats itself across various parts of the essay. The most pervasive and exploitative evil that Akshay talks about in this essay is in the third part where he delineates in detail the system of indigo plantation that was prevalent in these rural pockets of power. The root of evil, in this case, was the representative of the master class, the petty bourgeois *sahib* representative of the colonial system, whose unbridled and illicit greed for wealth had devastating effects on the rural economy of Bengal in the nineteenth century. Interestingly, Akshay places the notion of the sovereign self at the heart of this problem. The fact that the farmer was forced to cultivate and trade in indigo rather than other cash crops that would sustain his physical, social, cultural, or emotional needs and was completely divested of his sovereign will, the right to his body and soul, was a trope that Akshay was using in the third section of his essay. The *nilkar saheb* who has completely annihilated the will of the farmer by force and strategy becomes in the essay *swadhikarer samrat swarup* (as if the emperor of sovereignty)[77] or *swadhikarer ekadhipati swarup* (as if the sole owner of sovereignty)[78] claiming, in philosophical terms, all rights to the body and mind of the farmer. Akshay strikes at the heart of the project with the tool of affect by declaring clearly that the production of indigo was not the desire of the farmers (he uses the word *manas*,[79] a derivative of the word *mon*, thereby creating an easy correlation between the heart and the mind), and that it was a direct encroachment on their sovereignty. The farmer knows how to till and his land is his only treasure, the sole hope of his survival: 'Which sovereign self would want to commit suicide by giving up on his acquired treasure? But does he have a choice?'[80] Subsequently, as the farmer is forced to surrender to the whim of the colonizer, Akshay laments that the farmer 'strikes the plough into his heart'.[81]

It is interesting how Akshay would use the platform of this essay to train his critique on the category of the *bhadralok*. This critique, in the third part of the essay, is more nuanced and complex than is immediately apparent. I have mentioned at various moments in the book how Akshay's location within the category of the urban *bhadralok* was fraught at multiple levels. Although, as an intellectual, his milieu would be that of the upper-class, elite, urban gentry of Calcutta, his indifferent training and subsequent discursive practice would steer his instincts towards the margins of society, the smaller subjects of history, the non-*bhadralok* category of people. There was a subtle liminality in his class location, and thus it was perhaps possible for him to view the category of the *bhadralok* from a distance. However, that is not to say that Akshay failed to acknowledge the contribution and importance of such intellectual influences as Iswarchandra Vidyasagar or Debendranath Tagore in his life and works.[82] Nevertheless, one could say that there was a certain unease in Akshay about his class location, and a consequent anxiety in terms of the dynamics of collusion between the colonizer and the *bhadralok* class. In this essay, for instance, he critiques the *bhadralok* employees of the indigo merchant:

> What would I say about the character of the employees of the indigo merchant? The common people are aware. They are known as bhadraloks, but if one were to consider their behaviour it would be absolutely improper to call them so. The limit of their knowledge is basic mathematics, neither are they interested in acquiring knowledge, nor would they be educated in ethics. Who would be unaware of the behaviour of those without *vidya* and *dharma*?[83]

Of course, Akshay here is speaking not of the upper echelons of the *bhadralok* category, but of the class of clerks or *keranis*.[84] An admonition of the lower ranks of *bhadralok* officials within the bureaucracy, or those that made their way up by guile or dishonesty, was a common trope used by the upper-class *bhadralok* to set themselves apart from the less privileged specimens of an identical group.[85] More often than not, such a critique coming from the creamy layer of the *bhadralok* category was unfair, considering that the lower category of the *bhadralok* would rarely wield the agency or power of the former. I would say that in spite of the unease in Akshay about his location within this upper section of the *bhadralok*, his discursive instincts were largely formulated from within this elite category. Thus, even when he admonishes the native *bhadralok* representative within colonial bureaucracy, he chooses its lowest rung for his sharpest words, and carefully glosses over the role of the elite *bhadralok*. What I am trying to suggest here is that Akshay, as the editor of the *Tattwabodhini* (or even otherwise), was rarely inclined to personal attacks or direct confrontations. If he were to take on the upper-class *bhadralok* as his adversary, he would inevitably have to train his invective on people he personally knew. Likewise, if he were to place someone from the colonizer class as a foil to John Bethune whom he so admired, he had to name and confront the person directly. Akshay, on the other hand, was more comfortable in talking about a class as a whole, or a section of it as a homogeneity, a faceless and nameless collection of people. One could easily read this as Akshay's peculiar strategy (unlike most of his contemporaries) of articulating disaffection. While the problem at hand would reach the reading public and initiate debate and discussion, it would rarely incite hatred or unrest among them against a particular person. Akshay is also strategically careful in creating the necessary division between the good and the bad colonizer. In a piece that is so consistently critical of the class of the colonizer Akshay would unambiguously put in a sentence such as, 'The decent Englishmen of good character do not indulge in indigo trade',[86] thereby clearly setting apart a section of the ruling class as benevolent and therefore different.

In the end, Akshay appeals to the affective instincts of both his countrymen and the colonizers alike. The tone of disaffection is pervasive across the three parts of the essay – directed through various agents at the colonizer and the failure of polity. His tone of critique, however, does not take the route from disaffection to forms of disruption. He uses the affective as a form of critique to persuade those with more agency to participate in the transformation of the polity towards the emergence of a cohesive *janasamaj*. He calls upon the *iccha* (desire) of the people to change the condition of the *swadesh* – calls upon their affective instincts of *utsaha* (enthusiasm), *anurag* (affection or attachment), and *yatna* (care) for the emancipation of the nation from its present state. Likewise, instead of a militant call for subverting the administrative order, Akshay urges the colonial master or the *rajpurush* to perform his duties with more *manajog* (attention) and *daya* (compassion).

Conclusion: Akshay Dutta, *Tattwabodhini Patrika*, and the Public Sphere

To conclude, I would contend that under the editorship of Akshay Dutta, the *Tattwabodhini Patrika* attempted to be an instrument of inclusive public engagement both in terms of its pedagogic intent and in the formation and dissemination of public opinion. In most discussions on the nature and formation of public culture in nineteenth-century Bengal, the *Tattwabodhini* is mentioned as one of the foundational instruments of intellectual engagement among the elite Calcutta *bhadralok*, particularly as the organ of the Brahmo Samaj. This, I would say, is to take a narrow view of things. Most historians would view the *Tattwabodhini* as a periodical that was founded under the aegis of Debendranath Tagore and subsequently carried forward by notable editors, all of them important intellectuals of the time. However, curiously, in the same way as most historians of nineteenth-century Bengal would want to see a significant ideological fissure between the pre-Bankim and the post-Bankim eras, there is a peculiar prejudice towards the *Bangadarshan* over such a periodical as the *Tattwabodhini* in terms of its role in the formation of the public sphere, and its scope and penetration among the educated, common public of Bengal. As Samarpita Mitra unambiguously asserts in her book: 'Bankim's *Baṅgadarśan* in a way marks the very first moment in the crafting of the Bengali public sphere.'[87] Immediately earlier Mitra has also provided her readers with a definition of the public sphere: 'The Bengali intelligentsia envisioned the formation of the public sphere primarily in terms of a literary sphere and public activism as modern literariness. In their imagination, this public sphere was to embody the nation's life (*jātīya jīban*).'[88] The two important markers here are those of 'activism' and 'literariness', and how the two would come together in the formation of a public sphere. Interestingly, both the *Tattwabodhini Patrika* and its first editor, Akshay Dutta, are only cursorily mentioned in Mitra's book.[89] I would contend that in an otherwise fine analysis of the literary culture of the time, Mitra, like Sartori, is foregrounding the notion of activism as one of the principal aims of the development of a public culture. As I have discussed in the previous chapter, it is possible to discover pedagogic and discursive similarities between the writings of Akshay and Bankim. It is not difficult to compare the basic tenets of Akshay's *Dharmaniti*, for example, with Bankim's *Dharmatattwa* in terms of a map of activism that they foreground, and none of their kinds of activism may be confused with militant nationalism. In my opinion, a close reading of the *Tattwabodhini*, particularly under the editorship of Akshay Dutta, could easily reveal it to be a precursor of the pedagogic intent of the *Bangadarshan* and the periodicals that followed. Both in terms of the intention of *lokasiksha* (education of the masses) and an involvement of the *janasamaj* (public sphere) in the larger social and historical context of the lived life of the times, the *Tattwabodhini* and its first editor had played a crucial role, as I have tried to show in this chapter. In terms of 'literariness', it is possible to argue that Akshay, as the editor of the *Tattwabodhini*, was less inclined to literary genres and practices, and therefore the 'literary' value of the *Bangadarshan* under Bankim's editorship was more pronounced and the periodical had a stronger inclination towards creative pieces. However, if one were to allow some latitude to the implications of the word 'literature', and not consider only 'creative writing' as its domain, the *Tattwabodhini* would easily fit into the rubric. Anindita Ghosh, for example, clearly considers the *Tattwabodhini* to be a literary journal. In her analysis, the intention of the Tattwabodhini Sabha was 'to improve Bengali literary and religious life', and the *Tattwabodhini Patrika* 'was held in high repute for its uncompromising standards, producing well-researched articles on physiology, history, and biographies, apart from various translations of the Vedas'.[90] Similarly, Tithi Bhattacharya has also noted how authors such as Michael Madhusudan Dutt and Rabindranath Tagore had made their first forays into the literary world in the pages of the *Tattwabodhini*.[91] Evidently, the *Tattwabodhini* under Akshay Dutta had its fair share of both literature and activism in its pages.

It is also perhaps fair to claim that Akshay's *Tattwabodhini* was more serious in its tone and content than Bankim's *Bangadarshan*. It is important to understand that Akshay was taking up the task of editorship of a periodical, and taking up the cudgels of trying to ascribe a framework to native public opinion in a colonized society at least three decades before Bankim. Both the pedagogy and the epistemology was still unknown to him and he chose to address a *janasamaj* a large part of which was still unsure about methods of comprehending polity, let alone formulate methods of resistance. One would say that Akshay was taking early steps that were later followed by Bankim at a time when the idea of a reading public had already been consolidated. And it is difficult to deny that in its time under Akshay, *Tattwabodhini* had gained immense popularity and the circulation of the periodical is a testament to its reception among the common public. My intention here is not to initiate a debate on the comparative popularity or importance of these periodicals. What I am arguing is that there is an unfair bit of neglect in the way a claim may be made for the *Bangadarshan* being the foundational instrument of the Bengali public sphere. One has to browse through the various pieces, mostly written by Akshay, spread across the issues of the *Tattwabodhini* to understand how the editor was not only addressing the common public, but also carefully pushing them towards having an informed opinion: in 'Bharatvarsher Sahit Anyanya Desher Purbakalin Banijya Bibaran' he is writing of the global nature of regional entrepreneurship and the cosmopolitanism of India's past;[92] 'Hindukalejer Siksha Pranali', for example, is a critique of the contemporary courses taught in the Hindu College, and emphasizes the need for a more rigorous humanities education along with the sciences;[93] 'Surapan' is a moral narrative on the evils of drinking;[94] 'Kalikatar Bartaman Durabastha' is a long piece on the civic deficiencies of the city of Calcutta.[95] These are only a few examples that would emphasize how Akshay Dutta was using the space of a periodical, primarily meant for the dissemination of the Brahma Dharma, as a secular tool for the formulation of public opinion and for initiating a framework of public culture in colonial Bengal. The subversion of the rhetoric of colonial governance was not always immediately apparent, nor was there any implicit militant nationalism in the editor's intention. There was, however, a strong sense of selfhood and identity, an urgency for consolidating an opinion in both the public and the counterpublic about the sense of culture that was to be a curious mix of the modern and the premodern, consistent strategies of veiled disaffection. But over and above all of this there was a rational urge in Akshay for the emancipation of the people of Bharatvarsha, across class and caste, and a deep-rooted sense of *swadesh* that is always apparent in his writings.

Notes

1. See, for example, Partha Chatterjee, *The Nation and Its Fragments: Colonial and Postcolonial Histories* (New Jersey: Princeton University Press, 1993); Andrew Sartori, *Bengal in Global Concept History: Culturalism in the Age of Capital* (Chicago: The University of Chicago Press, 2008); or Kris Manjapra, *Age of Entanglement: German and Indian Intellectuals Across Empire* (Cambridge, MA: Harvard University Press, 2014).

2. George Combe, *The Constitution of Man Considered in Relation to External Objects* (Cambridge: Cambridge University Press, 2009).

3. Akshay Dutta, *Bahyavastur Sahit Manabprakritir Sammandha Vichar*, in *Akshaykumar Dutta Rachana Sangraha*, vol. 1, ed. Swapan Basu (Kolkata: Paschimbanga Bangla Academy, 2008), pp. 116–118.

4. Combe, *The Constitution of Man*, pp. 7–8.

5. Dutta, *Bahyavastu*, pp. 116.

6. James Poskett, *Materials of the Mind: Phrenology, Race, and the Global History of Science, 1815–1920* (Chicago: The University of Chicago Press, 2019), p. 178.

7. Ibid., p. 182.

8. However, Akshay's biographer Nakurchandra Biswas writes that Akshay had met Cally Coomar Das in Debendranath Tagore's drawing room where the latter seems to have said about the former, 'I see a crown of intellect over his forehead.' See Nakurchandra Biswas, *Akshay-Charit* (Calcutta: Adi Brahmosamaj Press, 1891), p. 53.

9. Ibid., p. 186.

10. Combe, *The Constitution of Man*, p. 145. Earlier in the book Combe illustrates his method and dependence on the science of phrenology:

   > … man is an animal – moral – and intellectual being. To discover the adaptation of these parts of his nature to his external circumstances, we must first know what are his various animal, moral, and intellectual powers themselves. Phrenology gives us a view of them, drawn from observation; and as I have verified the inductions of that science, so as to satisfy myself that it is the most complete and correct exposition of the Nature of Man which has yet been given, I adopt its classification of faculties as the basis of the subsequent observations.

   Ibid., 34.

11. Ibid., p. 144. Of course, Combe asserts soon after that the European 'whose brains possess a favourable development of the moral and intellectual organs' is superior to Hindoos and native Americans 'whose brains are inferior' Ibid., p. 154.

12. Dutta, *Bahyavastu*, pp. 181–183. Also see Combe, *The Constitution of Man*, pp. 146–147.

13. Combe, *The Constitution of Man*, p. 239.

14. Ibid., p. 155.

15. This moral framework that upholds *buddhivritti* and *dharmapravritti* and sets it aside from *nikkrista pravritti* is the one that Akshay has used throughout, from *Bahyavastu*, through *Charupath* to *Dharmaniti*.

16. Dutta, *Bahyavastu*, pp. 237–238. For a more detailed analysis of the lives of this particular class of people, see Sumit Chakrabarti, 'The Sahib Writer in Calcutta: A Different Discourse', in *The Calcutta Kerani and the London Clerk in the Nineteenth Century: Life, Labour, Latitude* (London: Routledge, 2021), pp. 88–112.

17. Dutta, *Bahyavastu*, p. 178.

18. Ibid., p. 179.

19. Combe, *The Constitution of Man*, p. 233.

20. Ibid.

21. Dutta, *Bahyavastu*, pp. 237–238. For a detailed analysis on the subject and the causes for the dissolution of the Union Bank, see Blair B. King, 'The Fall of the Union Bank', in *Partner in Empire: Dwarkanath Tagore and the Age of Enterprise in Eastern India* (Berkeley: University of California Press, 1976), pp. 198–229.

22. Combe, *The Constitution of Man*, p. 234.

23. Dutta, *Bahyavastu*, p. 218.

24. Ibid., pp. 218–219.

25. Ibid., p. 219.

26. Ibid., p. 220.

27. Ibid., p. 174.

28. Emily Apter, *The Translation Zone: A New Comparative Literature* (Princeton and Oxford: Princeton University Press, 2006), p. 5.

29. The native speaker of Bengali will not fail to notice the subtle but obvious difference between the words *buddhi* and *buddhivritti*. While the former could merely mean either intelligence or intellect, the latter has a wider and more philosophical connotation that immediately encompasses the affective within its fold. With *buddhi* one can solve a mathematical problem, or resolve a problem rationally. *Buddhivritti*, on the other hand, will be linked to a more holistic sense of good (*mangalkari* or *hitakari*) that would have a relevance for the community or the *janasamaj*.

30. As quoted in Tanya Agathocleous, *Disaffected: Emotion, Sedition, and Colonial Law in the Anglosphere* (Ithaca and London: Cornell University Press, 2021), p. 2.

31. Ibid., p. x.

32. Ibid., p. 8.

33. Ibid., p. 9.

34. See, for example, Bhabanicharan Bandopadhyay, *Kalikata Kamalalaya* (Calcutta: Ranjan Publishing House, 1823/1937); Bhabanicharan Bandopadhyay, *Naba Babu Bilas* (Calcutta: Subarnarekha, 1825/1979); Tekchand Thakur, *Aalaler Ghorer Dulal* (Kolkata: Bangiya Sahitya Parishat, 1858/1999).

35. The pages of the *Tattwabodhini* were peppered with various dialogues and debates on religion, from the interpretation of the Vedas, or introducing minor religious sects, to debates on conversion, or the path to *dharma*.

36. See, for example, 'Hindukalejer Siksha Pranali', *Tattwabodhini Patrika* 4, no. 86, Ashwin 1772 Saka, pp. 92–99.

37. See, for example, 'Modirapan', *Tattwabodhini Patrika* 2, issue 13, Bhadra 1766 Saka, pp. 97–98; 'Pandosh', *Tattwabodhini Patrika* 4, no. 84, Sraban 1772 Saka, pp. 55–59.

38. Agathocleous borrows the term and the concept of 'counterpublic' from Michael Warner, *Publics and Counterpublics* (New York: Zone Books, 2002).

39. Agathocleous, *Disaffected*, pp. 15–16.

40. Ibid., p. 16.

41. The Vernacular Press Act of 1878 was perhaps a late realization and reaction to this complex nature of the counterpublics and their affective constituency.

42. See Akshay Kumar Dutta, *Bharatvarshiya Upashak Sampraday*, vols. 1 and 2 (Kolkata: Karuna Prakashani, 1870 and 1883).

43. For the popularity and circulation figures of the periodical, see Biswas, *Akshay-Charit*, pp. 25–26.

44. See the discussion in Chapter 1.

45. *Tattwabodhini Patrika*, no. 4, Agrahayan 1765 Saka, p. 27.

46. *Tattwabodhini Patrika* 3, no. 73, Bhadra 1771 Saka, p. 83.

47. Ibid., p. 84.

48. Ibid., p. 85.

49. *Tattwabodhini Patrika* 3, no. 69, Baisakh 1771 Saka, p. 1.

50. Ibid.

51. Ibid., p. 2.

52. Tanya Agathocleous, *Disaffected*, p. 27.

53. See, for example, Rammohun's *Letter on English Education* to Lord Amherst in December 1823 (see Sophia Dobson Collet, *The Life and Letters of Raja Rammohun Roy*, ed. Hem Chandra Sarkar [Calcutta: A. C. Sarkar, 1914], p. 107) and his letter to J. Crawford against the government imposition of religious distinctions in the judicial system in August 1828 (see Collet, *The Life and Letters of Raja Rammohun Roy*, pp. 153–154); he also wrote letters to the *Bengal Hurkaru* in 1823 (see Collet, *The Life and Letters of Raja Rammohun Roy*, p. 56). Notable epistolary exchanges by Vidyasagar include

Letter and Report to F. J. Mouat, Secretary to the Council of Education (1850), Note on Vernacular Education (1854), or letter to R. B. Chapman Esquire, Secretary to the Board of Revenue, on the question of alienation of *devatra* property (1866). For more examples, see Indramitra, *Karunasagar Vidyasagar* (Calcutta: Ananda Publishers, 1969), pp. 705–807.

54. *Tattwabodhini Patrika* 3, no. 69, Baisakh 1771 Saka, p. 2.

55. Ibid., p. 3.

56. Ibid., pp. 3–4.

57. See, for example, ibid., pp. 4–9 and pp. 9–12.

58. See, for example, *Tattwabodhini Patrika* 1, no. 97, Bhadra 1773 Saka, pp. 67–82.

59. Agathocleous, *Disaffected*, p. 28.

60. It was only towards the later years of the nineteenth century that the vernacular press emerged as a veritable monster for the ruling class. Tanya Agathocleous discusses the trials and court proceedings around the vernacular press in some detail in her book. See, for example, 'Affectation: The Aesthete and the Babu on Trial', in *Disaffected*, pp. 33–70.

61. See P. N. Bose and H. W. B. Moreno, *A Hundred Years of the Bengali Press* (Calcutta: The Central Press, 1920), p. 26.

62. Ibid., p. 10.

63. For another reference to this meeting, see Partha Chatterjee, *Our Modernity* (Rotterdam: SEPHIS, 1997), pp. 14–15.

64. As quoted in Bose and Moreno, *A Hundred Years of the Bengali Press*, pp. 47–48.

65. See Rajat Ray, *Urban Roots of Indian Nationalism* (New Delhi: Vikas Publishing House, 1979), p. 17.

66. The essay appeared in the *Tattwabodhini Patrika* 4, no. 81, Baisakh issue (pp. 5–12), 4, no. 84, the Sraban issue (pp. 49–55), and 4, no. 88, Agrahayan issue (pp. 115–121) in 1772 Saka or 1850.

67. *Tattwabodhini Patrika* 4, no. 81, Baisakh 1772 Saka, p. 5.

68. Ibid.

69. Ibid., p. 7.

70. Ibid.

71. Ibid.

72. Ibid., p. 11.

73. *Tattwabodhini Patrika* 4, no. 84, Sraban 1772 Saka, p. 50.

74. Ibid.

75. Ibid., pp. 54–55.

76. Ibid., p. 55.

77. *Tattwabodhini Patrika* 4, no. 88, Sraban 1772 Saka, p. 115.

78. Ibid., p. 116.

79. Ibid.

80. Ibid.

81. Ibid., p. 117.

82. One example of this is his acknowledgement of both Vidyasagar and Debendranath in the introduction to the first volume of *Bahyavastu*: 'I gratefully acknowledge that Iswarchandra Vidyasagar and Debendranath Tagore have taken great pains in suggesting emendations to the manuscript and that I consider to be a particular favour.' See Dutta, *Bahyavastur Sahit Manabprakritir Sammandha Vichar*, p. 118.

83. *Tattwabodhini Patrika* 4, no. 88, Sraban 1772 Saka, p. 118.

84. For a detailed discussion on this, see Sumit Chakrabarti, *The Calcutta Kerani and the London Clerk* (London: Routledge, 2021), pp. 26–39.

85. A classic example of this is of course the character of Muchiram Gur created by Bankimchandra. See Bankimchandra Chattopadhyay, *Muchiram Gurer Jibancharit* (Calcutta: Bangiya Sahitya Parishat, 1884/1945).

86. *Tattwabodhini Patrika* 4, no. 88, Sraban 1772 Saka, p. 118.

87. Samarpita Mitra, *Periodicals, Readers and the Making of a Modern Literary Culture* (Leiden: Brill, 2020), p. 7.

88. Ibid.

89. See ibid. Akshay Dutta is mentioned twice and the *Tattwabodhini Patrika* about six times.

90. See Anindita Ghosh, *Power in Print* (New Delhi: Oxford University Press, 2006), p. 93.

91. See Tithi Bhattacharya, *The Sentinels of Culture* (New Delhi: Oxford University Press, 2005), p. 80.

92. *Tattwabodhini Patrika* 3, no. 78, Magh 1771 Saka, pp. 153–166.

93. *Tattwabodhini Patrika* 4, no. 86, Ashwin 1772 Saka, pp. 92–99.

94. *Tattwabodhini Patrika* 2, no. 111, Kartik 1774 Saka, pp. 73–75.

95. *Tattwabodhini Patrika* 4, no. 36, Sraban 1768 Saka, pp. 309–315.

6

Imagining Bharatvarsha

Identity, History, Nationhood

Partha Chatterjee ends his short piece *Our Modernity* with a few specific remarks on how the nature or fashioning of post-colonial modernity in India would necessarily be different from the larger and more general template of modernity that has emerged from continental Europe.[1] In the first place, the native subject is always a consumer and not the producer of modernity. It is inevitable, therefore, that to ascertain one's subjecthood within the narrative of history the post-colonial subject must look backwards into an independent and creative past. Chatterjee asserts that it is 'superfluous to call this an imagined past, because pasts are always imagined'.[2] I shall come back to this point about the relationship between imagination and the past in greater detail later in the chapter. Second, unlike the model of prioritizing the present over the past that Kant delineates in 'What Is Enlightenment?'[3] as the model for the progress of western modernity, Chatterjee notices how the post-colonial model of modernity in India is predicated on an escape from the present to the past. Chatterjee considers Rajnarayan Basu's *Sekal ar Ekal*[4] to be a formative text in this regard. He concludes, therefore, that 'the very modality of our coping with modernity [is] radically different from the historically evolved modes of Western modernity'.[5] Third, it is also an imperative, according to Chatterjee, that in fashioning post-colonial modes of modernity the subject needed to 'reject the modernities established by others'.[6] Chatterjee argues that from the position of the colonized subject it was rarely possible to imagine or believe in a template of universal modernity, a 'domain of free discourse, unfettered by differences of race or nationality'.[7] In spite of these differences with the general or universal template of modernity that Chatterjee points out here, the narrative of Indian modernity has traced a fraught and complicated path that may not have been as 'radically different' as he claims in the essay.

Viswa Patir Viswa-Rachana

One of the principal questions in terms of social polity that was foremost in the mind of the nineteenth-century Bengali intellectual was undoubtedly that of modernity. Whether to accept the template of modernity foisted on the native by the colonizer or to reframe the idea of modernity through indigenous links to a glorious past (along with its obvious orientalist implications) were questions that could not be easily answered. In fact, in terms of claiming the right to one's history, or culture, or identity – the colonized space gave rise to too many questions that needed to be addressed simultaneously for a narrative to take shape: 'Was western modernity the one singular way to the emancipation of a people?' 'Are the terms "western modernity" and "colonial modernity" interchangeable?' 'Is colonial modernity, in spite of its naturally exploitative character better than a superstitious, regressive, and almost equally exploitative indigenous social polity?' 'Does one foreground and use the past as a template to counter the present native society or colonial modernity or both?' It is not difficult to realize that these questions easily flow into each other, and it is not always possible to distinguish clearly between them while addressing the idea of selfhood on the one hand and the future of the community or *janasamaj* as a whole on the other. The other obviously related question that also needs to be addressed simultaneously is that of history, of how to articulate or represent the idea of the history of a people or a nation that is passing through a prolonged phase of colonial rule.

As I have elaborated in the previous chapters, Akshay Dutta had spent most of his working life grappling with these issues of the articulation of identity for the Bengali (and the Indian) individual, and trying to revive a cultural narrative for the *janasamaj* culling influences from the past and reading them along with and often against the grain of the narratives foregrounded by the colonizer. In an interesting article, titled 'Susikshita o Asikshita Loker Sukher Taratamya' (The Difference in the Pleasure Principle of the Well-Educated and the Uneducated), published in the third volume of *Charupath*, he broaches, for example, the question of history in a curiously roundabout manner.[8] He begins by suggesting that the uneducated are guided, throughout their life span, by the lowly instincts (*nikkrista pravritti*) mostly directed towards physical labour, while the life of the mind eludes them: 'His professional duties are his primary concern, and mostly his conversations are related to the present time and related events.'[9] By indicating that the uneducated lives in the 'present time' (*bartaman kal*), Akshay insinuates, of course, that the person has no sense of history or a past. Akshay continues that this person is as much ignorant of the world that he inhabits as he is of the universe in general. In the course of the piece, the reader will be gradually aware of what entails for the author the idea of an educated person – it is to know about the making of the universe by the lord of the universe (*viswa patir viswa-rachana*). The essay then veers towards the idea of education that is complex at many levels. In the first place, by referring to a pre-ordained idea of the universe with its set of natural laws that through a continuous process of evolution and change govern the physical, the mental, the phenomenal, and the existential spaces of existence (*sarva-shastra-sammandhiya*),[10] Akshay is clearly setting his idea of education apart from the dominant narrative of progress foregrounded by colonial modernity. At the same time, however, he summarily dismisses the many forms of indigenous knowledge that the uneducated tend to believe in their ignorance. Akshay writes:

> [The uneducated] believe that all the rules as written in indigenous *shastras*, all the rituals as indicated in their culture are the best. They believe that the dated path that their ancestors have traced is beyond compare. Even if such a path is rather irrational and thoroughly incongruous it must be beyond change. To see the faults in one's race and the qualities in another is beyond him.[11]

He continues his critique of the indigenous belief that a training in grammar means true education, that astrology and astronomy are interchangeable, or that the imaginary history enumerated in the Puranas is true history. He also insists emphatically that the narrative in the Puranas about the existence of the seven seas is absolutely false.[12] The educated person, on the other hand, is able to rationally comprehend the separate and distinct laws of the universe meant for the separate faculties of humankind. He does not consider a certain god to be the arbiter of a certain disease, or consider that a certain man's curse will ruin another, but that there is an abiding set of rules, universally true and ordained by the *parameshwar*, that is the driving force of the universe. The truly educated person is the one who can 'in his imagination envision and assimilate the entire universe'.[13]

There is a rather complex dynamic at work here, and this needs to be carefully unpacked. It is important to notice in Akshay's formulation of *viswa patir viswa-rachana* an implicit yet firm movement away from the Hegelian universal. Akshay's essentialism in imagining a *parameshwar* as the engineer of the universe, the one who has set down the rules – natural or otherwise – is a subtle resistance to the selective Eurocentric modernity that is at the heart of the colonial model of progress. The transcendental signified engendered by the presence of the *parameshwar* undercuts any other trope of dominance or hegemony and, in a way, democratizes the idea of education. In the previous chapter I have discussed in some detail how Akshay had trained his critique on the colonial master class in terms of their civic and administrative duties towards the citizens of the colonized space. Likewise, in this piece there is a sharp critique of the dogma that is intrinsic to the civic and societal life of the native subject mired in tradition and superstition, faith in the unscientific, and the rejection of the larger rubric of what constitutes the modern. This modernity, the one that opens up the space for a dialogue with other cultures and forms of existence, although loosely based on the rational and scientific framework of the Eurocentric model, is open to switching back and forth in time, thereby upsetting the basic premise of progress as a temporally one-way process, a movement forward. With the abstract form of the *parameshwar* as the abiding principle of this model, it divests colonial modernity of its assumed superiority, while at the same time continuously reminding the native of the pitfalls of indigenous discourses. Akshay, here, is not talking of imitation, of foregrounding one culture at the expense of another, but a sustained and informed engagement with other forms of knowledge. In the course of the discussions that will follow in this chapter, we will see how Akshay uses the past as a tool, and dream as a strategy, to unpack an alternative discourse of the modern.

History as Imagination: Akshay's *Swapnadarshan*

Each of the three sections of the third volume of Akshay Dutta's *Charupath* begins with a dream vision: 'Swapnadarshan – Vidyabishayak' (a dream vision about knowledge) in the first section; 'Swapnadarshan – Kirtibishayak' (a dream vision about achievements) in the second section; and 'Swapnadarshan – Nyaybishayak' (a dream vision about justice) in the third section.[14] In each of these pieces the author has fallen asleep while ruminating philosophically about the ways and aspects of the universe and enters a dream world. It unfolds through a commingling of the past and the present, and through a comparatist strategy that has global implications, the state of affairs in the Bharatvarsha of the present. Taken together, these three pieces may be read as a receptacle of Akshay's idea of progress that brings together the notions of modernity, history, and culture. In a sense, this dream vision contains an ethical framework that takes note of the past as a point of reference and hints at a possible assimilationist globality for a future Bharatvarsha. The three markers that Akshay chooses for his dream vision – those of knowledge, achievement, and justice – are directly commensurate with the idea of progress or modernity that the colonizer condones. What a close reading will reveal, however, is how Akshay deviates strategically from the western model, not through a subversion of their narrative, but through a continuous reading against the grain of the standard and validated narrative of the master class.

Each of these heterotopic spaces is egalitarian in terms of representation and democratic in terms of race. As Akshay enters the 'forest of education' (*vidyaranya*), in the first vision he encounters the huge trees of *kavya* (poetry) and *jyotish* (astronomy). The tree of astronomy is connected at its roots to the ancient and productive mother-tree of mathematics. The deity of *vidya* points out to him:

> Trees and plants from all nations have been brought and planted here. Some seeds of *jyotish* (astronomy) and *ganit* (mathematics) have been brought from your nation. Notice how people from different races have assembled in this garden to nurture these trees and plants with enthusiasm and care! And people from your nation should be reprimanded. All those trees that were assigned to them for nurture have either dried up or been ruined.[15]

The author then roams around to see the trees of physiology, chemistry, and medicine and subsequently wonders about the qualities an individual needs to possess to be an inhabitant of this forest. He realizes that one must be divested of the qualities of greed, lust, and drinking to be able to stake a claim. But one must also possess the qualities of *sraddha* (respect), *yatna* (effort), *daya* (compassion), *bhakti* (devotion), *kshama* (pardon), *ahimsa* (non-violence), and *maitree* (friendship) to be able to acquire *vidya* and be a part of this place.

In order that a person might be an achiever or *kirtiman*, Akshay writes in the second piece on *kirti*, he must first eschew the invitations of *ajnan* (lack of knowledge), *alasya* (laziness), and *amod* (entertainment). In order that one may hear the clarion call of the deity of *kirti*, the person has to be in possession of *unnata-buddhi* (higher intellect). Akshay then speaks about three categories of achievers who have been able to make their places in this part of the universe – the ones who are achievers in the realm of leadership and administration, poets, and men of letters. In this realm he recognizes the heroes of Bharatvarsha, the Kauravas and the Pandavas. However, the pride of place does not belong to them, but to those hailing from foreign lands – Alexander, Caesar, Hannibal, and others. However, the ones who are the most celebrated in this second realm are the poets. Two ancient poets are seated on decorated thrones, Valmiki and Homer. Alongside Valmiki, Akshay recognizes the figures of Magha, Bharavi, Bhavabhuti, and Bharatchandra. With Homer are seated such great poets as Virgil, Dante, Milton, Shakespeare, and Byron. It is at this confluence of the greatest poets of the world that Akshay overhears a conversation between Valmiki and Kalidasa:

> The young generation of our race does not celebrate us as it celebrates poets from other races. However, what is heartening is that the learned folk from other races have realized our stature and give us proper respect ... Incidentally, therefore, some of the recent scholars from our part of the world have begun to show some interest in our work.[16]

Among the men of letters, Akshay discovered in this realm the likes of Aryabhatta, Varahamihira, Brahmagupta, and Bhaskaracharya. Aryabhatta, among them, suddenly pointed towards some foreign scholars and started addressing the author:

> Earlier no one realized my potential, and instead of faith, they expressed disdain for my work. However, these friends from foreign lands have followed my path and given fruition to my labour.[17]

Akshay enquired about the identity of these foreign scholars and came to know that they were Copernicus, Galileo, and Newton. Akshay also mentions that he saw the likes of Vedavyas, Sankaracharya, Plato, and Pythagorus among these men of letters. Towards the end of this vision, however, Akshay notes how *kirti*, in spite of its great potential for the uplift of mankind, must be subservient to *dharma* – the most important among all qualities.

The third section of the dream vision begins with the descent of the god of justice on earth. Immediately he calls for the legal papers and property documents of the citizens. As the flame from his wand touches these documents, all that has been falsified or manipulated is scorched. Sometimes entire documents are destroyed by the flame. The author is caught by surprise when entire documents from some of the important courts of justice, including almost all the documents from the Insolvent Courts, are completely destroyed in this flame.[18] In this mayhem Akshay witnesses how some of the rich and respected citizens are reduced to utter penury, while those who would struggle to make ends meet receive substantial parts of such property and begin to lead decent lives. Akshay writes:

> Except those who had acquired *dharma*, *vidya* or *bishaya-buddhi* (the just awareness of right to property), everyone else was mortified at the sight of the wand of justice. These pure souls were then gathered into groups. Those with *dharma* were in the first group, those with *vidya* in the second, and those with *bishaya-buddhi* were clubbed in the third group.

Akshay then goes on to explain the logic of inclusion into each of these categories. The first category was peopled by those with cheerful countenances, eyes full of empathy, *karunya swavab*. One look at them would fill a person with joy and love. The author is surprised to discover that even brahmins and pundits with great pride in their learning were driven away to accommodate apparently lesser mortals into this group. As for the second category, those who had acquired knowledge merely from secondary sources or were not in possession of critical minds, could barely find their place here. The author is surprised to notice that some authors of Bengali books who had expected to find a place in this category were summarily rejected. However, the lord of justice gives them hope:

> You have chosen the right path to glory and to serve your nation. The spread of knowledge is impossible without proper training. But you have to educate yourselves some more, so that you may achieve your goal. All that you write lack unity, depth of thought, and contain errors. Especially some write on subjects on which you require more knowledge and research. If you rectify these you will succeed.[19]

Even in this category Akshay notices some brahmin pundits unable to make the cut, and how they are forced to accept that those lower in caste status are chosen over them. The third category had many aspirants, but among them only a few who had the three qualities of enterprise, industriousness, and efficiency, along with the necessary quality of *dharma-raksha* (to have followed the path of *dharma* in terms of not causing pain to others due to selfishness, not having accepted bribes, and not having forfeited the teachings of their individual gurus), were admitted.

Akshay concludes his three-part dream vision with a few interesting observations that need some critical analysis in terms of how the *janasamaj* would construe an identity and selfhood for itself. In the first place, he says that those who have all the three qualities of *dharma*, *vidya*, and *bishaya-buddhi* (*tri-guna sampanna*) were the foremost in the society: 'In this universe they are obeyed by all (*sarva-manya*), venerated (*param-pujya*), and the foremost of human beings (*pradhan manush*).'[20] In this context, Akshay trains his critique on the colonial officers who have none of these qualities and have yet been part of the administration. But in his dream vision they are justly reprimanded:

> What do I say about the insult of certain English officers. In spite of their many misdeeds they had survived due to luck and cunning. But now, in the face of the wand of justice they are humiliated and insulted, and their places given to deserving others.[21]

Akshay then moves on to an instrumentalist vision for society, one that would consolidate the narrative of a well-formed society or *samaj*. If one is born, then one must work for the world (*sangsar*); if one is educated, it is for the betterment of the world (*jagater upakar*). From the world he moves his focus towards the family – the need of every householder to provide nutritious food (*upadeya anna*), clean clothes (*pavitra vastra*), and a well-maintained home (*pariskrita bati*). If the householder refuses to perform these tasks, or is reluctant towards such well-being of the family, he is disobeying the rules laid down by the *parameshwar*. Once again, towards the end of his dream vision Akshay seems to be trying to consolidate the idea of the *brahmanistha grihastha*, one who would work towards both self-improvement (*atma hita*) and the benefit of the world (*sangsarer upakar*).[22]

A crucial question to ask here would be whether, through such a dream vision, Akshay Dutta is foregrounding for his readers an alternative model of sovereignty and selfhood as early as 1859 (the year of publication of the third volume of *Charupath*). In the introductory chapter, 'Whose Imagined Community', to his book *The Nation and Its Fragments*, Partha Chatterjee asserts how 'anticolonial nationalism creates its own domain of sovereignty within colonial society well before it begins its political battle with the imperial power'.[23] However, Chatterjee's model is based on a clearly marked binary between the domains of the spiritual and the material within the social institutions. He argues how, particularly towards the latter half of the nineteenth century, or the proper nationalist phase, the spiritual, which deals with the myriad aspects of *dharma* (not used in the narrow sense of religion), belonged to the inner domain of the colonized subject and was resistant to narratives of change or reform suggested by the colonizer. Of course, that did not mean that the spiritual domain was not changing from inside. Chatterjee writes how it was within the spiritual domain that 'nationalism launches its most powerful, creative, and historically significant project: to fashion a "modern" national culture that is nevertheless not Western'.[24] The material domain was on the outside, dealing with economy, science, technology, and governance, 'a domain where the West had proved its superiority and the East had succumbed'.[25] The 'imagined community', argues Chatterjee, therefore unfolds necessarily in the spiritual domain. It is within this inner realm where the foreigner has no right of passage that the sovereignty of the nation is manifested. Also, it is at this moment of the articulation of selfhood that Chatterjee posits the difference between the state and the nation. He speaks of literature, art, and the family as spaces within the inner domain used for the articulation of sovereignty and selfhood, independent in many ways from the machinations of state power and its manifestations. But, according to him, there is a necessary disconnect here: 'If the nation is an imagined community and if nations must also take the form of states, then our theoretical language must allow us to talk about community and state at the same time.'[26]

I would argue, however, that for someone like Akshay Dutta, the idea of the 'imagined community' clearly went beyond the realm of the private (or the inner domain) and assimilated the public life of the colonized Bengali subject. Whereas it is possible to imagine such compartmentalization of the inner and outer domains, the nature of community and social living would naturally allow a fair bit of flux between the two. Akshay's instrumentalist understanding of the nature and function of human life, subservient to the larger vision of the *parameshwar*, easily brings together the ideas of *samaj*, *sangsar*, and *jagat*. The community, the family, and the universe naturally involve the domains of both the private and the public. Likewise, the *pradhan manush* (obviously imagined as the sovereign) will be *tri-guna sampanna*. If we are to understand *dharma* as the *guna* that belongs largely or wholly to the domain of the private, the other two qualities of *vidya* and *bishaya-buddhi* would very much be part of the outer or the public domain. Thus, the abstraction of the inner domain, either in the form of imagining ways of practising *dharma* or through the forms of art or literature, is complemented, in Akshay's view of the world, by the very material manifestations of education and finance – two institutional practices that have an immediate connect to western modernity and its forms of administration. It is no doubt easier to imagine the 'imagined' as belonging to a domain of abstraction, either as a world of pre-modern practices with intonations of the sacred and the traditional or to contain it within the domain of the purely 'cultural' as forms of art or literature that have no immediate bearing to the empirical functions of the empire. Likewise, confining each of the material and the spiritual, that is the public and the private, within their separate domains of functioning would help locate the category of the 'sovereign as imagined community' within the form of the nation and not involve it as a player in the functioning of the state. In a sense, the conceptual framework of the various forms of proto-nationalisms will easily be assimilated within such an idea of the imagined nation, and therefore literary works such as Bankim's *Anandamath*[27] (1882) or Tagore's *Ghare Baire*[28] (1916) become repeated and often overused examples of the manifestation of an imagined nation within the Bengali intellectual domain of the late nineteenth or the early twentieth centuries. Akshay's *Swapnadarshan*, however, belongs to a different form of imagining the sovereign self, not as any kind of esoteric proto-national category of imagining a nation-state, but in terms of the quotidian everydayness of lived experience that draws its moral and ethical determinants from a pre-existent template of a historically and culturally defined idea of the *samaj*.

In the context of reading Akshay's work, written around the middle years of the nineteenth century, I find the derivative model somewhat problematic. In the first place, as most historians agree, rampant tendencies of proto-nationalism based on the model of European polity were a phenomenon of the later years of the nineteenth century. I find Swarupa Gupta's idea of using the concept of the *samaj* as an analytical tool quite helpful. Gupta replaces the 'modular' idea of nationalism with 'indigenous unities and origins, which fed into constructions of nationhood'.[29] While not divesting culture from polity, Gupta looks at the idea of a subterranean unity within the thematic ramifications of the ideas of race, caste, and nation, subsequently reading the nations 'as a cultural entity historically rooted in the evolution of *samaj*'.[30] Gupta also weaves into this framework of the *samaj* the connection between history and *jati* that collates indigenous forms of epistemology with the notion of unity through cultural identity and moral and ethical commonalities:

> As the term could imply both division (multifacetedness) and unity (overarching nature), *jati* was unique in acting as a site for forging unity alongside, and in contention with bonds of caste, class, clan, micro-region and ethnic category. It provides a heuristic field for seeing how interactions between multiple scales of identity were negotiated and mediated by the literati in their discourse on nationhood envisioned through *samaj*.[31]

It is such heuristic practice that Akshay deftly weaves into his three dream visions. The idea of culture as both embedded organically and manifested in practice is at the core of the three categories that Akshay chooses as the content of his dreams – *vidya*, *kirti*, and *nyay*. All the three qualities are seen as existent historically within the cultural narrative of Bengali identity, while the need for continuous practice is also emphasized. The blueprint towards achieving the desired condition of being *sarva-manya* and *param-pujyu* is mapped through a network of ethical and moral qualities that emerge from a foundational system of cultural practice that dates back to a traditional past and is quite independent of the templates produced by colonial modernity – *sraddha*, *yatna*, *daya*, *bhakti*, *kshama*, *ahimsa*, *maitree*, *karunya swavab*. In fact, it may be fairly claimed that Akshay sees a lack of all these qualities within the colonial enterprise and its manifestations of modernity, and thus claims a separate space for indigenous cultural praxis. There is a traditional framework of historically informed moral routine implicit in these qualities that will be instrumental in re-establishing the lost glory of a *jati*. As Gupta argues, the notion of *jati* is linked with both the quest 'for an indigenous history'[32] and a 'process of self-definition, as well as the conceptualization of a wider social and cultural universe within which diverse groups could be included'.[33] A part of such an attempt by Akshay was to be as inclusive and diverse as possible in his discussions on the religious sects of India in both the pages of the *Tattwabodhini Patrika* and his two-volume *Bharatvarshiya*

Upashak Sampraday. Likewise, the reader will not fail to notice how the entire project of the dream visions assimilates within the utopic space a global connect reiterating a continuity of intellectual exchange, a glorious tradition of science, technology, and literature, and the need to redefine selfhood through the exploration of a rich indigenous tradition and its global reach and possibilities of assimilation and syncretism through the connecting principle of *viswa patir viswa-rachana.* The abiding trope in these essays is not one of subservience or imitation, but one of collaboration and exchange, as Aryabhatta's attitude towards Copernicus, Galileo, and Newton seems to suggest.[34] Through the three tracts, Akshay is clearly and singularly addressing the Bengali *jati* and assimilating in the discussion a conception of both the nation and the world. The immediate and essentializing presence of the colonial narrative is implicitly relegated to the margins. It is crucial to notice in this context that the dream space becomes one of consolidating primarily a material identity through an exploration of the cultural dynamic harking back to a past and emphasizing the narratives of education, achievement, and justice. Therefore, it is possible to say that the way Akshay intervenes into the space of dream histories and imagined communities is unlike the way Partha Chatterjee frames the inner and outer, or the spiritual and material domains. There is a conscious effort in Akshay to emphasize the materiality of cultural history in the context of indigenous attempts to elicit a narrative of Bengali selfhood in the colonial context.

Bhudeb's Dream History: A Necessary Comparison

More or less contemporaries, both Bhudeb Mukhopadhyay and Akshay Dutta were writing important tracts towards a definition of Bengali identity in the nineteenth century and carving out a template of the sovereign self with a commensurate history within the space of colonial modernity. A comparison between their writings is both necessary and inevitable. Both of them have been editors of influential periodicals, have written moral and cultural guidebooks in the vernacular for their readership, and have consistently tried to elicit a historical narrative of the indigenous people while they themselves were suitably trained in the discourses of western modernity. What is more topical in the present context is that both of them have written dream narratives that envision a roadmap for the future Bharatvarsha.[35] While Akshay writes his three-part *Swapnadarshan*, Bhudeb writes a tract titled *Swapnalabdha Bharatvarsher Itihas*.[36] Bhudeb's counterfactual dream history begins at the battle of Panipat in 1761 when the Afghan warrior Ahmad Shah Abdali is comprehensively defeated by the Marathas, leading to the young prince Ramchandra (of Shivaji's lineage) assuming the throne in Delhi. Although both are dream visions, and both refer to a certain historical narrative of a Bharatvarsha, there are some fundamental differences in their respective approaches to the project. Broadly speaking, Bhudeb's dream history talks about the larger scope and development of the society and polity of India in a space that develops towards a modern future for the nation. As Pradip Kumar Datta observes, Bhudeb's dream vision has a programmatic character: 'It lays out what the new basis of the nation will be, its constitution (with its hierarchy of fundamental and regulative principles), the nature of its education, commerce, international policy, and so on. The nation is dreamt in its details.'[37] Akshay, on the other hand, focuses on the crucial development of the character of the individual. His future vision of Bharatvarsha is modelled on the singular vision of the subject evolving into a *pradhan manush* invested with the three qualities of *dharma*, *vidya*, and *bishaya-buddhi*. His focus is on the building of the Bengali character, and his reference, somewhat different from Bhudeb's, is the past glory of the Hindu *jati*, and how through the rigours of discipline and practice it was possible to emulate the achievements of the ancients.

However, there is an interesting disconnect that needs to be pointed out here. If one were to carefully unpack the entire oeuvre of the two authors, a striking paradox will reveal itself. In *Swapnalabdha Bharatvarsher Itihas*, Bhudeb imagines a polity that is symptomatic of the emergence of a modern Bharatvarsha where Hindus and Muslims co-exist as fellow inhabitants of the society in perfect harmony with each other. He calls the Muslims the foster-child of Bharatbhumi.[38] He writes:

> Although Bharatbhumi is the original motherland of the Hindu *jati*, although it were the Hindus who were born of her womb, still the Muslims are not strangers, she has been fostering them in her bosom for quite a while. So the Muslims are her foster children.[39]

In the course of the text, Bhudeb gives his readers many examples of Hindu–Muslim unity in this new Bharatvarsha of his dreams. He warns that their strife will only help the foreign powers to multiply their profits.[40] He witnesses the brahmin pronouncing, 'He who is Ram is also Rahim, there is only one God', while the Muslim says, 'We are all sons of the one Father, just wearing different sets of clothes'.[41] There is also this certain character, simply called the 'Bengali', who declares, 'The one who is Satyapir is also Satyanarayan'.[42] It is interesting to witness such a dream vision unfold in Bhudeb's imagination of the nation. A staunch brahmin throughout his life, Bhudeb's views on society or the administration of the *samaj* was hardly liberal. Deeply traditionalist, casteist, and Brahminical in most of his writings, Bhudeb's views on the Hindu *samaj* were unequivocally hierarchical, with the brahmin, as the superior being, at the helm of affairs. His criticism of Vidyasagar's attempts at widow remarriage were not unknown: 'Bhudeb was deeply respectful of the Brahminical qualities such as virtue, benevolence, mettle, simplicity, erudition and others in Vidyasagar; however, he thought that the widow remarriage movement would cause harm to his *samaj*.'[43] Likewise, in his essay 'Samajik Prakriti – Hindusamaj', he declares how the English have ruled India peacefully for such a long time due to the peace-loving nature of the Hindus, and that such inclination towards peace is an intrinsic quality in them. In the same vein he continues how certain Muslims in Bombay created a great commotion when a certain author had not praised their prophet Muhammad enough, and how the Bengali Muslims had also joined in.[44] Further on in the same essay he declares, 'The Brahmin *jati* is the ideal of the Hindu samaj,' and lays down the qualities that makes the brahmin superior to the rest of his race: *pavitrata* (purity), *dharmaviruta* (religiosity), *atmasanyam* (self-restraint), *kshama* (pardon), *daya* (compassion), *dhairya* (patience), and so on.[45] Many such examples are strewn across the body of Bhudeb's work. On the other hand, Akshay, the more liberal and anti-casteist, would clearly denounce the period of Muslim rule in India as one of repression and incarceration.[46] Interestingly, in his *Swapnadarshan*, Akshay makes no mention of this Hindu–Muslim binary in his conception of a future citizenry. Although Akshay also mentions the qualities such as *kshama, daya, sraddha, yatna*, and so on, all commensurate with Bhudeb's ideals for the Hindu brahmin, the former views them more as generic human qualities than belonging to a certain caste or class or religion. One might say that in his dream vision, the transformation from the imaginary nation to the imaginary state was less political for Akshay than for Bhudeb. While Bhudeb, in spite of his clearly casteist and Hindu supremacist view, was envisioning a modernity that was cosmopolitan, Akshay's, in spite of his more liberal and egalitarian views, would seem to be more conservative and much less political in its import.

From *Jati* to *Jagat*: An Important Turn

In an essay on Bhudeb, Pradip Kumar Datta makes an interesting distinction between Bhudeb's conception of the historical and that of others such as Akshay Dutta or Rajendralal Mitra. He argues how Akshay and Rajendralal were following the model foregrounded by such Orientalists as H. T. Colebrooke, a revivalist model that privileges the ancient past as the basis for a cultural legitimacy that needed to be retraced as a template for asserting an indigenous selfhood.[47] Bhudeb, on the other hand, Datta argues, was envisioning an 'alternative modern' that was to elicit its narrative of representation from within the moment of colonial modernity, and through refashioning the relationship between the Hindus and the Muslims not according to the Hindu–Muslim–Christian periodization of the history of India, but through an immediate need for positing a narrative of harmonious and inclusive indigeneity against colonial rule. Datta is of the opinion that *Swapnalabdha Bharatvarsher Itihas* 'inaugurates a new idea of the nation that is modern because it operates on the basis of a new legitimacy'.[48] I would agree with Datta in this contention about the different narratives of culture and selfhood that Akshay and Bhudeb had assumed as their strategies for inaugurating their versions of the modern. However, in spite of such a difference in the framework for articulating the future of Bharatvarsha, there was a discernible movement in both of them towards opening up the scope of their respective epistemologies towards the world. Both of them were writing tracts on social and cultural practice as well as their own versions of utopic dream narratives, each of which was opening up the conception of a modern selfhood towards a global engagement.

In *Swapnalabdha Bharatvarsher Itihas*, for example, Bhudeb lays down an elaborate plan for the acquirement of knowledge, language, technology, and techniques of warfare from across the globe. The new state will train its youth to visit foreign lands and make them understand how travelling across the seas or seeking out the company of foreigners (*mlechha sangsarga*) is not prohibited in the *shastra*s.[49] In the inimitably sexist style common to many of his contemporaries, Bhudeb says through the voice of Bajirao:

> If we do not travel, see foreign lands – are forever restricted to the
> confines of our homes – then our nature will be like women. We shall
> never be self-sufficient, and in the same way as women are subdued
> by men, our countrymen will be subdued by foreigners. Hence I have

decided on these three methods: first, about two hundred able foreign soldiers have to be employed for teaching warfare; second, another one hundred will be employed for building warships; third, around three hundred young men from our land should be sent to foreign lands at the cost of the exchequer to learn their languages and acquire their knowledge.[50]

In this new Bharatvarsha born after the counterfactual Third Battle of Panipat, the plan for education is also elaborate. At the centre of the city of Kanauj there is a university where all the ancient languages – Sanskrit, Greek, Latin, Arabic – are taught. Students throng this centre of learning not only from Bharatvarsha, but also from Arabia, Persia, and Turkey, and even from Germany and Russia. The library in this centre of learning has almost all the texts from all these parts of the world.[51]

Likewise, there is an identical reaching out towards the global in Akshay's imagining of the historical. The only subtle difference in their respective epistemologies was in the method of collaboration or acquirement. Bhudeb's method, one would contend, is one of the acquirement of new learning, of building a whole new epistemology that is born out of a careful selection of models, methods, and strategies that have been mastered by foreigners over centuries. The consolidation of an indigenous modernity would require a successful acquirement and amalgamation of all those methodologies that were to be collated from across the globe. Akshay's method, on the other hand, presumes an implicit superiority of the ancients of the land, and is more about collaboration through an engagement that was a priori and only stultified by the recent recalcitrance due to colonial modernity. In 'Swapnadarshan – Kirtbishayak', for example, he writes:

I saw Vedavyas and Sankaracharya and Plato and Pythagoras. Initially they were at the centre of the congregation, but later, unable to withstand the illumined faces of some new authors from the Western part of the globe, they moved to one side.[52]

In general, in his dream vision Akshay would make no qualitative distinction between ancient and modern knowledge systems, or between the east and the west. Likewise, he would always discover a collaborative intent between intellectuals from across the globe, with praise, exchange, and respect for each other. The value judgement is clearly based on ethical and moral binaries such as laziness and industriousness, or greed versus generosity, or excess against temperance, but rarely is there a racial spin to such judgement. However, there is an interesting fourfold structure to Akshay's epistemic model. The 'Kirti Niketan' (which could be roughly translated as the 'House of Achievements'), or the seat of Kirtidevi, has four gates of entry. Akshay writes how 'the most important intellectuals from the four parts of the globe entered through the four gates',[53] without making any hierarchical distinction either between the parts of the globe or in the order of entry. He also specifies four material objects that were necessary to stake one's claim at the gates of the Kirti Niketan: someone carried a lethal sword, another a well-authored book, one a telescope, and someone an armillary sphere.[54] That is to say, each of these material objects was instrumental in foregrounding a particular vocation commensurate with both the arts and sciences from the ancient times as well as modern innovations in technology and expansion that would lead to the creation and sustenance of global networks – warfare and colonialism, acquirement of knowledge, geographical explorations, or astronomical calculations.

In both Akshay and Bhudeb, therefore, there was an intended trajectory from *jati* to *jagat*, although their attitudes to the intended goal were ideologically different. None of them would, however, engage in any direct confrontation with the colonial government, nor provoke disaffection that was evident in the growing militant nationalism of the later part of the nineteenth century. Akshay had slowly retracted from public life, while Bhudeb was an employee of the colonial government for most of his working life. However, it is evident that both of them felt the imperative to underscore a historical narrative of Bengali selfhood – either as a continuity from the ancients to the modern or as a beginning that had to be set apart from the Hegelian framework of a Eurocentric and therefore subservient discourse. An easy method of doing this was to foreground the notion of culture, of imagining and promoting the perception of the Bengali *jati* as a cultural unit that needed to reinvent itself, or rewrite its history as culture, a trope that would immediately divest itself of its immediate colonial legacy and view their identity as either a continuity from the ancient past or one that has congealed with the history of Muslim presence in India and Bengal in terms of cultural similarities and exchange due to sustained affinity. Swarupa Gupta seems to argue along similar lines of culture as history when she discusses the notion of Bengali identity in the context of the Hindu *mela*:[55]

Present disunity posited against the *jati*'s past explained the connection between identity and history. The re-imagination of the Bengali self, and dreams of future unity therefore coalesced in a quest for history, where the past, present and future of the *jati* interlocked to give a new expression to notions of identity.[56]

At the same time, it was an imperative both of modernity as a network of influences and for the reconstitution of the Bengali self as capable of imagining beyond the immediate discourse of colonial modernity that the *jati* had to turn its face towards the *jagat*. Through connecting, or reassembling, or revisiting, or reformulating discursive and epistemological strands, intellectuals such as Bhudeb and Akshay were continuously opening up the question of identity, more specifically cultural identity, towards an engagement with the world.

Time, History, and the *Mahapurush*

Another interesting aspect that would emerge in the way either Bhudeb or Akshay was approaching the question of modernity was how they handled the notion of time. The writing of a history, any history, presumes grappling with the idea of time. Of course, this becomes more complicated when colonialism as a sustained narrative intervenes and therefore complicates how a nation will write its history. The *jati* to *jagat* narrative that I have elaborated above is naturally complicated by the way the history of Bharatvarsha in general, and say the Bengali race in particular, was continuously being qualified by the discourse of colonial modernity in almost every aspect of lived experience. From the intervention into everyday cultural practice through the introduction of clock-time, for example, to the larger canvas of how a race or a people would locate their identity or write their histories – the influence of colonial practice was everywhere.[57] To think about time was therefore an important aspect of writing about the *jati*. It is in this context that in his essay on Bhudeb, Pradip Kumar Dutta discusses the 'magisterial conception of historical time', in which 'the agent seeks to carefully adjudicate between tendencies of a given time in order to isolate, select, and develop particular ones'.[58] Although in *Swapnalabdha Bharatvarsher Itihas* the author as agent chooses to develop his counterfactual narrative in terms of a modernity that presumes both a Hindu–Muslim unity and the implicit subordination of the European colonizer,

Bhudeb was intensely aware of how the temporal perspectives of the historical narrative were largely controlled, in the real sense, by powerful individual forces within the empire. Therefore, although the dream narrative and its projected historiography had their peculiar temporal framework, Bhudeb had little doubt that 'the subject of human intervention actually underlines the fact that the empire produces the time which shapes the world of the Bengali'.[59] It is perhaps due to this awareness of the agency invested by colonial power to an individual that Bhudeb, towards the end of his essays on society (*Samajik Prabandha*), feels the need for a *mahapurush* (or a Great Man) who would bail Bharatvarsha out of its current historical trajectory and lay the foundation for the beginning of a new historical narrative. The 'magistracy over time'[60] that has been the prerogative of the master class, only to be claimed by the native in incidental utopic narratives of dream histories, could only be finally claimed, thought Bhudeb, by the arrival of such a *mahapurush*. The final chapter of his *Samajik Prabandha* deals with the notion of *kartavya* or duty and begins with the section titled 'Kartavyanirnay – Netripratiksha' (Determining Responsibility – Waiting for the Leader). In this section he begins his argument with how native education in the hands of the colonizer has only been imitative in nature, and how, since the respective social, cultural, and intellectual viewpoints of the colonizer and the colonized are incommensurate, such imitation of their knowledge will not be able to produce a new Bharatvarsha. For this, Bhudeb insists, Bharatvarsha needs a *swadeshiya mahapurush* or an indigenous Great Man.[61] He then goes on to list the qualities of such a *mahapurush*: he will be self-sacrificing in nature and seek only the sympathy of his own people (*swajatiya*); he will discover the means towards uniting his countrymen; he will include in his teachings the knowledge of his indigenous predecessors; his ideology should be a summary of both shastric and scientific knowledge; like the sun, he will assimilate, but not annihilate, the previously existing indigenous stars and comets. Along with these qualities the *mahapurush* will also possess intellect, erudition, eloquence, and extreme magnanimity.[62] At the end of the essay he writes how Bharatvarsha is waiting for a *netripurushottam* (the Supreme Leader) from its own *jati*.[63]

This is where, I suppose, there is another subtle difference between the respective approaches of Akshay and Bhudeb. Akshay's approach to the entire dynamic of modernity was through revisiting the past as a template of cultural and ethical superiority, and a more evolved Aryan civilization that already had a global lookout and was connected to the world through continuous exchange in the sciences and the arts as also through travel and commerce.[64]

But there was also a deeply nurtured belief in the *epistemic* superiority of the Europeans. In the *Bharatvarshiya Upashak Sampraday*, for example, he argues how many philosophers in the recent past have tried to interpret the ancient Vedantic texts through *tika*s and *vasya*s. Many of these philosophers 'were born with fresh seeds of intelligence. Only if they had followed the correct path of investigation and traversed the pure trajectory of the sciences then Bharatbhumi would have, like Europe, become a paradise'.[65] Bharatvarsha, he regrets, needed a Francis Bacon to achieve this epistemic rigour.[66] However, for Akshay, the figure of Rammohun Roy has always remained as a model of what constitutes ideal Bengali selfhood. While Bhudeb eagerly waited for his indigenous *mahapurush* figure, Akshay had already discovered all the necessary qualities of such a *mahapurush* in Rammohun. Strewn across the oeuvre of his work are praises for Rammohun, and even as he was writing his final book, the *Bharatvarshiya Upashak Sampraday*, the figure of Rammohun remained an abiding and venerated presence. Akshay sees Rammohun to be a figure who has been a presence in the imaginative geography of the nineteenth-century Bengali subject: 'You have the sobriquet Raja. The lifeless earth is not your kingdom. You have the right over an expansive imagination.'[67] Akshay insists that the Hindu traditionalists who had reigned supreme in the minds of the common people were now replaced by the figure of Rammohun. He was therefore the king of kings (*rajar raja*).[68] And it is through Rammohun that Akshay foregrounds the move towards modernity and establishes a connection with the rest of the world: 'You are not only the friend of the people of Bharatvarsha, you are the friend of the world (*jagater bandhu*).'[69] It may be said that for Akshay, the template of developing a historiography for Bharatvarsha was far more complex than Bhudeb's. In the first place his movement towards a new Bharatvarsha (or Bengal) was comprehensively backed by ancient or pre-modern systems of knowledge; second, such knowledge had to both assimilate western forms of scholarship and be filtered through the systematic and streamlined epistemological frameworks that were largely European; third, his *mahapurush* figure of Raja Rammohun Roy was a perfect example of the kind of the complex assimilation of epistemologies that Akshay envisioned in terms of Rammohun's location in time (at the cusp of the pre-modern and the modern), his global value system, and his complex relationship with traditional shastric disciplines. In the final section of this chapter I will further explore the nature and implications of this complexity with a brief reference to Akshay's final work, the two-volume *Bharatvarshiya Upashak Sampraday*.

Bharatvarshiya Upashak Sampraday: Jati, Samaj, and the History of the Hindus

Akshay had planned the composition of *Bharatvarshiya Upashak Sampraday* as a three-volume discourse but could only complete the first two volumes in his lifetime. Roughly speaking, it is a detailed discourse on the religious sects in India, based on both his readings of other source materials on the subject and painstaking empirical research.[70] Haraprasad Shastri has also claimed that Akshay had read up all possible sources in English, German, French, Latin, and Bengali for writing the introduction to the two volumes of this work.[71] On the completion of the second volume, Akshay was congratulated by intellectuals across the globe, including Max Muller, Monier Monier-Williams, Rajnarayan Basu, and Rajendralal Mitra, among others.[72] Other than a description and occasional critique of many and varied major and minor religious sects, each of the two volumes contains a lengthy introduction (*upakramanika*) where Akshay debates on and discusses the foundational bases of the Hindus in Bharatvarsha through a series of scattered reflections on their language, race, faith, belief system, religious, literary and cultural texts, social practices, and reaction to colonialism and modernity, among others. In spite of the praise heaped on this text across time and space, the reader does not fail to notice the scattered, haphazard, and often incomplete nature of the discussions that Akshay undertakes in these two lengthy introductions to the volumes. In fact, often there is a clear disconnect between the subject matter of the main texts and the discourses in the introduction. A possible reason for this would be Akshay's steadily failing health and the often ad hoc manner in which he attempted to complete the work. Towards the end of the *upakramanika* of his second volume, Akshay regrets how his health has prevented him from reading, writing, thinking, hearing, or undertaking any physical or mental labour. He laments how he was unable to revisit, revise, or even copy-edit the printed version of the text. When a thought occurred to him and did not leave, he persuaded random people to write for him, or visited friends and requested that they write for him. Likewise, he has sometimes dictated to untrained minds or woken his household help up at midnight and dictated parts of the text.[73] Thus, it is somewhat difficult to read the two *upakramanikas* in the two volumes of *Bharatvarshiya Upashak Sampraday* as an organic whole that seamlessly unpacks Akshay's project in the volumes. As I have mentioned earlier, the two *upakramanikas* straddle various issues and debates – some of which are beyond my expertise and not germane to the present discussion. I will, therefore, lift and briefly discuss elements from the *upakramanikas* that try to constitute a history of the Hindu *jati* and have some bearing to the present context of my discussion.

Imagining a *Jati*

Akshay begins the *upakramanika* of the first volume of *Bharatvarshiya Upashak Sampraday* with the simple claim that the Hindus were not the original inhabitants of Bharatvarsha and had come from elsewhere.[74] He argues, referring extensively to such sources as J. C. Prichard's *Researches into the Physical History of Man* and A. Weber's *Modern Investigations on Ancient India*, how the Hindus who settled in India were of Aryan origin, and that the ancient religion of the Aryans was the primary form of Hinduism. It was through a complex period of evolution in terms of settlement, cultural relations, and forms of worship that the Hindus accustomed themselves to what was Bharatvarsha. Akshay argues that a sense of history was, however, inherent in them, and the idea of *jatiya dharma* (racial characteristics) of the inhabitants of Bharatvarsha could be traced through the Vedas, the Smritis, the Puranas, and the Tantras. He writes:

> History is grafted in the Vedas, the Smritis, the Puranas, and the Tantras. One has to read with care. The Vedas and the Samhitas are the earliest accounts of Hinduism in Bharatvarsha., the Brahmanas and the Aranyaks constitute the second period, the Kalpa-Sutras and the Smriti-Samhitas constitute the third period, while the Puranas and the Tantras delineate the fourth period.[75]

Akshay argues, therefore, how through an unravelling and development of social polity a continuous process of historical narrativization was present from the earliest moment of settlement of the Hindus in Bharatvarsha. He is full of praise for the medicinal expertise of the earliest Hindu settlers, contending that they often surpassed European methods of treatment.[76] Subsequently, he refers to passages from the *Rigveda Samhita* to argue how there was a holistic account of the existing social polity evident in its pages:

> They would build cities and towns to live in; plough the land and produce crops; they would have governments for the necessary functioning of

the state; they would produce weapons and jewellery; ... the repetitive
mention of such subjects as seafaring and merchants, travellers and inns,
medicine and treatment bear testimony to the progress of the Hindu-
samaj during the times of the Samhita.[77]

Akshay also argues how, once the basic needs of the Hindu *samaj* in terms of
its polity, structure, worship, and other necessities were taken care of, it moved
towards a rational exploration of questions centred around human existence
and the uniqueness of the universe. This was the time of the composition of
the Upanishads – written by intelligent and perceptive people across time.[78] It
is in this context that Akshay broaches the question of epistemology, arguing
how the templates of knowledge were systematized (*pranalibaddha*) through
the Upanishads.[79] The debates addressed in the Upanishads, Akshay argues,
also bear testimony to the diverse ideas and ideologies that were assimilated
within the knowledge system of Bharatvarsha and invested in it a plurality
that was intellectually stimulating and also opened newer and evolved
perspectives about lived experience.[80] Akshay would also try to assimilate
the diversity of intellectual thinking in Bharatvarsha through two almost
contradictory perspectives, both of which were part of the Upanishadic
system. On the one hand, he argues that the acquirement of knowledge is
dependent on both *buddhi* and *dharmaniti* and coordination between these
necessary qualities; on the other hand, he refers to a Persian saying that it
is impossible to unravel the meaning of the universe through the practice of
rationality and quotes from the Upanishad that the universe is both unknown
and unknowable.[81]

The *upakramanika* continues into the second volume and becomes more
voluminous as Akshay was perhaps trying to pack all his complex thoughts,
ideological positions, and beliefs into it. As he moves from one strain of
thought to another, the *upakramanika* sometimes reads like his personal
diary where he puts down his thoughts for the day. Through much of the
second *upakramanika*, we find Akshay carefully locating the Hindu *shastra*s
within a space of dialogue and exchange with European knowledge systems,
particularly with those of the Greeks and the Romans. For example, Akshay
argues that the Sankhya claim that 'matter cannot be produced from non-
matter' was accepted by such philosophers as Aristotle and Lucretius.[82]
Likewise, he thinks that if one would read the works of Pythagoras, they
would be under the illusion that they were studying the Hindu *shastra*s.[83]
Akshay agrees in such instances with H. H. Wilson and H. T. Colebrooke

that it was probable that the Greeks had acquired such knowledge from the Hindus and not the other way round.[84] Likewise, he considers Kalidasa to be the greatest of all poets in the world and discovers in the structure and descriptions in Kalidasa's poetry a pronounced Europeanism. However, his poetry is inflected by the bounty of Bharatbhumi, and thereby he transcends the greatest of poets, including Shakespeare, Milton, Byron, and Valmiki.[85] This second *upakramanika* is largely informed by the works of Orientalist scholars and argues about the progressivist dynamic of the early Hindu *samaj* as compared to the present state of superstition and regression. It speaks of how the *puratan samaj* endorsed widow remarriage and inter-caste and love marriages unlike the current dispensation that not only lacked such qualities but endorsed child marriages and kulinism instead.[86] Books on mathematics and medicine travelled from Bharatvarsha to the Arab nations, and then through Egypt to the rest of Europe.[87] Likewise, the earlier *samaj* had not only spread across the world (*bhumandaley*) knowledge, *dharma*, and medicine, but it also taught them entertainment in the form of music and sports such as the game of chess (*satranch*).[88]

It is after such a detailed description of the *samaj* and the *jati* at the height of its excellence that Akshay returns to the present once again. In this last work of his, Akshay seems to be critical both of the present condition of the Hindu *jati* in its failure towards the structuring of a foundationalist epistemology in terms of polity and of the colonizer for having failed its subjects as the sovereign. From the lament 'Shei Hindu ekhon ei Hindu!' (That Hindu is now this Hindu!)[89] that critiques both the loss of valour (*virya*) and values (*dharma*) Akshay turns towards questioning the civilizational ethic of the ruler class:

> If under the watch of a king who is civilized and takes pride in his civilization the state of the peoples' minds are reduced to such depravity, it is a shame for the king, for his state, and for the civilization itself.[90]

He describes his contemporary society as a disease-ridden society of dwarves,[91] a people who have even lost their voices to cry, and concludes that the only solution was for England to show compassion (*daya prakash*).[92] In an almost desperate apostrophe to England, he writes:

> And England! You and your brethren have in the past expectantly sought the favour of Bharatbhumi, and this noble queen of yore, now

reduced to wretchedness, is pitiably crying at your feet. Now, England! Do what is just. Shower your science-nurtured compassion, consider the time, space, and people and do the needful, set aside your ruler-self (*rajbhab*) and show your motherly-self (*matribhab*) to your subjects, and if possible revive this listless Bharatbhumi and wipe its tears.[93]

Akshay ends the *upakramanika* to the second volume with a similar regret that the countrymen of Rammohun Ray have been reduced to a subhuman race (*naradham jati*).[94]

To conclude, it is crucial to try and understand how Akshay Dutta envisioned the idea of a Bharatvarsha where the idea of selfhood and sovereignty was related to the notions of both *jati* and *jagat*. It is important to read Akshay's work as a continuity, from the days when he was the editor of the *Tattwabodhini Patrika* till the moment when he was writing the second volume of the *Bharatvarshiya Upashak Sampraday*, to be able to comprehend the many ideological contradictions that he was straddling across his writing career. No doubt the *upakramanika* to the second volume of the *Bharatvarshiya Upashak Sampraday* ends on a note of despondency, a loss of hope in the potential of both the *samaj* and the *jati*, but the reader needs to understand that he was writing the volumes in a state of extreme physical pain and mental duress. It is staccato and lacks an organic structure. He was also, possibly, trying to collate all the ideological strands that had influenced him from his early days as a scholar. As I have discussed in the first chapter, Akshay's eclectic milieu and nineteenth-century Bengali identitarianism were unfolding themselves through manifold influences – cultural and counter-cultural, rendering the dynamic of representation in a state of continuous flux. In this chapter, for example, I have tried to read comparatively the kinds of differing paradigms of historical understanding that Bhudeb and Akshay as contemporaries represented. I would contend that Akshay was trying to expand the horizon of his debate about culture as history and looking for a narrative that would embrace the ideas of *jati* and *jagat* together. As I have argued along the lines of Swarupa Gupta's contention, for Akshay the notion of the *jati* would contain within it the heterogeneity of caste, class, clan, region, and ethnicity. The consistent use of the word 'Hindu', problematic and sectarian as it is, was also perhaps used to represent the wide heterogeneity of a geographical and cultural space that that could not otherwise be brought together.[95] Akshay's was a more empirical approach than Bhudeb's, for example, and he could not take refuge like the latter within an imaginary political. The secular praxis of Akshay's works, his scientific and rational approach to questions of polity and nationhood, may not be over-emphasized. His idea of the *mahapurush* was Rammohun Roy, a figure he keeps going back to. The cosmopolitanism of Rammohun and his rationalism and scientism were also deeply ingrained in Akshay, along with his engagement with the interpretations of Hindu texts. That is why, as I have argued, Akshay's historiography was a complex mix of influences, and he was aware of these contradictory strands. His idea of the Hindu was racially inflected, the inhabitants of Bharatvarsha who were looking out towards the world. It is a symptom of Akshay's expansive imagination that leads him to call Rammohun *jagater bandhu*. The notion of *dharma*, for him, was always divested of ritualistic engagement and based on the sociocultural qualities of *upachikirsha*, *bhakti*, and *nyayparata*. Likewise, the *pradhan manush* of society was one invested with the qualities of *dharma*, *vidya*, and *bishaya buddhi* – all leading towards the imagination of a modern polity but reasonably different from the tropes of colonial modernity. His final call towards England was not assimilationist in its import, not one where the soul of Bharatvarsha merges with that of its colonial master. It was clearly one of *daya* (compassion) that reminds one immediately of Rammohun, in this case pleading with the colonizer for sustenance and good governance. Akshay's regret, inflected by Europe or the west, was the lack of an epistemology within contemporary indigenous knowledge practices. For him the idea of Bengali selfhood, and a search for history or identity, had to strike that balance between culling a cultural narrative from the ancient past and incorporating within it an epistemology that was both global and cosmopolitan in its narrative of progress.

Notes

1. Partha Chatterjee, *Our Modernity* (Rotterdam: SEPHIS, 1997), pp. 19–20.
2. Ibid., p. 20.
3. Immanuel Kant, 'An Answer to the Question: What Is Enlightenment?' (1784), in *What Is Enlightenment? Eighteenth-Century Answers and Twentieth-Century Questions*, ed. James Schmidt, 1st ed. (California: University of California Press, 1996), pp. 58–64.
4. See Rajnarayan Basu, *Sekal ar Ekal* (Calcutta: Kalikinkar Chakrabarty, 1874).
5. Chatterjee, *Our Modernity*, p. 20.

6. Ibid.
7. Ibid., p. 14.
8. See 'Susikshita o Asikshita Loker Sukher Taratamya', in *Charupath*, vol. 3, in Swapan Basu (ed.), *Akshaykumar Dutta Rachana Sangraha*, vol. 1 (Kolkata: Paschimbanga Bangla Academy, 2008), pp. 379–383.
9. Ibid., p. 379.
10. Ibid., p. 380.
11. Ibid.
12. Ibid., p. 381.
13. Ibid., p. 382.
14. See Akshay Kumar Dutta, *Charupath*, vol. 3, in *Akshaykumar Dutta Rachana Sangraha*, ed. Swapan Basu, vol. 1 (Kolkata: Paschimbanga Bangla Academy, 2008), pp. 361–378.
15. See 'Swapnadarshan – Vidyabishayak' in ibid., p. 363.
16. See 'Swapnadarshan – Kirtibishayak' in ibid., p. 370.
17. Ibid., p. 371.
18. See 'Swapnadarshan – Nyaybishayak' in ibid., p. 375.
19. Ibid., p. 377.
20. Ibid.
21. Ibid., p. 378. It is interesting to note, though, that Akshay Dutta does not specify the racial identity of those that replaced these undeserving officers. This could be another example of how he eluded the disaffection clause I have elaborated in the previous chapter.
22. Ibid.
23. See Partha Chatterjee, *The Nation and Its Fragments* (Princeton, NJ: Princeton University Press, 1993), p. 6.
24. Ibid.
25. Ibid.
26. Ibid., p. 11.
27. See Bankimchandra Chattopadhyay, *Anandamath*, in *Bankim Rachanabali*, vol. 1 (Calcutta: Sahitya Samsad, 1953), pp. 715–788.
28. See Rabindranath Tagore, *Ghare Baire*, in *Rabindra Upanyas-Sangraha* (Kolkata: Visvabharati Granthanvibhag, 1990), pp. 843–966.
29. See Swarupa Gupta, *Notions of Nationhood in Bengal* (Leiden and Boston: Brill, 2009), p. 6.
30. Ibid., p. 7.
31. Ibid., p. 94.
32. Ibid.

33. Ibid., p. 93.

34. See 'Swapnadarshan – Kirtibishayak', in Dutta, *Charupath*, vol. 3, p. 370.

35. The dream narrative or the writing of imaginary history was an interesting movement against the grain of the contemporary practice of writing the history of Bengal or India in the vernacular. One is reminded of such books as Iswarchandra Vidyasagar, *Banglar Itihas* (Calcutta: Sanskrit Press, 1853); Tarinicharan Bandopadhyay, *Bharatvarsher Itihas*, vol. 1 (Calcutta: Sanskrit Press Depository, 1858); Krishnachandra Ray, *Bharatvarsher Itihas, Ingrejder Adhikarkal* (Calcutta: J. C. Chatterjee, 1859); Kshirodchandra Raychaudhuri, *Samagra Bharater Sangkhipta Itihas* (Calcutta: n.p., 1876); among others.

36. At the very beginning Bhudeb writes how while he was helping a relative write a history of India (possibly meaning Ramgati Nyayratna writing *Bharatvarsher Sangkhipta Itihas*), he was inspired to write this dream history while wondering how the narrative of history would have been if the third battle of Panipat had ended differently. See the introduction to Bhudeb Mukhopadhyay, *Swapnalabdha Bharatvarsher Itihas* (Hooghly: Kashinath Bhattacharya, 1895).

37. See Pradip Kumar Datta, 'A Nineteenth-Century Romance of Counterfactual Time', in *History in the Vernacular*, ed. Raziuddin Aquil and Partha Chatterjee (Ranikhet: Permanent Black, 2012), p. 459.

38. See Mukhopadhyay, *Swapnalabdha Bharatvarsher Itihas*, p. 6. Whereas the Hindus are born of her womb (*garbhajata*), the Muslims are fostered by Bharatvarsha (*stanyapalita*). Bhudeb wonders, 'Is it not possible to imagine a brotherhood between the *garbhajata* and the *stanyapalita*?'

39. Ibid., p. 6.

40. Ibid., p. 7.

41. Ibid., p. 10.

42. Ibid., p. 11.

43. See Kumardeb Mukhopadhyay, *Bhudeb Charit*, vol. 1 (Calcutta: India Press, 1917), p. 174. For a discussion on this, see also Alok Ray, *Unish Satak* (Kolkata: Prama Prakashani, 2012), p. 167.

44. See Bhudeb Mukhopadhyay, 'Samajik Prakriti – Hindusamaj', in *Prabandha Samagra*, ed. Manaswita Sanyal and Ranjan Bandopadhyay (Kolkata: Charchapad, 2010), pp. 146–147.

45. Ibid., p. 147.

46. Akshay Dutta, *Bharatvarshiya Upashak Sampraday*, vol. 2 (Kolkata: Karuna Prakashani, 2013; first published 1883 [Calcutta]), p. 157.

47. For Colebrooke's conception of the Hindus and ancient Indian texts and philosophy, see H. T. Colebrooke, *Miscellaneous Essays*, vols. 1 and 2 (London: W. H. Allen and Co., 1837).

48. Datta, 'A Nineteenth-Century Romance of Counterfactual Time', p. 455.

49. Mukhopadhyay, *Swapnalabdha Bharatvarsher Itihas*, p. 22.

50. Ibid., pp. 22–23.

51. Ibid., p. 30.

52. 'Swapnadarshan – Kirtibishayak' in Dutta, *Charupath*, vol. 3, p. 371.

53. Ibid., p. 369.

54. Ibid., p. 367. Akshay here uses the term 'goljantra' which is most likely the Bengali word for the armillary sphere. It was an astronomical instrument used in ancient India. The Indian equivalent of the armillary sphere was traditionally made using thin wooden strips. Nagendranath Basu asserts that the means of use and the function of the *goljantra* was quite similar to the western globe used in astronomy. Basu also writes that the detailed description and instructions for using the instrument may be found in such texts as the *Surya Siddhanta* and the *Siddhanta Shiromani* among others. For a discussion on this, see Nagendranath Basu, *Viswakosh*, vol. 5 (Calcutta: Viswakosh Karyalay, 1894), pp. 564–568.

55. For a detailed understanding of the ideology and purpose of the Hindu *mela*, see Jogesh Chandra Bagal, *Hindu Melar Itivritta* (Calcutta: Maitri, 1968).

56. Gupta, *Notions of Nationhood in Bengal*, p. 96.

57. For a detailed discussion on the handling of time and the politics of social and cultural practice around it, the idea of the traditional Kaliyuga vis-à-vis the 'renaissance', and the introduction of clock-time, see Sumit Sarkar, 'Renaissance and Kaliyuga: Time, Myth and History in Colonial Bengal' (pp. 186–215) and 'Kaliyuga, Chakri and Bhakti: Ramkrishna and His Times' (pp. 282–357) in *Writing Social History* (Delhi: Oxford University Press, 1997).

58. Datta, 'A Nineteenth-Century Romance of Counterfactual Time', p. 466.

59. Ibid.

60. Ibid., p. 468.

61. Bhudeb Mukhopadhyay, *Samajik Prabandha*, in *Prabandha Samagra*, ed. Manaswita Sanyal and Ranjan Bandopadhyay (Kolkata: Charchapad, 2010), p. 258.

62. Ibid., p. 259.

63. Ibid., p. 281.

64. See my detailed discussion on this in Chapter 3. See also Akshay's essay 'Prachin Hindudiger Samudrayatra', *Tattwabodhini Patrika* 3, no. 71, Asad, 1771 Saka, pp. 44–48.

65. Dutta, *Bharatvarshiya Upashak Sampraday*, vol. 2, p. 52.

66. Ibid.

67. Ibid., p. 34.

68. Ibid.

69. Ibid.

70. For the myriad sources that Akshay had read up, including and most importantly H. H. Wilson's *Sketch of the Religious Sects of the Hindus*, for his research, see the preface written by Baridbaran Ghosh in Dutta, *Bharatvarshiya Upashak Sampraday*, vol. 1, pp. iii–vii. See also, H. H. Wilson, *Sketch of the Religious Sects of the Hindus* (Calcutta: Bishop's College Press, 1846).

71. As quoted in the preface by Baridbaran Ghosh in Dutta, *Bharatvarshiya Upashak Sampraday*, vol 1, pp. v–vi.

72. See ibid., p. vi.

73. For an account of such a random manner of composition, see Dutta, *Bharatvarshiya Upashak Sampraday*, vol. 2, pp. 313–314. Also, his trusted household help, Sriram, was formerly a pundit in a Bengali school, and would help Akshay read and write. A brief account of this may be found in Saradacharan Mitra, 'Akshaykumarke Jemon Dekhechhi', in *Dwisatajanmabarshe Akshaykumar Dutta*, ed. Tapas Bhowmik, *Korok Sahitya Patrika*, Kolkata, 2020, p. 267. Here Mitra claims that the *upakramanika* part of *Bharatvarshiya Upashak Sampraday* had been dictated by Akshay to Sriram. Incidentally, Saradacharan Mitra was an executor of Akshay's will, and had known him closely.

74. Dutta, *Bharatvarshiya Upashak Sampraday*, vol. 1, p. 1.

75. Ibid., p. 59.

76. Ibid., pp. 56–58.

77. Ibid., p. 79.

78. Ibid., pp. 103–112.

79. Ibid., p. 104.

80. Ibid., pp. 105–106.

81. Ibid., pp. 108–109.

82. Dutta, *Bharatvarshiya Upashak Sampraday*, vol. 2, p. 57.

83. Ibid.

84. See ibid., pp. 58–59.

85. Ibid., pp. 123–124.

86. Ibid., p. 65.

87. Ibid., p. 164.

88. Ibid., p. 168.

89. See ibid., pp. 153–157.

90. Ibid., p. 160.

91. Ibid.

92. Ibid., p. 161.

93. Ibid., pp. 166–167.

94. Ibid., p. 320.

95. Akshay is also quick to point out in the *upakramanika* of the second volume of *Bharatvarshiya Upashak Sampraday* that Emperor Akbar ordered translations of the *Ramayana*, the *Mahabharata*, the *Amarkosha*, the *Atharvaveda*, and possibly some Upanishads into Persian. His great grandchild had also, in 1657, ordered the translation of all Upanishads into Persian. See Dutta, *Bharatvarshiya Upashak Sampraday* vol. 2, p. 165.

Conclusion and Further Thoughts

It is inevitable, perhaps, as one winds up an article, a chapter, or a monograph, to reflect on the intention of the project. What it was that one had begun with, and what has after all been said. Also, the writing of history has this double-edged quality of betrayal. It is the continuous and keen sense of being haunted by what one is forgetting, or setting aside, or deliberately putting away as one 'remembers' through the act of writing. As I write the conclusion I also wonder how this book may have taken many directions, and how our ways of seeing are mostly inadequate to the task at hand.

The Science Worker and the Scientist

In what we may call the age of empire in the Indian subcontinent, the most significant methodological and epistemic changes within the polity germinated in the nineteenth century under the abiding and fraught influence of modernity. As a subject of history, therefore, the nineteenth century in India has attracted much attention from historians across the globe. There have been analyses of categories, epistemic shifts, significant cultural and political figures, and events that have shaped the trajectories of thinking about India as a pre-colonial, colonial, or post-colonial space, and these have had a significant influence on how the historian might begin to think of intellectual history of this period in the Indian subcontinent and its global implications, if at all. In his book *Horizons: A Global History of Science*, James Poskett recounts an event of some significance. It was in January 1897 that Jagadish Chandra Bose, as the first ever Indian scientist, was to deliver a talk on 'Electro-Magnetic Radiation' at the Royal Institution in London. Poskett writes:

> Well aware of the significance of the occasion, Bose concluded his lecture with an appeal to bridge the gap between European and Indian science. He expressed his sincere hope that 'at no distant time it shall neither be the West nor East, but both the East and the West, that will work together, each taking her share in extending the boundaries of knowledge, and bringing out the manifold blessings that follow in its train.' And with that, the audience rose to its feet in applause, eager to follow this enigmatic Indian physicist into the hidden world of electromagnetism.[1]

One is struck by the phrase 'each taking her share in extending the boundaries of knowledge' in Bose's speech. Speaking from within the machinations of colonial rule, Bose was imagining a more equal world of intellectual exchange and participation. It was an act of pushing the limits of 'knowledge' beyond the contours of power, beyond the discourses of colonial epistemic processes, and situating it in an open space of collaboration and mutual respect. Kris Manjapra has pointed out how figures such as Rabindranath Tagore and Jagadish Chandra Bose were opening up the world of knowledge exchange beyond the empire: 'Tagore's world travels as a Nobel Laureate and J C Bose's travels as a renowned physicist both helped claim a place for India in the world, outside the periphery of empire.'[2] It is through such hope in the powers of equality, collaboration, and connection, in the idea of intellectual exchange as a process that filters out the dynamics of inequalities, domination, or hegemony, that the idea of the 'global' is germinated. I would contend that there is a certain implicit naiveté within the idea of the global as well, where the historian and the scientist alike try to locate intellectual history within a space that overcomes, or has the possibility of overcoming, the ideas of state power or imperialism or racism or other forms of domination. It is this abiding faith in the powers of the intellectual process itself that I have tried to address in this book through the works of Akshay Dutta.

I hope to have been able to put my finger on the singular importance of Akshay Dutta as an intellectual in nineteenth-century Bengal in my arguments across this book. From within the closed recesses of a colonized space, Akshay becomes one of the notable examples of the commoner subject who emerged from the systematic discursive apparatus of knowledge production symptomatic of colonial modernity to look out towards the world. Not exactly the native elite, Akshay's intentions in foregrounding the importance of the vernacular, the necessity of basic science education, and rationalized spiritualism would have instilled hopes of emancipation in a section of the population who were barely even the 'small voices of history'.[3] The seeds of possibility that the likes of him had sowed in the middle years of the nineteenth century culminated in the hope that is reflected in the words of Jagadish Bose towards the end of the century. Another noted contemporary of Jagadish Bose, the scientist Prafulla Chandra Ray, begins the preface of his autobiography with a commensurate hope as Bose's:

> While a student at Edinburgh I found to my regret that every civilized country including Japan was adding to the world's stock of knowledge but that unhappy India was lagging behind. I dreamt a dream that, God willing, a time would come when she too would contribute her quota.[4]

As one of the pioneer scientists of modern India, this opening remark in his autobiography points towards not only a combination of faith and science in his individual discourse, but also the possibility of a global project of knowledge. The likes of Jagadish Bose and Prafulla Ray were brought up in a Calcutta whose intellectual and cultural milieu was shaped also by the likes of Akshay Dutta among other more illustrious personalities. Ray writes of the importance of the *Tattwabodhini Patrika* in the formative years of his life:

> Strange as it may appear, from my boyhood I was unconsciously drawn towards the Brahmo Samaj.... The *Tatwa Bodhini Patrika*, the organ of Adi Brahmo Samaj, adorned the shelves of my father's library. The writings and sermons of Debendranath Tagore, Keshab Chandra Sen, Rajnarain Basu, Ayodhyanath Pakrasi, and Akshay Kumar Datta and others imperceptibly prepared the groundwork of my faith.[5]

It was in the pages of the *Tattwabodhini Patrika* that Ray encountered the global debates on faith, religion, and the sciences. He recounts having read in the *Tattwabodhini* extracts from the writings of Francis William Newman and the correspondence between Frances Cobbe and Rajnarain Bose.[6] He was also introduced to the German school of Biblical criticism and *Life of Jesus* by David Friedrich Strauss in the pages of the *Tattwabodhini*.[7] Later on in his autobiography, Ray describes himself as 'a disciple of Epictetus, and admirer of Diogenes in the tub and of the Gymnosophists of the land of the five waters as described by Arrian and lately of Mahatma Gandhi in his loincloth, one whose motto in life has been plain living and high thinking....'[8] Put simply, all of this speaks of the eclecticism of the milieu and the discourse in which Ray discovered himself within a colonized space in the city of Calcutta in the second half of the nineteenth century.

The groundwork of faith that Ray refers to was often a combination of religion and science, uneasy bedfellows, but crucially instrumental in putting together a comprehensible, indigenous, and causal universe that would act as a shield against the almost teleological mechanism of the colonial epistemic force. It would not oppose, but stand guard, creating a narrative that was a combination of both native and foreign influences but inflected in a manner uniquely suited to the contingent moment in indigenous history. But one must understand that the imperceptible influences of such a shield would not begin in the laboratories of the Indian Association for the Cultivation of Science, or the classrooms of the Calcutta Medical College, or the corridors of the Hindu College. It would begin much earlier, through textbooks and exercises in the humble precincts of the vernacular school, and this is where figures such as Akshay Dutta have been crucial to this story. Ray recounts how 'Akshayakumar Datta was the first Bengali writer of note who enriched Bengali with translations from astronomy and natural philosophy'.[9] The likes of Akshay Dutta, Rajendralal Mitra, and Krishnamohan Banerjee were instrumental in shaping a Bengali scientific modernity that culled influences from across the globe but remained unique in its contingent indigeneity. It is due to their contributions that in later years, scientists such as Ray could infer with confidence that the 'period of borrowing and assimilation was naturally followed by the period of original productivity.... The impact of the West and the East has brought most striking results as far as the intellectual development of Bengal is concerned.'[10] But neither Akshay, nor Rajendralal, nor Krishnamohan was a scientist. Akshay, for example, only wrote textbooks for schools, or short tracts in the *Tattwabodhini Patrika*, or books such as *Bahyabastur Sahit Manabprakritir Sammandha Vichar* as a quasi-scientific moral tract that did not require specialist knowledge to understand. Neither was he a specialist himself, but merely, as I have called him, a science worker. As I was writing the second chapter of this book, I often wondered how this curious trajectory of the flowering of modern science education within the indigenous space of nineteenth-century Bengal and the individual narratives of such science workers, the barely remembered voices of reform, their influences and methods could be another fascinating story to explore.

Science and Religion: The Question of the Hindu Nation

There is another idea that I have only cursorily explored in these chapters – the notion of Hindu Bharatvarsha. In the context of Akshay Dutta and his *Bharatvarshiya Upashak Sampraday* and some of the works of Bhudeb Mukhopadhyay and Bankimchandra Chattopadhyay, among others, this had the potential to become a lengthy, fraught, and widely open discourse. The flow of my thoughts in this book prevented me from exploring this further. To go back once again to Prafulla Chandra Ray's autobiography, this is what he had to say about the time of his youth:

> There was ferment all around. A new world had been opened out; new aspirations were awakened. Roused from a period of stupor and stagnation young Bengal began to realise that there were immense possibilities in the Hindu nation.[11]

One needs to understand that this idea of the Hindu nation that Ray talks about here is one that is conceptually adhering more to the idea of society or *samaj* than polity.[12] The examples that immediately follow in Ray's autobiography make this amply clear: the flourishing of patriotic literature; political associations and newspapers that had an affective role and gave expression to people's 'feelings'; the opening of schools and colleges in the interior parts of Bengal, and the role of the middle class in this; the awareness of the need for science education; and so on. There is nothing overtly religious or Hindu about the demands that Ray is making of the nation space, but lamenting the indolence of a race that was once vigorously enterprising and intellectually motivated. The word 'Hindu', the reader would immediately understand, determined less a religious identity set apart from Islam or Christianity, but stood more for the people who were the inhabitants of 'Hindustan', or the geographical space that was not Europe. There is both an imperial and a global dynamic at work here. The sense is of the empire having stultified progress and intellect by using science education as merely an instrumentalist, basic, and profit-making project. On the other hand, the larger geographical space of Europe was expanding its horizons by newer inventions in science that the native subject was moving away from. One is immediately reminded of Akshay's lament in the *upakramanika* of the second volume of *Bharatvarshiya Upashak Sampraday*: 'Shei Hindu ekhon ei Hindu!' (That Hindu is now this Hindu!).[13] Like Akshay, as for Prafulla Ray, it was a question of the loss of both valour and values as a race or *jati* when 'the Hindu intellect lying dormant and fallow for ages, was overgrown with rank weeds and brambles'.[14] Clearly, there is a commonality in thinking about the Hindu *jati* if one traces the trajectory from Akshay and Bhudeb, through Bankim, to what one reads in the autobiography of one of the pioneer scientists of colonial Bengal, although I would say that Ray thinks more like Akshay and Bhudeb and less like Bankim.[15] One is tempted to explore, however, the relationship between science education, scientific progress, and its relevance to the questions of *jati* and *swadesh*, religious practice and rationalism, and how the baton was taken up from the science workers by practising scientists as opportunities for the native subject opened up. There are many studies on the subject of the development of native scientific practice in colonial and post-colonial India, but I am tempted to think of the not so tenuous link between the science worker and the scientist, and of the possible personal collaborations in terms of exchange of resources and ideas. In the third annual lecture in the memory of David Hare, Akshay was already proposing a roadmap for the native scientist:

> I wait with hope for that happy day when the people of Bharatvarsha equipped with their own intelligence and capability will build ships, bridges, steam engines and succeed in industrial development with the help of material produced indigenously.[16]

It was this hope that was beginning to be fulfilled by native scientists and engineers in the latter years of the nineteenth century. Akshay Dutta was reclusive, and by the time higher education in science was taking off in India towards the latter years of the nineteenth century, he was severely unwell. However, the possibilities of such collaborations would open newer ways of thinking about the common pursuit of the disinterested science worker writing textbooks and primers in the vernacular and the ambitious scientist working in the modern laboratory, or the geologist going on field trips, or the engineer and the medical practitioner working on their vocation, and thereby the framing of a native scientific ethos.

The *Samaj* or the Nation

Almost throughout my argument in this book, I have tried to focus on Akshay Dutta's interest in the *samaj*, roughly translated as the native community, and how his idea of indigenous geographical space was predicated less on polity and geographical boundaries and more on the relationship between the householder and his milieu. The notions of *karunya-swavab*, *lokahita*, and *paropakar* were central to Akshay's discourses on both education and the idea of a new or reformed Bharatvarsha. Likewise, he has spoken about *swaparibar swarup swadeshiya lok* (people from the same land are like one family) and *amader sakaler sadharan grihaswarup Bharatvarsha* (Bharatvarsha as the commonplace household for all of us).[17] In spite of the considerable influence and assimilation of European thought in much of Akshay's work, the concept of the nation as a singularly political space was never firmly situated in his discourse. His imagination of Bharatvarsha as a family and the geographical space as a receptacle (*adhar*)[18] or 'like a home' (*grihaswarup*)[19] was symptomatic of a kind of pre-modern indigeneity that set his vision significantly apart from the nationalist rhetoric of the latter half of the century. He describes the space of the nation as paradise-like (*bhuswarga swarup*), and a person who is away from his *swadesh* will remember it, Akshay writes, not as a geopolitical space, but as a space that is imagined in terms of his favourite river, or tree, or the space of celebration (*utsab bhumi*), or the land of his best friend, or the loving faces of dear ones at home (*nija-niketanastha murtimati pritiswarup manohar mukha-mandal*).[20] What one feels for one's land, Akshay says, is *premamay bhava* (a feeling of love),[21] emphatically undercutting the politics around the more utilitarian and functional conception of the nation-state. It is rather difficult to find, if at all, the word 'nation' (in terms of such inflections as *jatiya* or *rashtriya* or *jatiyatabad*, and so on, although it is not difficult to find such phrases as *Hindu jati*) in Akshay's writings. He would mostly use words such as *swadesh* or *matribhumi* or *Bharatbhumi*, although the word 'nation' was never unfamiliar to him from his reading of European texts as well as the works of some of his contemporaries.

Years later, fifteen years after Akshay's death, in 1901, we witness Rabindranath Tagore broaching the idea of the nation in his essay 'Prachya o Paschatya Sabhyata':

The word 'nation' does not exist in our language, nor in our country. It is only recently due to European education that we have been excessively indulgent to the importance of the national. But its ideals are not in our hearts. Our history, our *dharma*, our society, our homes, do not accept the importance of nation building. The place Europe assigns to freedom, we assign to liberty. We do not accept the greatness of any kind of freedom other than the freedom of the *atman*.[22]

Immediately following this, Rabindranath refers to the notion of the *brahmanistha grihastha*, the familiar Brahmo idea of the godly householder (a familiar trope in Akshay's writings), and insists that it is both more difficult and nobler to follow the ideals of such a householder than that of a nationalist.[23] Rabindranath argues about the intrinsic nature of 'Hindusavyata' (Hindu civilization),[24] something that is predicated not on the idea of the unity of this geographical space as a state, but on the inherent quality of the *samaj*. Towards the end of his essay Rabindranath writes:

> At the root of our Hindu civilization is the *samaj*, while at the root of European civilization is the principle of the state.... But if we believe that the European model of building a nation is the sole nature of civilization and the singular aim of humanity, then our understanding is at fault.[25]

Rabindranath's emphasis on the *samaj* as the driving force of identity for the people of Bharatvarsha is somewhat contrary to Christopher Bayly's argument that after the 1857 mutiny the 'experience of British invasion and of humiliation by the new breed of post-mutiny white expatriates created amongst the Indian elites a clearer sense of the need for political revival through the creation of a national community'.[26] Rabindranath was imagining a Bharatvarsha that was not commensurate with what Bayly has imagined as the homogeneous response of the Indian elite towards the need for a 'national' polity. Rabindranath was clearly rejecting the idea of the nation for the model of the *samaj* that is foregrounded throughout Akshay's works. He emphasizes how the idea of the political in Britain is predicated on the notion of monarchy. On the contrary, the idea of *desh* in Bharatvarsha is predicated on the idea of the *samaj*: 'That is why he have not done much for national freedom, but fervently guarded our social independence (*samajik swadhinata*).'[27] Rabindranath calls it *samajlakshmi*[28] and declares, 'I believe in *swadesh*, I respect *atmashakti*.'[29] The reader will remember that when Akshay was speaking of the idea of *samanjasya* or coordination between the various qualities of the human subject, his model of responsibility began with the self and moved through the world towards the *parameshwar*.[30] In a similar vein Rabindranath writes: 'The Hindu dharma has laid down the path for everyone to move beyond one's home and community to participate in the feelings of the world,' and this would lead to the well-being (*mangal*) of the world.[31] In fact, it is quite possible that Rabindranath had read Akshay's *Bharatvarshiya Upashak Sampraday*, as soon after he refers to the eclecticism and *samanjasya* between such minor religious sects as the Nanakpanthis, the Kabirpanthis, and the lower rungs of the Vaishnavas, all of whom are discussed in Akshay's book.[32] I deliberately draw this connection between Akshay Dutta and Rabindranath Tagore to emphasize how the great cultural and political upheaval of the latter years of the nineteenth century and the early years of the twentieth that led to the quick and almost meteoric rise of nationalist tendencies in their many forms was not able to foreclose a dialogue that was still being opened up on the fringes of the colonial space. It was the clearing of a space for an alternative narrative of self-representation, that of the *samaj* and not the nation. In most of my arguments throughout the chapters in this book, I have tried to foreground this necessary characteristic of Akshay's works. Of course he was not unique or singular in thinking of the representation of the native people in terms of the *samaj* or community. What I am arguing is that there has been a dogged consistency throughout Akshay's oeuvre in his insistence on the importance of the *samaj* as an antidote to colonial epistemic violence, from the middle years of the nineteenth century till his last work, and this needs to be noted. There is little doubt that Akshay was profoundly influenced by European thinkers, by enlightenment rationalism, by the idea of scientific progress. In his own way, he was a facilitator for the spread of such thoughts. But that does not necessarily consolidate a corollary that Akshay subscribed to the novel framework of nationalism. The politics in Akshay's writings, if one has to unpack it, has to be understood in terms of the inherent heuristic pattern that was an intrinsic part of it. His influences made him think about frameworks, but his lack of formal training also gave him a natural freedom to go beyond. As I have shown in the last two chapters, his search for a representative narrative for Bharatvarsha extended its search towards eclectic forms of engagement with the discipline of history, while being firmly rooted to the need for an essential connection with the *samaj* around him. By referring to Rabindranath, I am suggesting the continuation of this dialogue, of this notion of identity as a *samaj* rather than a nation that was necessary in the early years of the twentieth century as well, and how this narrative was perhaps also useful during the rebellion against the division of Bengal around 1905. Swarupa Gupta has thrown considerable light on the idea of the *samaj* in her book *Notions of Nationhood*,[33] but there still remains the possibility of a close reading of texts and textual practice from the middle of the nineteenth century till the second decade of the twentieth to understand the ways in which this dialogue continued vis-à-vis the idea of India as a nation. In my close reading of some of the texts of Akshay Dutta in this book, I have tried to highlight this peculiar and significant foregrounding of the indigenous community as a unit, however tentative, of the idea of both unity and resistance on the one hand and the immense possibility of global assimilation on the other. In Akshay's works there is no cancelling out of Europe or the rest of the world. There is only the continuous and conscious reminder of a well-formed and existing polity that need not be side-stepped as one welcomes global engagement.

Is Akshay Dutta a Figure in Global History?

I am asking this question for the second time in this book. The first time I asked this question was in the third chapter, when I introduced the framework of global intellectual history into my argument. As I have tried to closely read some of Akshay's works, written about his engagement with modes and processes of historical and cultural development in nineteenth-century Bengal, and tried to understand the breadth of his debt to both foreign and native influences, this question has only become more complex and somewhat uncertain. In many cases, a book does not give its author a closure, and this has been one for me. The range of the global, global history, or global intellectual history is wide enough, and open enough, to accommodate a whole gamut of overtures and strategies of representation, resistance, or difference. As I have shown in my arguments, Akshay both addresses and fits into the notion of the global comfortably in terms of some of his ideological strategies and his location within a certain narrative of contemporary intellectual practice. In the third chapter I have examined, using the model put forward by Samuel Moyn and Andrew Sartori in *Global Intellectual History*, how Akshay was in a sense acting as both an object and agent of history.[34] By all means, it is possible to raise the questions whether what Akshay was writing was history at all, or whether such history could be accommodated within the disciplinary practices of modelling colonial or post-colonial forms of historiography.

These are valid questions, and I have tried to address them in this book. What is crucial however is that the synthetic nature of global history ('the call for global history comes as a call for inclusiveness, for a broader vision')[35] has opened up the necessary wherewithal with which to make claims for Akshay as a historian. In the words of Sebastian Conrad, the 'ascendancy of modern historical scholarship ... was the work of many authors around the world, responding to their various needs and interests. Historical knowledge changed in response to an increasingly integrated world'.[36] Quite specifically, Akshay had his own ideology and interest. However we choose to see global history – as an 'all-in' version, or as connections and entanglements, or as a form of global integration – it is possible to fit Akshay's ideas into the system.[37] What Akshay brings into the fold of global history is his ability to constantly push the limits of the historical towards the possibility of questioning the authenticity or rigidity of its epistemic boundaries. It is easy to mark the European tendencies in Akshay's writings, to mention by name his ideological influences and mentors. Yet the process through which Akshay culled his thoughts together into a narrative had its heuristic principles that went beyond disciplinary boundaries. I would contend that if one were to carefully unpack the strategic mores in Akshay's writings, it would seem that he was advocating or foregrounding a global history of the Bengali *samaj* as a contrapuntal move against the continuous and epistemic pressures of a narrative of the national. For Akshay, the *samaj* would provide a fluid yet formal framework of writing about the past, present, and future. That such a move was effective is evident from the fact that Rabindranath picks up this strand and posits it directly against the national in his writings a few years later. Akshay's idea of the *samaj* is both more inclusive (therefore global) and set apart from the idea of the national. *Swadesh* for him was a set of common values of assimilation, engagement, and connections, with a view towards a rational understanding of the universe and in praise of the *parameshwar*. It was an open space where the past commingled with the present, the foreign with the indigenous, in order that an emancipated, modern polity would emerge in the form of a more equal and inclusive *samaj* free of superstitions and dogma, and exposed to scientific developments across the world. Akshay was clearly writing about his own space, Bharatvarsha, with an awareness of global movements. As Conrad puts it, global history 'is often more a matter of writing a history of demarcated (i.e., non-"global") spaces, but with an awareness of global connections and structural conditions'.[38] It can perhaps be argued that the idea of Bharatvarsha in Akshay's writings was less a geographical space and more ideational or emotive in its intent, a hermeneutic and evolving idea of unity or togetherness. This same sentiment can be discerned in Rabindranath a few decades later. In his essay 'Purba o Paschim' published in 1908, he talks about the idea of a 'MahaBharatvarsha' and immediately evokes Rammohun Roy as a pioneer of such effort: 'In the present times some of the most revered figures of our country have dedicated their lives towards the assimilation of the west and the east. One example is Rammohun Roy. Once he stood alone to unite Bharatvarsha with the world on the basis of humanity.'[39] Does this not remind us immediately of Akshay's celebration of Rammohun as a figure for a new and emergent Bharatvarsha, and of the world, multiple times in his work? From the period of his days as the editor of the *Tattwabodhini Patrika* till his last work, *Bharatvarshiya Upashak Sampraday*, Akshay has posited Rammohun as an intellectual for the world. In the *upakramanika* of the second volume of the *Bharatvarshiya Upasak Sampraday* Akshay writes about Rammohun, 'You are beyond your time. Why only time? You are beyond your country,'[40] and he discusses the impact of Rammohun as an intellectual across the globe. It is interesting to note what Rabindranath writes about Rammohun later in his essay:

> The main reason why Rammohun Roy could assimilate the spirit of the west was because the west did not overwhelm him; there was no weakness on his part. He stood on the grounds of his foundation and collected objects from the outside. He was not unaware of where the richness of Bharatvarsha was, and he had made that his own; thus he had the wherewithal to judge all that he had collected from other places; he did not lose his sense of judgment and struck with wonder collect everything from the outside.[41]

One wonders if these words were not true of Akshay Dutta as well, his ardent admirer. Rammohun had travelled the world; Akshay had never left his native soil. Yet there was in him a capacity to imagine the global. It would be a wonderful enterprise to trace the patterns of the global in the *janasamaj* from the middle of the nineteenth till well into the twentieth century in Bengal, and examine if an imagining of a 'global *samaj*' was more intrinsic to the spirit of Bharatvarsha than imagining the 'national'.

Finally, I hope to have created some space for Akshay Dutta within the larger templates of engagement with the figures of nineteenth-century Bengal. I have felt the need to see him as an important presence in situating the enterprise of indigenous modernity within the global map. As Sebastian Conrad has argued, it was inevitable that the rest of the world would engage with European cosmologies while trying to discover ways of interpreting their pasts because of the multiple modes of domination of the world that was engendered by Europe. I agree with Conrad in his contention that '[h]istorians increasingly took their cue from historical narratives grounded in the nineteenth-century ascendancy of a liberal world order and were predicated on the nation as the driving force of history and on a general notion of "modernization"'.[42] Only that I have slightly differed in my arguments in this book. I have tried to examine if the replacement of the word 'nation' by the word *samaj*, particularly in the works of Akshay Dutta, could engender the possibility of opening up the space of representation towards a more global, ecumenical, and therefore a less derivative form of attempting to write the history of a time, a space, and a people. As I emphasize, Akshay was not unique in his claim, but he was an important voice who needs to be heard and written about as part of the larger enterprise of talking about Bengal in the nineteenth century.

Notes

1. James Poskett, *Horizons: A Global History of Science* (New Delhi: Viking, 2022), p. 238.
2. Kris Manjapra, 'Knowledgeable Internationalism and the Swadeshi Movement, 1903–1921', *Economic and Political Weekly* 47, no. 42 (20 October 2012): 59.
3. As I have discussed earlier in this book, I borrow this phrase from Ranajit Guha. See Ranajit Guha, *The Small Voice of History: Collected Essays*, ed. Partha Chatterjee (New Delhi: Permanent Black, 2002).
4. Prafulla Chandra Ray, *Life and Experiences of a Bengali Chemist*, vol. 1 (Calcutta: The Asiatic Society, 1932/1996), p. v.
5. Ibid., p. 30.
6. Ibid.
7. Ibid.
8. Ibid., pp. 55–56.
9. Ibid., p. 146.
10. Ibid. The important influence of Swadeshi internationalism and the consequent opening up of a political geography quite independent of

colonial knowledge production also needs to be accounted for here. The significant links with the world beyond the colony, particularly the collaborative endeavours with Germany and Japan, were also significant pointers towards the building up of an anti-colonial *nationalism* that went beyond the fluidity of the principles of an indigenous *samaj*. The likes of Prasanta Chandra Mahalanobis or Meghnad Saha to whom the like of Prafulla Chandra Ray passed on the baton were in a way the product of a nation-building process that was initiated by the mechanism of Swadeshi internationalism. For a more detailed perspective on this, see Manjapra, 'Knowledgeable Internationalism and the Swadeshi Movement, 1903–1921', pp. 53–62.

11. Ibid., p. 147.

12. As Prathama Banerjee has recently argued:

> Modernity arrived in the colony via colonial conquest. To placate this experience of political humiliation, colonial intellectuals began claiming that the nation's true history lay not in the vagaries of politics but in the deep continuities of *samaj* or native society. The national self was a deeply social self, unperturbed by surface ripples like foreign invasion and regime change.

See Prathama Banerjee, *Elementary Aspects of the Political: Histories from the Global South* (Durham and London: Duke University Press, 2020).

13. Akshay Dutta, *Bharatvarshiya Upashak Sampraday*, vol. 2 (Kolkata: Karuna Prakashani, 1883/2013), pp. 153–157.

14. Ray, *Life and Experiences of a Bengali Chemist*, vol. 1, p. 147.

15. It is interesting to discover that Prafulla Chandra Ray's autobiography does not mention Bankimchandra at all. Also, for an informed discussion on the differing views of Bankim and Bhudeb regarding Hinduism and Islam, see Amiya P. Sen, *Hindu Revivalism in Bengal, 1872–1905: Some Essays in Interpretation* (New Delhi: Oxford University Press, 1993), pp. 83–128.

16. Akshay Dutta, 'Hare Saheber Nam Swaranartha Tritiya Sambatsarik Sabhar Baktrita', in *Akshaykumar Dutta Rachana Sangraha*, vol. 1, ed. Swapan Basu (Calcutta: Pashchimbanga Bangla Academy, 2008), p. 111.

17. See Akshay Dutta's brief essay 'Janma-bhumi', in *Akshaykumar Dutta Rachana Sangraha*, vol. 1, ed. Swapan Basu (Calcutta: Pashchimbanga Bangla Academy, 2008), p. 351.

18. Ibid.

19. Ibid.

20. Ibid.

21. Ibid.

22. Rabindranath Tagore, 'Prachya o Paschatya Sabhyata', in *Sangkalan* (Calcutta: Visvabharati Granthanvibhag, 2000), p. 44. I have deliberately kept the word *dharma* untranslated. The immediately obvious English translation, 'religion', will not capture the wider meaning that Tagore has intended here.

23. Ibid.

24. Ibid.

25. Ibid., p. 45.

26. Christopher Bayly, *The Birth of the Modern World, 1780–1914: Global Connections and Comparisons* (Oxford: Blackwell Publishing, 2004), p. 217.

27. Rabindranath Tagore, 'Swadeshi Samaj', in *Sangkalan* (Calcutta: Visvabharati Granthanvibhag, 2000), p. 56.

28. Ibid., p. 57.

29. Ibid., p. 60.

30. Akshay Dutta, *Bahyabastur Sahit Manabprakritir Sammandha Vichar*, in *Akshaykumar Dutta Rachana Sangraha*, vol. 1, ed. Swapan Basu (Kolkata: Paschimbanga Bangla Academy, 2008), p. 158.

31. Tagore, 'Swadeshi Samaj', p. 61. One is immediately reminded of Akshay's emphasis on the idea of *aihik paratrik mangal*.

32. Ibid., p. 64.

33. Swarupa Gupta, *Notions of Nationhood in Bengal: Perspectives on Samaj, c. 1867–1905* (Leiden and Boston: Brill, 2009).

34. Samuel Moyn and Andrew Sartori (eds), *Global Intellectual History* (New York: Columbia University Press, 2013), p. 5.

35. Sebastian Conrad, *What Is Global History?* (Princeton, NJ: Princeton University Press, 2016), p. 5.

36. Ibid., p. 28.

37. For the various versions of global history, see Sebastian Conrad, *What Is Global History?* (Princeton, NJ: Princeton University Press, 2016), pp. 6–11.

38. Conrad, *What Is Global History?*, p. 12.

39. Rabindranath Tagore, 'Purba o Paschim', in *Sangkalan* (Calcutta: Visvabharati Granthanvibhag, 2000), pp. 75–76.

40. Dutta, *Bharatvarshiya Upashak Sampraday*, vol. 2, p. 36.

41. Tagore, 'Purba o Paschim', pp. 78–79.

42. Conrad, *What Is Global History?*, p. 25.

Bibliography

Primary Sources

Chattopadhyay, Bankimchandra. *Bankim Rachanabali*. Edited by R. Jogeshchandra Bagal. Vol. 1. Calcutta: Sahitya Samsad, 1953.

———. *Bankim Rachanabali*. Edited by Jogeshchandra Bagal. Vol. 2. Calcutta: Sahitya Samsad, 1954.

———. *Muchiram Gurer Jibancharit*. Edited by Brajendranath Bandopadhyay and Sajanikanta Das. Calcutta: Bangiya Sahitya Parishad. First published 1884.

Dutta, Akshay K. *Bahyavastur Sahit Manub Prakritir Sammandha Vichar*, vols. 1–2. In *Akshaykumar Dutta Rachana Sangraha*, edited by Swapan Basu, vol. 1, pp. 113–316. Kolkata: Paschimbanga Bangla Academy, 2008.

———. 'Bartaman Byabahar'. *Tattwabodhini Patrika* 3, no. 73 (1849): 83–85. https://fid4sa-repository.ub.uni-heidelberg.de/1300/ (accessed on 22 September 2021).

———. 'Bharatvarsher Sahit Onanyo Desher Purbakalin Banijya Bibaran'. Part 1. *Tattwabodhini Patrika* 3, no. 78 (1849): 153–166. https://fid4sa-repository.ub.uni-heidelberg.de/1300/ (accessed on 3 February 2022).

———. 'Bharatvarsher Sahit Onanyo Desher Purbakalin Banijya Bibaran'. Part 2. *Tattwabodhini Patrika* 4, no. 85 (1850): 68–76. https://fid4sa-repository.ub.uni-heidelberg.de/1317/ (accessed on 3 February 2022).

———. *Bharatvarshiya Upashak Sampraday*. Vol. 1. Kolkata : Karuna Prakashani, 2015. First published 1870 (Calcutta).

———. *Bharatvarshiya Upashak Sampraday*. Vol. 2. Kolkata : Karuna Prakashani, 2013. First published 1883 (Calcutta).

———. 'Brahmo Samajer Baktrita'. *Tattwabodhini Patrika* 2, no. 17 (1844): 135–137. https://fid4sa-repository.ub.uni-heidelberg.de/1271/ (accessed on 14 March 2021).

———. *Charupath*, vols. 1–3. In *Akshaykumar Dutta Rachana Sangraha*, edited by Swapan Basu, vol. 1, pp. 317–384. Kolkata: Paschimbanga Bangla Academy, 2008.

———. *Dharmaniti*. In *Akshaykumar Dutta Rachana Sangraha*, edited by Swapan Basu, vol. 1, pp. 431–528. Kolkata: Paschimbanga Bangla Academy, 2008.

———. 'Editorial'. *Tattwabodhini Patrika* 1, no. 4 (1843): 25–28. https://fid4sa-repository.ub.uni-heidelberg.de/1250/ (accessed on 12 January 2022).

———. 'Editorial'. *Tattwabodhini Patrika* 2, no. 13 (1844): 97–98. https://fid4sa-repository.ub.uni-heidelberg.de/1271/ (accessed on 9 June 2021).

———. 'The First Yearly Lecture of the Brahmo Samaj'. *Tattwabodhini Patrika* 1, no. 103 (1851): 146–150. https://fid4sa-repository.ub.uni-heidelberg.de/1266/ (accessed on 31 August 2022).

———. 'Hindukalejer Siksha Pranali'. *Tattwabodhini Patrika* 4, no. 86, Ashwin, 1772 Saka (1850): 92–99. https://fid4sa-repository.ub.uni-heidelberg.de/1317/ (accessed on 25 May 2021).

———. 'Kalikatar Bartaman Durabastha'. *Tattwabodhini Patrika* 4, no. 36 (1846): 309–315. https://fid4sa-repository.ub.uni-heidelberg.de/1308/ (accessed on 15 June 2021).

———. 'Nitijnan'. *Tattwabodhini Patrika* 2, no. 17 (1844): 138–139. https://fid4sa-repository.ub.uni-heidelberg.de/1271/ (accessed on 4 December 2021).

———. 'Pandosh'. *Tattwabodhini Patrika* 4, no. 84 (1850): 55–59. https://fid4sa-repository.ub.uni-heidelberg.de/1317/ (accessed on 20 February 2022).

———. 'Palligramastha Prajader Durabastha'. *Tattwabodhini Patrika* 4, no. 81 (1850): 5–12. https://fid4sa-repository.ub.uni-heidelberg.de/1317/ (accessed on 17 October 2020).

———. 'Palligramastha Prajader Durabastha'. *Tattwabodhini Patrika* 4, no. 84 (1850): 49–55. https://fid4sa-repository.ub.uni-heidelberg.de/1317/ (accessed on 17 October 2020).

———. 'Palligramastha Prajader Durabastha'. *Tattwabodhini Patrika* 4, no. 88 (1850): 115–121. https://fid4sa-repository.ub.uni-heidelberg.de/1317/ (accessed on 17 October 2020).

———. 'Prachin Hindudiger Samudra Jatra'. *Tattwabodhini Patrika* 3, no. 71 (1849): 44–48. https://fid4sa-repository.ub.uni-heidelberg.de/1300/ (accessed on 31 March 2021).

————. *Prachin Hindudiger Samudrajatra o Banijyabistar* or *Sea Voyage and Commerce of the Ancient Hindus*. Edited by Rajaninath Dutta. Calcutta: Sanskrit Press Depository, 1901.

————. 'Surapan'. *Tattwabodhini Patrika* 2, no. 111 (1852) : 73–75. https://fid4sa-repository.ub.uni-heidelberg.de/1284/ (accessed on 7 April 2021).

————. 'Swadeshiya Bhasay Bidyabhash'. *Tattwabodhini Patrika* 3, no. 69 (1849): 1–4, https://fid4sa-repository.ub.uni-heidelberg.de/1300/ (accessed on 19 November 2020).

————. 'Upashak Sampradaya: Shibnarayani'. *Tattwabodhini Patrika* 2, no. 112 (1852): 89–93. https://fid4sa-repository.ub.uni-heidelberg.de/1284/ (accessed on 28 January 2021).

————. 'Vaishnava Sampraday'. *Tattwabodhini Patrika* 3, no. 69 (1849): 9–12, https://fid4sa-repository.ub.uni-heidelberg.de/1300/ (accessed on 25 February 2022).

Tagore, Kshitindranath. 'Brahmodharmabijer Abhibyakti'. *Tattwabodhini Patrika* 3, Kalpa 19 (1913): 24–27. https://fid4sa repository.ub.uni-heidelberg. de/1299/ (accessed on 29 May 2021).

Mukhopadhyay, Bhudeb. *Swapnalabdha Bharatvarsher Itihas*. Hooghly: Published by Kashinath Bhattacharya, 1895.

————. *Prabandha Samagra*. Edited by Manaswita Sanyal and Ranjan Bandopadhyay. Kolkata: Charchapad, 2010.

Roy, Rammohun. *The Precepts of Jesus: The Guide to Peace and Happiness, Extracted from the Books of the New Testament Ascribed to the Four Evangelists. With translations into Sanskrit and Bengali*. Calcutta: Baptist Mission Press, 1820.

————. *A Second Defence of the Monotheistical System of the Veds: In Reply to An Apology for the Present State of Hindoo Worship*. Calcutta: n.p., 1817.

————. *Translation of the Céna Upanishad: One of the Chapters of the Sáma Véda; According to the Gloss of the Celebrated Shancaráchárya: Establishing the Unity and the Sole Omnipotence of the Supreme Being: and that He Alone is the Object of Worship*. Calcutta: Hindoostanee Press, 1816.

————. *Translation of an Abridgment of the Vedant, Or Resolution of All the Veds; the Most Celebrated and Revered Work of Brahminical Theology; Establishing the Unity of the Supreme Being; and that He Alone is the Object of Propitiation and Worship*. Calcutta: Publisher not mentioned, 1816.

————. *Tuhfatul Muwahhiddin or a Gift to Deists*. Edited by Maulvi Obaidullah El Obaide. Calcutta: Adi Brahmo Samaj, 1889.

Secondary Sources

Agathocleous, Tanya. *Disaffected: Emotion, Sedition, and Colonial Law in the Anglosphere*. Ithaca: Cornell University Press, 2021.

Apter, Emily. *The Translation Zone: A New Comparative Literature*. Princeton: Princeton University Press, 2006.

Aquil, Raziuddin and Partha Chatterjee, eds. *History in the Vernacular*. Ranikhet: Permanent Black, 2012.

Arnold, David. *Science, Technology and Medicine in Colonial India*. The New Cambridge History of India, vol. 3. Cambridge: Cambridge University Press, 2002.

Arnold, Matthew. *Culture and Anarchy*. London: Smith, Elder & Co., 1869. Reprinted with an introduction and notes by Jane Garnett. New York: Oxford University Press, 2006.

Asif, Manan Ahmed. *The Loss of Hindustan: The Invention of India*. Cambridge, MA: Harvard University Press, 2020.

Aurobindo, Sri. *Isha Upanishad. The Complete Works of Sri Aurobindo*. Vol. 17. Pondicherry: Sri Aurobindo Ashram Press, 2003.

Bagal, Jogesh Chandra. *Hindu Melar Itibritta*. Calcutta: Maitri, 1968.

Bandopadhyay, Bhabanicharan. *Kalikata Kamalalaya*. Calcutta: Ranjan Publishing House, 1936. First published 1823.

———. *Naba Babu Bilas*. Calcutta: Subarnarekha, 1979. First published 1825.

Bandopadhyay, Tarinicharan. *Bharatbarsher Itihas*. Vol. 1. Calcutta: Sanskrit Press Depository, 1858.

Banerjee, Milinda. '"All This Is Indeed Brahman": Rammohun Roy and a "Global" History of the Rights-Bearing Self'. *Asian Review of World Histories* 3, no. 1 (2015): 81–112. https://doi.org/10.12773/arwh.2015.3.1.081.

Banerjee, Prathama. *Elementary Aspects of the Political: Histories from the Global South*. Durham: Duke University Press, 2021.

Banerjee, Sumanta. *The Parlour and the Streets: Elite and Popular Culture in Nineteenth Century Calcutta*. Calcutta: Seagull Books, 1998.

Barua, Subrata. 'Akshaykumar Datter Bijnanmanaskata'. In *Dwisatajanmabarshe Akshaykumar Dutta*, edited by Tapas Bhowmik, *Korok Sahitya Patrika*, January–April 2020, pp. 67–71.

Basalla, George. 'The Spread of Western Science'. *Science* 156, no. 3775 (1967): 611–622. DOI: 10.1126/science.156.3775.611.

Bastin, John. 'Sir Stamford Ruffles and John Crawfurd's Idea of Colonizing the Malay Archipelago'. *Journal of the Malayan Branch of the Royal Asiatic Society* 26, no. 1 (1953): 81–85.

Basu, Nagendranath. *Biswakosh*. Vol. 5. Calcutta: Biswakosh Karyalay, 1894.

Basu, Rajnarayan. *Sekal ar Ekal*. Calcutta: Alokananda Publishers, 2012. First published 1874 by Kalikinkar Chakrabarty.

Bayly, Christopher A. *The Birth of the Modern World, 1780–1914: Global Connections and Comparisons*. Oxford: Blackwell Publishing, 2004.

Bhabha, Homi K. *The Location of Culture*. London: Routledge, 1994.

Bhattacharya, Asitkumar. *Akshaykumar Dutta Ebong Unish Sataker Banglay Dharma o Samajchinta*. Kolkata: K. P. Bagchi and Co, 2007.

Bhattacharya, Buddhadeb. *Bangasahitye Bijnan*. Calcutta: Bangiya Bijnan Parishad, 1960.

Bhattacharya, Rameshwar. *Shibayan*. Calcutta: Sutabihari Ray, 1903.

Bhattacharya, Ramkrishna. 'Rammohun Roy as Translator of the Upanishads'. 2006. https://www.researchgate.net/publication/308777209 (accessed on 22 August 2020).

———. 'Rationalism in Bengal: An Overview'. *Psyche and Society* 10, no. 1 (2012): 43–51.

Bhattacharya, Tithi. *The Sentinels of Culture: Class, Education, and the Colonial Intellectual in Bengal (1848–85)*. New Delhi: Oxford University Press, 2005.

Bhowmik, Dwijendra, ed. *Akshaykumar o Vidyasagar*. *Swarantar*. Kolkata: n.p., 2021.

Biswas, Nakurchandra. *Akshay-Charit or An Illustrated Life of the Late Babu Akshay Kumar Dutta*. Calcutta: Adi Brahmosamaj Press, 1891.

Bose, P. N. and H. W. B. Moreno. *A Hundred Years of the Bengali Press: Being a History of the Bengali Newspapers from Their Inception to the Present Day*. Calcutta: The Central Press, 1920.

Bruck, Mary T. 'Mary Somerville, Mathematician and Astronomer of Underused Talents'. *Journal of the British Astronomical Association* 106, no. 4 (1996): 201–206.

Carey, Felix. *Bidyaharabali. Orthat Europiya Sarbbagrahya Tabat Ayurvedshilpabidyadi Mulgranthaabali*. Calcutta: Calcutta School Book Society, 1819.

Chakrabarti, Sumit. *The Calcutta Kerani and the London Clerk in the Nineteenth Century: Life, Labour, Latitude*. London: Routledge, 2021.

Chakrabarty, Dipesh. *Provincializing Europe: Postcolonial Thought and Historical Difference*. Princeton, NJ: Princeton University Press, 2000.

Chatterjee, Partha. *Nationalist Thought and the Colonial World: A Derivative Discourse*. London: Zed Books, 1986.

———. *The Nation and Its Fragments: Colonial and Postcolonial Histories*. Princeton, NJ: Princeton University Press, 1993.

———. *Our Modernity*. Rotterdam: SEPHIS, 1997.

Chatterji, Joya. *Bengal Divided: Hindu Communalism and Partition, 1932–1947*. Cambridge: Cambridge University Press, 1994/2002.

Christian Ministers of Various Denominations, ed. *The Calcutta Christian Observer*. Vol. III. January–December 1834. Calcutta: The Baptist Mission Press, 1834.

Colebrooke, Henry T. *Miscellaneous Essays*. Vols. 1 and 2. London: W. H. Allen and Co, 1837.

Collet, Sophia Dobson. *The Life and Letters of Raja Rammohun Roy*. Edited by Hem Chandra Sarkar. Calcutta: A. C. Sarkar, 1914.

Combe, George. *The Constitution of Man Considered in Relation to External Objects*. Cambridge: Cambridge University Press, 2009. First published 1828 by John Anderson jun (Edinburgh).

———. *On the Relation Between Science and Religion*. Cambridge: Cambridge University Press, 2009. First published 1857 by Maclachlan and Stewart (Edinburgh).

Comte, Auguste. *A General View of Positivism*. Cambridge: Cambridge University Press, 2009. First published 1865 by Trübner and Co (London).

Connolly, Peter, ed. *Perspectives on Indian Religion: Papers in Honour of Karel Werner*. Delhi: Sri Satguru, 1986.

Cooper, Frederick. *Colonialism in Question: Theory, Knowledge, History*. Berkeley: University of California Press, 2005.

Conrad, Sebastian. *What Is Global History?* Princeton: Princeton University Press, 2016.

Drayton, Richard. 'Science, Medicine, and the British Empire'. In *Historiography*, edited by Robin W. Winks, pp. 264–276. Vol. 5 of *The Oxford History of the British Empire*. New York: Oxford University Press, 1999.

Ghosh, Anindita. *Power in Print: Popular Publishing and the Politics of Language and Culture in a Colonial Society, 1778–1905*. New Delhi: Oxford University Press, 2006.

Ghosh, Benoy. *Samayikpatre Banglar Samajchitra: Tattwabodhini Patrika*. Vol. 4. 1963. Reprint, Kolkata: Prakash Bhavan, 2016.

Ghosh, Tapobrata. *Je Bhabe Bankim Pori*. Kolkata: Tobu, 2014.

Guha, Ranajit. *Daya: Rammohon Ray o Amader Adhunikata*. Kolkata: Talpata, 2012.

———. *Dominance Without Hegemony: History and Power in Colonial India*. Cambridge, MA: Harvard University Press, 1997.

———. *An Indian Historiography of India: A Nineteenth-Century Agenda and Its Implications*. Calcutta: K. P. Bagchi, 1988.

———. *The Small Voice of History: Collected Essays*. Edited by Partha Chatterjee. New Delhi: Permanent Black, 2002.

Gupta, Abhijit. 'The Calcutta School-Book Society and the Production of Knowledge'. *English Studies in Africa* 57, no. 1 (2014): 55–65.

———. 'Popular Printing and Intellectual Property in Colonial Bengal'. *Thesis Eleven* 113, no. 1 (2012): 32–44.

Gupta, Swarupa. *Notions of Nationhood in Bengal: Perspectives on Samaj c.1867–1905*. Leiden: Brill, 2009.

Harle, John. *Ganitanka: Harley's Arithmetic For the Use of Bengalee Schools*. Chinsurah: School Press, 1819.

Hatcher, Brian. *Bourgeois Hinduism, or the Faith of the Modern Vedantists: Rare Discourses from Early Colonial Bengal*. New York: Oxford University Press, 2008.

———. 'Bourgeois Vedanta: The Colonial Roots of Middle-Class Hinduism'. *Journal of the American Academy of Religion* 75, no. 2 (2007): 298–323.

———. *Eclecticism and Modern Hindu Discourse*. New York: Oxford University Press, 1999.

———. *Hinduism Before Reform*. Cambridge, MA: Harvard University Press, 2020.

———. *Idioms of Improvement: Vidyasagar and Cultural Encounter in Bengal*. New Delhi: Oxford University Press, 1996.

———. *Vidyasagar: The Life and After-life of an Eminent Indian*. New Delhi: Routledge, 2014.

Heeren, Arnold H. L. *Historical Researches into the Politics, Intercourse, and Trade of the Principal Nations of Antiquity*. Vol. 1. Delhi: Daya Publishing House, 1985. First printed 1846 by Henry G. Bohn.

Howell, Arthur. *Education in British India, prior to 1854, and in 1870–71*. Calcutta: Office of the Superintendent of Government Printing, 1872.

Indramitra [pseud.]. *Karunasagar Vidyasagar*. Kolkata: Ananda Publishers, 2014.

Jagadananda, Swami, ed. *Gita*. Translated by Swami Jagadiswarananda. Calcutta: Udbodhan Karyalaya, 1961.

Jagadiswarananda, Swami, ed. and trans. *Sri Sri Chandi*. Calcutta: Udbodhan Karyalaya, 1962.

Jha, Saktinath. *Phakir Lalon Sai: Desh Kaal Ebong Shilpa*. Kolkata: Sambad, 1995.

Kant, Immanuel. 'An Answer to the Question: What Is Enlightenment?' In *What Is Enlightenment? Eighteenth-Century Answers and Twentieth-Century Questions*, edited by James Schmidt, pp. 58–64. California: University of California Press, 1996.

Kaviraj, Sudipta. *The Unhappy Consciousness: Bankimchandra Chattopadhyay and the Formation of Nationalist Discourse in India*. Delhi: Oxford University Press, 1995.

Kling, Blair B. *Partner in Empire: Dwarkanath Tagore and the Age of Enterprise in Eastern India*. Berkeley: University of California Press, 1976.

Kopf, David. *The Brahmo Samaj and the Shaping of the Modern Indian Mind*. Princeton, NJ: Princeton University Press, 1979.

Kumar, Deepak. *Science and the Raj: A Study of British India*. 2nd ed. New Delhi: Oxford University Press, 2006

Lahiri, Ashish. *Akshaykumar Dutta: Andhar Rate Ekla Pathik*. 2nd ed. Kolkata: Dey's Publishing, 2019.

Lawson, John. *Pasvabali*. Calcutta: Calcutta School Book Society, 1828.

Lushington, Charles. *The History, Design and Present State of the Religious, Benevolent and Charitable Institutions Founded by the British in Calcutta and Its Vicinity*. Calcutta: Hindostanee Press, 1824.

Mack, John. *Principles of Chemistry, Kimiya Vidyar Sar*. Vol. 1. Serampore: Serampore Mission Press, 1834.

Maharaj, Ayon. *Infinite Paths to Infinite Reality: Sri Ramakrishna and Cross-Cultural Philosophy of Religion*. New York: Oxford University Press, 2018.

Manjapra, Kris. *Age of Entanglement: German and Indian Intellectuals Across Empire*. Cambridge, MA: Harvard University Press, 2014.

———. 'Knowledgeable Internationalism and the Swadeshi Movement, 1903–1921'. *Economic and Political Weekly* 47, no. 42 (2012): 53–62.

Marshman, John C. *Jyotish ebang Goladhyay, or Treatise on Astronomy and Geography*. Calcutta: Mission Press for the Calcutta School Book Society, 1819.

Matthews, Steven. *Theology and Science in the Thought of Francis Bacon*. Aldershot: Ashgate, 2008.

McLeod, Roy M. 'On Visiting the "Moving Metropolis": Reflections on the Architecture of Imperial Science'. In *Scientific Colonialism: A Cross-Cultural*

Comparison, edited by Nathan Reingold and Marc Rothenberg, pp. 217–249. Washington DC: Smithsonian Institution Press, 1987.

Mitra, Samarpita. *Periodicals, Readers and the Making of a Modern Literary Culture: Bengal at the Turn of the Twentieth Century*. Leiden: Brill, 2020.

Mitra, Saradacharan. 'Akshaykumarke Jemon Dekhechhi'. In *Dwisatajanmabarshe Akshaykumar Dutta*, edited by Tapas Bhowmik, *Korok Sahitya Patrika*, Janaury–April 2020, pp. 265–270.

Moyn, Samuel and Andrew Sartori, eds. *Global Intellectual History*. New York: Columbia University Press, 2013.

Mozoomdar, Protap C. *The Faith and Progress of the Brahmo Somaj*. Calcutta: Calcutta Central Press, 1882.

Mukherjee, Amitabha. *Reform and Regeneration in Bengal, 1774–1823*. Calcutta: Rabindra Bharati Universit, 1968.

Mukhopadhyay, Kumardeb. *Bhudeb Charit*. Vol. 1. Calcutta: India Press, 1917.

Olivelle, Patrick. *The Early Upanishads: Annotated Text and Translation*. Oxford: Oxford University Press, 1998.

Pearce, William H. *Bhugol Brittanta. Geography, Interspersed with Information Historical and Miscellaneous*. Calcutta: Mission Press for the Calcutta School Book Society, 1819.

Pearson. John D. *Bhugol ebang Jyotish Ityadi Bishaye Kathapakathan. Dialogues on Geography, Astronomy, &c, for the Use of Schools*. Calcutta: Calcutta School Book Society Press, 1824.

Poskett, James. *Horizons: A Global History of Science*. New Delhi: Viking, 2022.

———. *Materials of the Mind: Phrenology, Race, and the Global History of Science, 1815–1920*. Chicago: The University of Chicago Press, 2019.

Prakash, Gyan. *Another Reason: Science and the Imagination of Modern India*. Princeton, NJ: Princeton University Press, 1999.

Prichard, James C. *Researches into the Physical History of Mankind*. London: Sherwood, Gilbert and Piper, 1836.

Ray, Alok. *Bankim-Maneesha*. Kolkata: Ebong Mushayera, 2014.

———. *Unish Satak*. Kolkata: Prama Prakashani, 2014.

———. *Unish Satake Nabajagaran: Swarup Sandhan*. Kolkata: Akshar Prakashani, 2019.

Ray, Krishnachandra. *Bharatbarsher Itihas, Ingrejder Adhikarkal*. Calcutta: Published by J. C. Chatterjee, 1859.

Ray, Mahendranath. *Srijukta Babu Akshay Kumar Datter Jiban-Brittanta*. Calcutta: Sanskrit Jantrer Pustakalaya, 1885.

Ray, Prafulla Chandra. *Life and Experiences of a Bengali Chemist*. Vol. 1. Calcutta: The Asiatic Society, 1996. First published 1932 by Chuckervertty, Chatterjee & Co., Ltd (Calcutta).

Ray, Rajat. *Urban Roots of Indian Nationalism: Pressure Groups and Conflict of Interests in Calcutta City Politics, 1875–1939*. New Delhi: Vikas Publishing House, 1979.

Raychaudhuri, Kshirodchandra. *Samagra Bharater Sangkhipta Itihas*. Calcutta: n.p., 1876.

Roberts, M. J. D. 2004. *Making English Morals: Voluntary Association and Moral Reform in England, 1787–1886*. Cambridge: Cambridge University Press, 2004.

Robertson, Bruce C. *Raja Rammohan Ray: The Father of Modern India*. New Delhi: Oxford University Press, 1999.

Sarkar, Benoy Kumar. *The Positive Background of Hindu Sociology: Introduction to Hindu Positivism*. Delhi: Motilal Banarasidass, 1985.

Sarkar, Pijushkanti. *Bismrita Abismrita Akshaykumar Dutta*. Vol. 1. Kolkata: Kabitika, 2020.

Sarkar, Sumit. *Writing Social History*. Delhi: Oxford University Press, 1997.

Sartori, Andrew. *Bengal in Global Concept History: Culturalism in the Age of Capital*. Chicago: The University of Chicago Press, 2008.

Sastri, Sivanath. *History of the Brahmo Samaj*. Vol. 1. Calcutta: Published by R. Chatterji, 1911.

———. *Ramtanu Lahiri o Tatkalin Bangosamaj*. Kolkata: New Age, 2009.

Sen, Amiya P. *Explorations in Modern Bengal c. 1800–1900: Essays on Religion, History and Culture*. Delhi: Primus Books, 2010.

———. *Hindu Revivalism in Bengal, 1872–1905: Some Essays in Interpretation*. New Delhi: Oxford University Press, 1993.

———. *Tattwabodhini Sabha and the Bengal Renaissance*. Calcutta: Sadharan Brahmo Samaj, 1979.

Sen, Atul Chandra, Sitanath Tattvabhushan, and Mahes Chandra Ghosh, eds. *Upanishads: Akhanda Sangskaran*. Calcutta: Haraf Prakashani, 1980.

Sen, Girishchandra. *Ekeshwarbadider Upohar*. Calcutta: Dharmatattva, 1899.

Sengupta, Prasad. 'Akshaykumar Datter Dharmabodh'. In *Dwisotojonmoborshe Akshaykumar Datta*, edited by Tapas Bhowmik, *Korok Sahitya Patrika*, January–April 2020, pp. 72–89.

Subrahmanyam, Sanjay. 'Global Intellectual History Beyond Hegel and Marx'. *History and Theory* 54, no. 2 (2015): 126–137.

Tagore, Debendranath. *Atmatatvabidya*. Calcutta: Tattabodhini Sabha Press, 1852.

———. *The Autobiography of Maharshi Devendranath Tagore*. Translated by Satyendranath Tagore and Indira Devi. London: Macmillan, 1914.

Tagore, Rabindranath. *Gora*. Vol. 2 of *Upanyas Samagra*. Kolkata: Sahityam, 2003. First published 1910.

———. *Rabindra Upanyas-Sangraha*. Kolkata: Visvabharati Granthanbibhag, 1990.

———. *Sangkalan*. Kolkata: Visvabharati Granthanbibhag, 2000. First published 1925.

Thakur, Tekchand. *Aalaler Gharer Dulal*. Edited by Brajendranath Bandopadhyay and Sajanikanta Das. Kolkata: Bangiya Sahitya Parishat, 1998. First published 1858.

Trivedi, Ramendrasundar. *Maya-puri*. Calcutta: Sahitya Parishat Mandir, 1910.

Vidyasagar, Iswarchandra. *Banglar Itihas*. Calcutta: Sanskrit Press, 1853.

Viswanathan, Gauri. *Masks of Conquest: Literary Study and British Rule in India*. New Delhi: Oxford University Press, 2004.

Warner, Michael. *Publics and Counterpublics*. New York: Zone Books, 2002.

Weber, Albrecht. *Modern Investigations on Ancient India*. Translated by Fanny Metcalfe. London: Williams and Norgate, 1857.

Wilson, Horace H. *Sketch of the Religious Sects of the Hindus*. Calcutta: Bishop's College Press, 1846.

Yates, William. *Padarthahidyasar, Orthat Balokdiger Padartbosikkharthoy Kothopokothon*. Calcutta: Calcutta School Book Society Press, 1824

Zastoupil, Lynn. 'Defining Christians, Making Britons: Rammohun Roy and the Unitarians'. *Victorian Studies* 44, no. 2 (2002): 215–243.

Index